THE
ANIMAL WELFARE
HANDBOOK

THE
ANIMAL WELFARE
HANDBOOK

Caroline E. Clough and Barry Kew

FOURTH ESTATE · *London*

First published in 1993 by
Fourth Estate Limited
289 Westbourne Grove, London W11 2QA

Copyright © Caroline E. Clough & Barry Kew, 1993

The right of Caroline E. Clough and Barry Kew
to be identified as the authors of this work has been
asserted by them in accordance with the Copyright,
Designs and Patents Act 1988.

All rights reserved. No part of this publication may be reproduced,
transmitted, stored in a retrieval system, in any form or by any
means, electronic, mechanical, photocopying, recording or otherwise,
without prior permission in writing from Fourth Estate Limited.

ISBN 1–85702–047–2

Typeset in Palatino 10/12pt by Last QT Word,
Aberdeenshire

Printed in Great Britain by Clays Ltd, St Ives plc

CONTENTS

ACKNOWLEDGEMENTS

The authors would like to thank the following for their invaluable assistance: the staffs of the organizations listed in the Directory, Helen Dore, Colin and Lis Howlett, Gill Langley, Paul and Marilyn Newton, Jon Wynne-Tyson, Superintendent Grant of the SSPCA, Stuart R. Harrop of the RSPCA, the North East Scotland Library Service, and all the many people who helped Caroline in the compilation of the original text.

Grateful thanks are due also, of course, to our families, Sue, Stuart, Charlotte and Rory, for their patience and understanding.

PREFACE

This *Handbook* is intended as an introductory guide to animal rights and animal welfare, not as a scientific or ethical treatise. Chapters 1–5 in Part One aim to acquaint the reader with the major areas of concern without attempting to define the most important issues. Nor is each area covered in detail, for this would have meant that every chapter would have become a book in its own right and would also repeat what is already available in the literature on the subject (see Chapter Seven: Resources [page 139]). Neither is it encyclopaedic, for almost every day yet another (ab)use of animals is exposed.

The information has been collected from a great many varied sources, with an attempt to do some justice to opposing viewpoints (although these are by no means aired exhaustively), and with references to selected major organizations listed at the end of sections and chapters. A more comprehensive Directory of Organizations will be found in Chapter Eight in Part Two. Other organizations referred to – which do not sit comfortably alongside those primarily concerned with animal rights and welfare, or which seek to promote the use of animals for various purposes – are listed in the Appendix [page 212].

The reader is strongly recommended to follow up all or any part of this *Handbook* with further reading on the subject as detailed in the Resources Chapter and with additional information which may be obtained from the listed organizations on request.

In order to avoid repetition – and for this reason only – the Royal Society for the Prevention of Cruelty to Animals (RSPCA) has been omitted from many of the Selected Animal Rights and Welfare Organizations listings shown at the end of sections and chapters. Readers should also note that the RSPCA operates in England and Wales. In Scotland, the respective Society is the Scottish SPCA (except for the Aberdeen area which is covered by the Aberdeen Association PCA); in Ulster, the USPCA performs a similar function, as does the ISPCA in the Republic of Ireland.

Page numbers shown in squared brackets refer throughout to pages in this *Handbook*.

INTRODUCTION

In this, the last decade of the twentieth century, it is generally thought that human society has attained a degree of civilized behaviour towards other animals. We seem to have come a long way from the gladiatorial shows of Ancient Rome in which, for instance, 5,000 animals were sacrificed in one day during the reign of Titus (AD 79–81). However, humans still indulge in public butchery of animals and it continues on an infinitely larger scale, but out of sight, in the slaughterhouses, fur farms and animal experimentation laboratories of the 'civilized' world. In fact, many would say that humans have *increased* the scope and magnitude of cruelty to animals, in parallel with advances in the sophistication of technology.

The past fifty years have seen the explosive growth worldwide of intensive livestock farming, animal experimentation, fur farming, and the further threat of extinction – already a large-scale reality – of many species through hunting and habitat destruction.

At the same time it is often argued that as humans have become more affluent we have developed higher ethical standards, and concern for animal welfare would seem to follow this general rule. Within the European Community (EC) the more affluent countries have tended to establish better, though by no means wholly satisfactory, animal-protection mechanisms. In Sweden, Germany and the Netherlands, for example, there is detailed and highly specific legislation concerning what is and what is not permitted in the treatment of animals. In the poorer countries, however, such as Greece, Italy and Spain, animal protection law is considerably more rudimentary and poorly defined. And there is little doubt that animal welfare is not a priority in the Third World where people are starving in their thousands (but see page 45), or in totalitarian countries where even basic human rights are denied.

In trying to determine the main focus of concern in animal welfare, many different conclusions can be reached. For some, the area most in need of urgent reform is animal experimentation, whilst others would argue that, by virtue of the vast number of animals used, livestock production and slaughter must top the agenda. Then there are wildlife concerns, such as the slaughter of kangaroos in Australia or pilot whales around the Faroe Isles. 'Country sports' are considered by many to need immediate reform or abolition, and the problems facing our domestic pet population are also seen as requiring prompt action.

A basic problem in trying to set priorities in animal welfare is that most people have their own personal preferences and prejudices which frequently prove very difficult to change. If emotion generally overrules logic in deciding what is and what is not important in animal welfare, in animal rights the opposite is more often the case. It is easier for most people to identify with the suffering of domesticated animals such as the dog and cat, or of animals which have media and soft toy appeal, like baby seals with their big brown eyes and fluffy faces, than with that of a laying hen in a battery cage. Organizations which raise funds through public sympathy have enough difficulties when appealing on behalf of the more attractive species, but those fighting for animals which do not arouse such strong, positive feelings can find raising public awareness considerably more strenuous. Taking the public beyond animal welfare and into the sphere of animal rights remains an undertaking of far greater magnitude.

Understanding the Terms

In consulting this *Handbook*, and in any additional reading or study of animal rights and welfare, the reader will undoubtedly come across a range of terms which, though not entirely unfamiliar, may not be fully understood. To maximize the reader's comprehension an explanation of the most commonly used of these – animal welfare, animal rights, conservation, vegetarian, vegan, organic, veganic, cruelty-free and animal-free – now follows.

Animal Welfare, Animal Rights and Conservation

Although these three terms may be seen as belonging together under the general canopy of animal concern, they differ in fundamental respects, as do the work and activities of the respective organizations. This is not to say, however, that all three causes cannot be subscribed to by one person. Such a comprehensive ethic belongs to the true, dark 'green'. (For an overview of the philosophical literature dealing with these differences see Chapter 1 in Magel (1989) [page 157]). Nowadays, conservation (and its range of organizations) is most often connected in the public's perception with certain green issues: where animals are considered, these tend to be wild animals. When we look at animal welfare and rights, however, our best introduction is by reference to domesticated, farmed and specially reared animals.

Animal Welfare

Whereas conservation has been a household word in the West for only the past two decades or so, animal welfare goes back for millennia: Pythagoras maintained about 500 BC that humans should treat animals well. But it was not until 1822 (and in England) that the first national law dealing specifically with cruelty to animals was passed – the Act to Prevent the Cruel and Improper Treatment of Cattle.

In modern times animal welfare has come to be recognized as a major concern of the British public. Members of Parliament receive more letters on the subject than on any other topic, and all political parties now mention animal welfare in their manifestos. On occasion it has also become a prominent media issue, with saturation coverage of judiciously selected (and conservation-tinted) events such as the disappearance of a friendly dolphin off the Northumbrian coast or the North Sea seal epidemic.

Generally, at the root of the animal welfare movement lies a conviction, reluctant or otherwise, that humans will never entirely relinquish making use of animals. Welfarists are therefore at pains to seek the *best possible* conditions for and treatment of those animals. For instance, welfarists are not necessarily against meat-eating or animal experimentation, as long as they consider that the animals in question are being treated 'humanely'. Welfarists are likely to be totally opposed to circuses, factory farming and some animal experiments (those which cause obvious pain or which are deemed 'unnecessary', such as cosmetic tests). Thus they are against certain types of animal use, only some of which they regard as constituting animal abuse.

Animal Rights

The animal rights movement has an altogether more radical agenda, one which flows primarily from the concept of universal justice. It was not until the early 1970s (and in the UK) that the term animal rights began to gain wide currency, helped along by the direct-action strategy of the Band of Mercy (which later became and continues to function as the Animal Liberation Front (ALF) [page 176]), and by the Oxford Group of philosophers and writers based at Oxford University. However, Thomas Taylor published (anonymously) *Vindication of the Rights of Brutes* as early as 1792 and Henry Salt's classic *Animals' Rights* was issued 100 years later, whilst between the two Abraham

Lincoln (1809–1865) wrote of being 'in favour of animal rights as well as human rights. That is the way of a whole human being.'

If the conservationist gives preference to wild animals and tends to value one species above another, and the welfarist promotes one animal-using system over another, the animal rightist respects all species and no such systems. Animal rights means the total abolition of animal use, which rightists claim is always animal abuse. If conservationists and welfarists are free-range food eaters or vegetarians, rightists are vegans. Nevertheless, one might find, for example, an anti-vivisectionist who is also a meat-eater, but such selective abolitionism is unrepresentative of animal rights in its purest and most coherent sense.

Rather than wishing to modify or reform animal-using practices, animal rightists demand an end to all animal-using practices, industries and recreations. A meeting-point for conservationists and rightists is possibly on the issue of land use where both oppose, though in different ways, the wholesale encroachment of humans into wild animal territories through overpopulation, industrialization and agriculture.

One of the problems faced by the animal rights movement is its extremist image, generated by certain sectors of the media, of a balaclava-clad, lentil-munching arsonist, which hinders efforts to promote a wider understanding of the fact that not all harms hurt. By 'painless' humiliation, degradation and confinement animals are also abused; above all, they suffer from humankind's attitude towards them. It is, then, not so much obvious cruelty that is challenged by the animal rights ethic as the near-universal human assumption that other species are here for our purposes (see Regan (1987) [page 154]).

Institutionalized philosophy decrees that we need to do things to and with animals in order to survive and make progress, and it is acceptable to do these things because animals are 'not like us', 'they don't feel pain as we do', 'they are "lower creatures"', 'they do not think like us', 'they have no souls'. Conversely, animal rights' 'hands-off' philosophy holds that any use of animals is not only unjust, cruel and unethical but outdated, and that real human progress can be made without the impoverishment of human character, by ending what Shaw termed 'man's slavery to the animals he exploits'.

Conservation
Campaigns run by organizations like Greenpeace [page 214] and the World Wide Fund for Nature (WWF) [page 217], often fronted by a

'Save the ...' slogan, are essentially conservationist, operating mostly from an anthropocentric, i.e. human-centred, viewpoint. This concentrates more on the notion of a species than on the reality of the individual animal which is being 'saved'.

A good example of how the conservationist stance can be at odds with animal rights is the dolphin-friendly tuna campaign of recent years. The conservationist concern has been that dolphins as a species could disappear, or their numbers be seriously depleted, if *certain* fishing practices (e.g. drift-netting) are allowed to continue. Those creatures which are presently endangered only on an individual level and not as a species, e.g. the tuna fish, are not taken into account by conservationists. In contrast, the animal rightist holds that all fishing practices are unacceptable. An important point here, however, is that the conservationist is not directly at odds with the welfarist, indeed conservationists are usually of welfarist persuasion with a genuine concern for animal suffering. But this is not the main thrust of the conservationist campaign which, at its most anthropocentric, considers it essential for endangered species to be saved 'for our children' to experience. Zoos, wildlife parks and dolphinaria [pages 24 and 5] often trade on this conservationist ethic in order to justify their keeping of animals in captivity as examples of a species rather than as creatures with their own inherent value (see Regan (1987) [page 154]). Circuses also now lay claim to a conservationist/educational role, arguing that audiences learn something positive from watching wild and semi-wild animals perform in the ring.

Another style of 'conservation' is that promoted by those who participate in country sports. Indeed, the International President of the WWF, the Duke of Edinburgh, is a keen shot, and one organization at least, the British Association for Shooting and Conservation [page 212], incorporates an apparent contradiction in its title. Operating under a banner of habitat conservation justifies killing some of the species to be 'saved' or 'ecologically managed' and ensures that there are always more to be shot or hunted. Anglers have also more strenuously of late claimed a conservation role for their practices (see Chapter One: Sports and Entertainment). Other conservationists will rescue a species from human exploitation, e.g. poaching, by creating a wildlife reserve. In doing so they come as close to an animal rights ethic as conservationists usually get.

By the use of conservation in either a manipulative or sincere manner (or both simultaneously), the conservationist lobby has made a vital impact on our collective consciousness and conscience. From an animal's point of view, it can be thanked for the growing awareness of our undeniable affinity with other (if only selected) species, and of the direct effect of human activity on their welfare. Greenpeace [page 214], Friends of the Earth [page 214] and other organizations have made obvious to politicians and the general public the human pressures, such as overpopulation, land wastage, rainforest destruction, greed, prestige- and power-seeking, etc., which contribute towards species' disappearance, endangerment and suffering. The growing public abhorrence of goods made from fur, ivory and reptile skins, and of the use of exotic species in animal experiments, is largely due to the work of conservationist as well as animal rights and welfare organizations.

Explained below are some other terms which are commonly used in connection with the three main movements outlined above.

Vegetarianism

Vegetarianism has two main strands; lacto-vegetarianism (sometimes referred to as lacto-ovo-vegetarianism) and veganism.

Lacto-vegetarians consume no meat, fish or fowl (flesh foods). They eat all other kinds of food except cheeses made using rennet from the calf's stomach. Fully vegetarian cheeses use a vegetarian rennet instead as their protein-breakdown agent. Many vegetarians also refuse to eat battery eggs or to wear certain animal products, e.g. leather. Basically, however, lacto-vegetarians boycott products derived directly from the slaughter of animals and fish.

Vegans adopt what might be termed advanced vegetarianism. Veganism is more comprehensive, a way of living which seeks to exclude, as far as is possible and practical, all forms of exploitation of animals for food, clothing or any other purpose. In dietary terms veganism dispenses with all animal produce including meat, fish, poultry, eggs, animal milks, honey and their derivatives. The Vegan Society [page 208] was formed in England in 1944 by a group of vegetarians who rejected what they saw as the ethical compromises implicit in lacto-vegetarianism and consequently decided to renounce the use of all animal products.

While it would appear that most people who become vegetarian do so out of a sense of ethical responsibility, the recent dramatic upswing in their number includes an increasing percentage of the population which is outraged by factory-farming methods and alarmed by the health risks associated with animal products. Bovine spongiform encephalitis (BSE), the so-called 'mad cow disease', did the meat industry few favours.

The vast majority of vegetarians and vegans are also opposed to all other non-dietary exploitation of animals: country sports, circuses, zoos, animal experimentation, and so on.

Cruelty-Free and Animal-Free

Ideally perhaps, these two terms, which are used to describe the status of certain products, should be interchangeable. However, 'cruelty-free' is currently used to refer to a product which has not been tested on animals, and 'animal-free' refers to a vegan product, i.e. one which has not been tested on animals and contains no animal ingredients. The shopper will often find such products flagged with a cruelty-free symbol (white rabbit) or a vegan/animal-free symbol (encircled green sunflower), respectively. Other products may carry a vegetarian symbol (green V-shaped seedling) denoting that they contain no calf rennet, battery eggs or ex-slaughter ingredients. The vegetarian symbol on cosmetics and toiletries also denotes non-animal-testing. (See British Union for the Abolition of Vivisection (BUAV) [page 180], Vegan Society [page 208] and Vegetarian Society [page 209]).

Organic and Veganic (Vegan–Organic)

While both terms signal a movement away from modern-day farming, with its use of agrochemicals and intensive systems, there is a vital difference between them which reverberates through any examination of relevant terms in animal rights and welfare. Both 'organic' and 'veganic' relate not just to products but more especially to land use, which is at the root of all farming systems. In our animal-based agriculture some 60 per cent of land in the UK is used to feed farm animals.

Organic agriculture, which relies upon fundamental rather than contemporary agrochemical methods, tends to be backward-looking, i.e. aiming to return to an older, more traditional style of food production, using free-range and extensive rather than intensive, factory methods. As the term is currently used, 'organic' usually implies an animal-based agriculture, incorporating the growing of crops (using animal manures) to feed to animals to feed to humans. On the other hand, 'veganic' (also referred to as vegan–organic) is an entirely non-animal system, using vegetable composting and green manuring techniques to maintain soil fertility and crop yield in growing food for direct human consumption. It is therefore the more land-use efficient of the two.

Convenient and often necessary as it is to deal, as above, with specific issues as if they were separate entities, it must be borne in mind that many areas of animal rights and welfare overlap and/or lead inevitably to a consideration of the others. A study of animal experimentation can quite naturally be extended to the subject of experiments on livestock, thence to farming systems, land use, hunting, effects on wildlife and thus to zoos, which have themselves been found to experiment upon animals.

Likewise, the subject of animals and how they are (ab)used by society should not be seen in isolation from other great issues of our time which, when their surfaces are scratched, reveal strong similarities to, and connections with, the way animals are exploited by humans. It is hardly an exaggeration to say that our civilization is founded upon the backs of animals. One might paraphrase Tolstoy and claim that, in the UK, people would do anything for animals except get off their backs. Non-human animals are still widely regarded as resources, there to be used for human 'benefit'. In such a wide-ranging role, they appear in human wars and war preparations, in rainforest-cleared grazings, in chemical pollutant research, on land which could be used instead to grow food for starving people, and on the piled-high plates of prosperous nations.

Like women and coloured races they are routinely exploited and discriminated against (often, tragically and perversely, by women and coloured races). Power is seductive and we all – including the 'lowest of the land' – have the ability and freedom to exert power over the weak, to feel a sense of superiority over other species. Non-human animals are at the bottom of the heap, the last base of victimization.

Those who use and abuse animals have claimed success for their endeavours but animal welfare and, to an even greater extent, animal rights recognize this as myth – a tradition of error – just as vegans are aware of the gruesome history of every animal product.

It has been said that as long as humans massacre animals we will massacre each other, that as long as vivisection exists so will disease, that random cruelty and violence will remain rife in a climate of institutionalized abuse and that justice will not be universal until the voiceless share its blessings.

PART ONE

Chapter One
SPORTS AND ENTERTAINMENT

These are probably the most diverse areas of animal abuse and the ones that are seen, even by the general public, as being the least justifiable, or not justifiable at all. The use of animals for human recreational purposes is considered as outdated and barbaric by its opponents. However, those involved in these pastimes claim that they are entertaining and educating the public or safeguarding traditional values and/or the countryside.

BULLFIGHTING

Bullfighting of various styles takes place in Spain – its country of origin – Portugal, parts of southern France, certain Central and South American countries and Russia, and is usually staged in purpose-built rings or arenas.

In the most commonly seen bullfight the bull, once in the ring, is 'warmed up' by toreadors who make it chase around the arena, while the matador may give several passes with the cape. The picador enters the ring on horseback and cuts deep into the bull's neck muscles with a sharp lance three or four times. Banderillos stick up to half a dozen barbed spikes (banderillas) into the bull's back, further cutting its muscles and nerves. The now bloodied, exhausted bull can no longer lift its head to full height.

The matador then takes over, encouraging the bull to charge at the cape. After several passes and twenty to thirty minutes after the start of the fight, the bull, while at a standstill in the centre of the ring, is meant to be killed by the thrust of the matador's sword at the base of the neck, between the shoulders and through to the heart (except in Portugal where the animal is often taken out of the ring to be slaughtered). If the matador is incompetent and makes several unsuccessful thrusts instead of a single *coup de grâce*, the kneeling bull will be killed by stabs of a dagger (puntilla) to the spinal cord. The bull's ears and tail are sometimes cut off and thrown to the crowd even though the animal may not be dead yet, just paralyzed. The thrust is practised by matadors on captive farm livestock in slaughterhouses, and thousands of young cattle are 'fought' by would-be matadors in makeshift arenas throughout bullfighting countries. Approximately 30,000 bulls are killed every year in Spanish bullfights, which are specifically excluded from the country's animal welfare laws.

Rights and Wrongs

Bullfighting is defended on the grounds that it is a traditional sport and an integral part of Spanish culture, and is supported as such by the Spanish government (which has established bullfight schools) and royal family. The matador is revered for his bravery and his grace under pressure, in what is probably the last direct confrontation of man and beast. The bullfight has of course been fêted in literature, couched in poetic and metaphorical terms. It is also lucrative, being a tourist attraction, involving many large stadia throughout the countries where it persists.

However, apart from the obvious cruelty and distress involved in the prolonged antagonizing of the bull during the fight, the animal is handicapped in a variety of ways prior to entering the ring: its horns are filed or cut down to impair judgement; vaseline is smeared in its eyes to blur vision; needles are stuck into its scrotum; it is beaten with sandbags; a nostril is plugged to interfere with its breathing; or it is given massive doses of epsom salts to induce diarrhoea, pain and lack of co-ordination. A bull may also be drugged to subdue it if too excitable or to stimulate it if too docile. The breeder's mark, a steel emblem, may be driven into the bull's back before the fight.

The picadors' horses are usually discarded racehorses or older animals at the end of their working lives. The bulls have been observed to gore them, or crush them against the walls of the ring; even though some horses are padded, these injuries are often fatal. Horses that survive a goring have been seen to be sewn up or to have their bowels stuffed back with straw before being forced back into the ring. Prior to entering the ring their vocal cords may be cut so that they cannot cry out, and they may be blindfolded, drugged and temporarily deafened by stuffing their ears with rags so that they will not be frightened by the sight and sound of the crowd.

If tourists were to boycott the bullrings (and their souvenirs), many of them would be forced to close down. There has been increased pressure on the Spanish government to abolish bullfighting since the country joined the EC [page 213]. Opinion polls conducted in Spain, including one by the Ministry of Culture, have indicated that over half the Spanish population is uninterested in bullfighting.

CETACEAN (DOLPHIN AND WHALE) DISPLAYS

In *The Rose-Tinted Menagerie* [page 139], William Johnson reports that between 1938 and 1980 the USA took a minimum of 1,500 live dolphins from the sea, and that between 1980 and 1990 Japan captured 500 for various amusement parks. Probably at least 2,700 bottlenose dolphins have been taken worldwide and 4,500 small-toothed whales are known to have been kept in captivity. Up to 50 per cent of these creatures are maimed or killed in the process of capture. Those surviving then have to face the further ordeal of transportation.

The history of the dolphin in captivity in the UK is not one of success. Figures from various UK reports are not consistent but some of these show that as many as 300 bottlenose dolphins and eight killer whales have been imported into the UK since 1962. According to the Klinowska Report (see below) there were 127 dolphin mortalities between 1965 and 1985. Of the fifty-seven imported between 1968 and 1983, thirty-eight have died after completing barely half of their natural twenty-five year lifespan. The whales have fared no better, with only one of the nine imported surviving, and the other eight living for less than one-sixth of their usual fifty to eighty years in the wild. Causes of death have included peritonitis and renal failure attributable to dirty and infected water; chlorine poisoning; heart failure (due to stress); physical attack (due to overcrowding); suicide (by ramming tank walls); and swallowing foreign objects thrown into the water by spectators. Out of twenty-four cetaceans known to have been born in Britain, twenty-two died as the result of miscarriages, stillbirths or premature births, or within weeks succumbed to disease or were drowned by their mothers.

In 1986 there were six dolphinaria in the UK, from a one-time total of thirty-six, with nineteen dolphins and two killer whales kept for display. Now only two dolphinaria remain and this would appear to be due in part to the 1986 government-commissioned review of the theory and practice of keeping dolphins and whales, conducted by Drs M. Klinowska and S. Brown of the University of Cambridge. As a result of the findings of this Report the Department of the Environment banned the import of bottlenose dolphins and killer whales until such time as the dolphinaria met the recommended standards. These included, for up to five dolphins (figures for killer whales in brackets): a minimum 1,000 (20,000) cubic metres; tanks not narrower than 7 (15) metres or shallower than 3.5 (7.5) metres, and at least one-third of the pool to be a minimum depth of 7 (15) metres. Failure to meet these standards after five years meant closure of the establishment.

Since 1984, the EC [page 213] has directed that cetaceans displayed in public must be kept only for breeding, research or education purposes: the Klinowska Report suggested that none of these criteria was met by UK dolphinaria. The report also criticized the lack of research facilities, the haphazard training programmes and the poor standard of report-keeping on the history and health of the animals.

Cetacea are also protected by the Convention on International Trade in Endangered Species (CITES) [page 213] which states (Order of Appendix 1) that an import licence may only be granted where: (1) the capture of the specimen will not have a harmful effect on the conservation of the species and (2) the applicant provides evidence that the intended recipient possesses adequate facilities for the species to carry out its natural behaviour, and to be properly cared for. The UK has signed this Convention and is thus supposed to adhere to the Orders.

Rights and Wrongs

The training of dolphins is designed to demonstrate the capabilities of the animals in an entertaining way, the tricks taught being extensions of their natural behaviour observed in the wild.

Dolphinaria owners believe that their education programmes, involving lectures to schools, and the content of the shows, justify keeping the animals in captivity. They have argued that 59 per cent of the British population have visited a zoo or safari park where dolphins and whales are kept, and that 68 per cent of visitors to the Windsor Safari Park go primarily to see the dolphinarium.

They also believe that the standards recommended for pool sizes by the Klinowska Report (see above) are unrealistic, making dolphins too expensive to display. Welfarists, however, argue that these animals are not suitable for captivity in the first place. Indeed, the keeping of any animal in captivity, unless for that individual animal's benefit, is anathema to the ethic behind the animal rights movement.

In the wild, dolphins travel in large family groups of up to 1,000, swimming at up to 60 km per hour and diving to depths of 300 metres, and all cetacea possess highly developed hearing used for communication and hunting. Dolphinaria cannot possibly emulate wild conditions. The concrete tanks used in captivity act like echo chambers, the animals becoming so bombarded with acoustic signals (and loud music) that they have to stop using their natural communicative behaviour; in time most of them (if they do not die naturally or commit suicide) become bored, distressed and lethargic. Many cannot be returned to the wild after this experience as their senses are so dulled that they would die of starvation through inability to hunt.

CIRCUSES

The training of animals for performance in circuses and exhibitions has a violent history. For centuries, the methods used were based on mastery enforced by goads and whips. The nineteenth-century wild-cat tamer, Van Amburgh, used a crowbar to train his animals, and beatings and burnings with hot irons were commonplace. The wildlife dealer Carl Hagenbach tried to lay down guidelines for more humane training methods in the latter half of the same century, but 100 years on many welfare groups claim that dubious taming and training methods are still used, involving fear, submission, deprivation and physical punishment.

Pressure was increased for new guidelines to control the usually cramped and squalid transportation of circus animals after three elephants from a British circus were kept chained up in a crate on a barge off Taiwan for two months in 1987 due to administrative complications. However, no new legislation has been implemented.

On site, circus animals may still spend up to twenty-three hours a day tethered, chained or caged. In the Zoo Licensing Act 1981 [page 122] some provision is made for the regulation of zoo animals' accommodation but the Performing Animals (Regulations) Act 1925 [page 109] is really only for registration purposes, with few provisions made for the welfare of circus animals. Thus their only protection lies in the general animal protection Acts [pages 105 and 111], and anyone can take out a licence to train animals and own a circus.

In Finland, under the anti-cruelty laws introduced in October 1986, circuses are not allowed to feature elephants or other big wild animals, and other countries – India, for example – have similar restrictions. Successful attempts have been made in the UK and elsewhere to promote circuses that do not have animal performers.

Rights and Wrongs

The Association of Circus Proprietors of Great Britain (ACP) [page 212], is the organization concerned with the promotion of circuses in the UK. In order to become a member a circus has to meet certain criteria relating to animal welfare, behavioural needs and accommodation. Only twelve circuses are members. (There are some twenty-five other non-member circuses, large and small). The ACP's members have agreed that in the UK Royal Society for the Prevention of Cruelty to Animals (RSPCA) [page 204] inspectors may have access at any reasonable time to ensure the welfare of the animals. However, the RSPCA claims that it is only invited to the rehearsal of animal acts and not to initial taming and training. It has no statutory right of entry.

Public interest in circuses is increasing in the UK (an estimated 3 million people visit a circus every year), with more large circuses touring the country now than at any time since 1945. The ACP promotes the circus as a unique family entertainment, claiming that the public should have the right to decide whether or not to attend.

The ACP also argues that the banning of circuses from council-owned sites may have a negative effect on animal welfare as non-member circuses of an inferior standard may use privately-owned sites. As landlord, the council can impose certain standards such as the use of exercise pens for the animals and regular veterinary inspections.

However, the training and dressing up of wild animals to perform tricks, for example elephants or bears standing on their heads, remains unnatural. It cannot be compared with the training of domesticated animals which extends a behaviour already present in their natural repertoire, such as pet dogs being taught to fetch sticks or sheep dogs to herd sheep. Given even the most humane training regime, there is still concern over the welfare of circus animals, especially large animals such as lions, tigers, and bears, which are kept in cramped cages (beast wagons) in which they travel long distances. There can be no doubt either, that training methods in some circuses, such as the beating of tigers in the Moscow State Circus, continue to be barbaric.

Moreover, circuses can serve to illustrate the animal rights maxim that not all harms hurt, as mentioned in the Introduction. The animals' humiliation, degradation and loss of freedom constitute a harm as great as the physical hurts incurred in their training. Anti-circus organizations continue to persuade Local Authorities to ban circuses from council-owned land, with over 150 local and district councils currently doing so.

STREET PERFORMERS

Individual animals have likewise been used in street entertainment for centuries, and performing bears – usually immature Himalayan bears captured as cubs – can still be seen on the streets in southern Europe, Turkey and India. Some of these animals are controlled by a knotted rope passed through a hole drilled in their palate and out of the nose. They are beaten to make them stand upright, and are forced to dance on hot metal trays.

Street entertainment using animals is now illegal in many countries but the laws are often flouted, as in the case of the chimpanzees and tiger cubs used by street photographers in Spanish tourist resorts. The photographers obtain chimpanzees or cubs at a few weeks old which are then de-clawed, de-toothed or given drugs and alcohol to subdue them. There have been cases of animals beaten by their owners, left in locked car boots, found in dustbins with their throats cut, or discarded at sea after they have become too big to manage.

FIGHTING

Although staged fights between animals were banned in 1835, their popularity appears to have undergone a resurgence in recent years. Badger baiting, cock fighting, dog fighting and dog and cat fighting (using stolen pet cats) have all been widely reported and several prosecutions have been secured. In May 1987 the Protection of Animals (Penalties) Act [page 126] increased the penalties for animal baiting and fighting to a maximum fine of £2,000 and/or up to six months in prison. Enormous secrecy surrounds these illegal activities, with fights being arranged at the last possible minute and look-outs employed to avoid detection. Large sums of money are staked on the outcome of the fights which are often videoed. The majority of people would not hesitate to condemn animal fighting or baiting and so there is little controversy involved.

BADGER BAITING

So many setts have been dug out in traditional badger-baiting areas like the Yorkshire coast that there is now a shortage of badgers there, and baiters are looking further south for a continued supply. Well-organized gangs raid the setts, taking the badgers to secret locations where they are kept before being forced to fight dogs.

There are several forms of badger baiting/fighting. In one, terriers are sent into a badger's sett while the men dig through the roof to expose the fight. Some of those involved have had affiliations with registered fox hunts which use 'terrier men' to extract a fox when it has gone to ground [page 17]. In another form, a captive badger is placed in a pit or chained up and set upon by fighting dogs. Sometimes the badger's jaw or back legs are broken to give the dogs a better chance. Yet another form is badger drawing when a badger is placed in a barrel or pipe and dogs are sent in to fight it. The winning dog is the fastest one to 'draw' the badger out of its hole.

Badgers have been protected to some extent by the Badgers Act 1973 [page 135] and the Wildlife and Countryside Act 1981 [page 120] but until the Badgers Act 1991 [page 128] their setts were not protected. It is now an offence to damage a badger sett or any part of it, to obstruct access or entrance to one (there are exemptions for fox hunts to stop up the sett lightly on the day of a hunt), to enter a dog into a badger sett, or to disturb a badger while it is in its sett. The Badgers (Further Protection) Act 1991 [page 129] gives courts the power to disqualify those who have been convicted of badger digging from keeping dogs.

COCK FIGHTING

Cock fighting is a very ancient sport and consists of encouraging two specially bred cocks to fight in a small ring until one is severely injured or dead. Metal spurs (some imported illegally from countries like Mexico where cock fighting is widespread) are attached to the birds' legs to increase the amount of damage one bird inflicts on the other.

DOG FIGHTING

In 1985 the first prosecution for dog fighting this century was brought at Cheshunt, Hertfordshire, when two men were gaoled for six months each. In 1991, an RSPCA raid resulted in the largest number of prosecutions ever brought in Britain for dog fighting, including six- month gaol sentences for the organizers of an event in Fife.

The favoured fighting dog is the American Pit Bull terrier of which over 1,000 were imported into the UK in 1986. By 1991, when the government banned any further imports, about 10,000 were living in this country. These dogs have been bred specifically for their aggression and ability to fight to the death, and are not recognized by the Kennel Club [page 215] in the UK.

After a series of near fatal attacks on adults and children by Pit Bulls, the government rushed through the Dangerous Dogs Act 1991 [page 127] which made it illegal to import or breed Pit Bull terriers (or Japanese Tosas, Fila Brazilieras and Dogo Argentinos) or to sell, exchange, give away, advertise, abandon or let them stray. Furthermore, dogs presently in the UK had to be registered and neutered by 30 November 1991 (extended to 1 March 1992), failure to do so resulting in the destruction of the dog.

Staffordshire and English Bull terriers are also used in dog fighting and there have been reports of family pets being stolen to fulfil the demand, and for breeding. Fighting dogs are trained to kill, with live animals used as bait, and they are fed a diet intended to instil bloodlust. To build up the dogs' stamina they are put on treadmills and encouraged to swing from pieces of wood by their teeth. Fights take place in 5-metre-square pits, carpeted to give the dogs a better grip, in barns, basements and even ships anchored offshore.

FIESTAS

There are around 10,000 annual fiestas in Spain, many of which celebrate religious festivals and date back to medieval times. Over 100 of them involve some animal ritual of gross cruelty.

The UK public was outraged in 1987 when it came to light, via the work of the Donkey Sanctuary [page 185] and a tabloid exposé, that the festival of the village of Villanueva de la Vera involved the riding of the oldest donkey by a fat man until the animal collapsed. A modified form of the spectacle continues under international surveillance by animal welfare organizations. In other fiestas a live goose is hung upside down and horsemen riding past it compete to pull off its head; calves are chased by tractors until they are crushed to death; chickens and geese are clubbed by blindfolded men; bulls have their horns wrapped in cloth and set alight and are then made to run until they drop; bulls have darts blown at them and bleed to death, or have their testicles cut off while they are still alive; goats are thrown from church towers after being milked at the crowd; and calves are thrown repeatedly from a platform which is progressively raised until they do not survive their fall.

FILMS AND VIDEOS

The Cinematograph Films (Animals) Act 1937 [page 112] and the Video Recordings Act 1984 [page 138] are aimed at preventing the distribution of films and videos which involve cruelty to animals during their making. The Protection of Animals Act 1911 [page 105] also offers some protection to animals used in films, but only those made in the UK, and the film industry in this country is relatively small. Most films come from the USA and many of those involving animals have been produced using methods which would be considered unacceptable in the UK. For example, in *Apocalypse Now* a live water buffalo was decapitated on-screen, and in *Pat Garrett and Billy the Kid* live hens were buried to the neck in sand for their heads to be 'shot' off (lighter fuel had been squirted in their eyes to keep them awake, whilst wires were wrapped around their necks to yank off their heads). The use of trip or running wires is obvious from a viewing of many films, especially westerns. (See Hall (1984) [page 152] for further examples).

The British Board of Film Classification is responsible for censoring scenes involving animal abuse, and the Royal Society for the Prevention of Cruelty to Animals (RSPCA) [page 204] has a consultative position within it. The American Humane Association has for many years been attempting to prevent cruelty on film sets but has been hampered by the complicated US laws which vary in different states, and by the small fines imposed upon directors and producers if and when a conviction can be obtained.

In the UK there have been complaints that television series like *All Creatures Great and Small* abuse the veterinary profession's reputation by using vets to administer drugs to create effects such as animals dying or being injured. It is also suspected that many scenes in natural history and wildlife programmes, depicting one animal attacking another, have been set up in order to save time waiting for nature to take its course. Other animals are bred especially to take part in such programmes.

Many animals in television studios and on sets are subjected to stress and humiliation, although some television companies claim to exercise a strict code of practice to ensure the welfare of these animals.

FISHING (ANGLING)

Fishing for pleasure is divided into coarse, game and sea angling and there are an estimated 3.5 million anglers in the UK. Coarse fishing is largely a competitive sport; the fish are caught, kept in nets, weighed at the end of the competition to see which angler has the biggest catch, and then returned to the water. Game fishing involves the catching of edible fish, such as trout and salmon, for the table. The bait used differs according to the preferences of the angler and the type of fishing. Live worms, fish and maggots are often used, as are artificial 'flies' made of coloured feathers and other materials.

The hook is taken into the mouth of the fish as it eats the bait, and is either swallowed or lodged in the mouthparts. The fish is then 'played' out of the water as the angler reels in the line, and killed by a blow or blows to the head. Fish and sharks caught by sea anglers are similarly despatched, although they are often killed by asphyxiation or by the severe injuries incurred in the catching.

Rights and Wrongs

Fishing is a traditional country sport. Many anglers do not accept that fish are capable of the sensation of pain, and therefore angling poses no great moral dilemma for them. In 1976 the Royal Society for the Prevention of Cruelty to Animals (RSPCA) [page 204] commissioned the independent Medway Report [page 140] on shooting and angling in an effort to reach some consistent position on these sports. The panel, comprising conservation, zoology, and field sports experts, concluded that if it is accepted that vertebrates other than humans can experience pain, then there appears to be no reason why fish should be excluded, as they possess similar sensory and transmission processes.

Many welfarists maintain that the injuries inflicted on the fish by the hook are unacceptable, as is the damage done to the sensitive epidermis by handling. In the case of coarse fishing the fish may suffer irreparable damage and become susceptible to disease and predators (e.g. while in keep-nets), so that when released they do not survive for long. In the cases of game and sea fishing there is grave concern over the methods of killing, especially by inexperienced anglers.

The RSPCA issues a Code of Practice for anglers, whilst urging them to review their appreciation of the sport in the light of the findings of the Medway Report. The Code encourages more humane treatment, such as the killing of game fish before attempting to remove the hook; the use of disgorgers of appropriate size for other fish; the use of barbless hooks, and the minimum handling of fish. It suggests also the gaining of proper knowledge on killing and on the use of tackle, to minimize the occurrences of broken lines which lead to fish still carrying hooks being set free. The RSPCA would like to see the authorities responsible for issuing fishing licences taking a more active part in the education of anglers, with information akin to its Code issued with the licence.

Anglers also claim to be guardians of the countryside by cleaning up the waterways and prosecuting polluters, but one of the biggest complaints against them, and one that has come from many quarters, is the discarding of fishing tackle such as broken lines and lead weights. Apart from the physical injuries sustained by animals and birds that become entangled in nylon line and hooks, discarded lead weights are picked up by swans as they collect grit from the river bed. Lead is toxic and when absorbed into the bloodstream leads to 'kinky' neck, paralysis of the neck muscles, swelling at the base of the neck, discoloration of the faeces and lethargy. The birds may take up to six weeks to die of starvation.

In 1983 the Royal Commission on Environmental Pollution concluded that lead from fishing weights was a major cause of mortality in Mute swans, estimating that approximately 3,500 of these swans every year were dying from lead poisoning alone. The numbers of other birds affected was unknown. In 1986 the Control of Pollution (Anglers' Lead Weights) Regulations attempted to control the use of lead weights, with the use of some sizes for coarse fishing being made illegal. Anglers who stockpiled lead shot prior to the regulations may still be using it, however. The welfare and conservationist organizations working in this area argue that a total ban on its use is the only solution, and even then it will take many years for the lead presently in the rivers and waterways to be cleaned up.

Another problem that has been highlighted is the removal of an estimated 1–3,000 lugworms a day from UK seashores, to be used for fishing bait. Lugworms are a valuable food source for low tidal feeding birds, such as oyster catchers and curlews.

HUNTING

DEER HUNTING

The hunting of mature stags (red deer) takes place from August to October, while youngsters (spring stags) are hunted during March and April, and hinds are hunted from November to February. There are three packs of hounds in Devon and Somerset which hunt red deer (estimated at about 200 killed every year) and one pack of buck hounds in the New Forest which hunts fallow bucks during September and again during November–March (the hunt claiming about five to six deer a year). There are some 1,000 subscribers to stag hunts nationally, with around 200 on average following the hunt on Exmoor.

The day's hunting starts with a hunt servant (the 'harbourer') going out early to locate good strong 'warrantable' deers for hunting. When the hunt meets at about 10.30 a.m., the riders and some of the more experienced hounds will split up the herd until a suitable stag is running alone. This may take some hours.

The selected deer may be hunted over many miles, for as long as seven hours, jumping all that comes before it, until it is exhausted and comes to a standstill, holding off the hounds with its antlers. When the hunt catches up, the stag is shot and its carcase and antlers are distributed to the followers and hounds.

In Northern Ireland 'carted' deer are hunted. These are captive deer, often de-antlered and castrated, which are released for the chase and then recaptured and kept for further hunts.

Rights and Wrongs

The British Field Sports Society (BFSS) [page 212] and other organizations believe that about one-third of deer herds must be culled every year to prevent the numbers rising to intolerable levels and to destroy sick or old deer, that hunting has a useful role in deer management, and that deer would be worse off if there was no hunting. Farmers who only tolerate deer on their farms because they provide 'sport', would kill more deer by shooting than are destroyed by the hunts. But pro-deer hunt farmers are a minority, and some already shoot deer to sell the venison. It is also claimed that hunting disperses deer and prevents intensive crop losses, yet when deer are aware of predators they gather in larger groups, only dispersing when the hunting season is over.

Often the huntsmen are not quick enough to get to the deer before the hounds, or the deer might be despatched by having its throat cut, which is illegal. The hunting of hinds is of special concern as they have no antlers to hold the hounds at bay and they may be pregnant and / or have a calf at foot which will be taken first by the hounds.

Buck hunting (fallow deer) in the New Forest is a very ancient sport and now takes place with the co-operation of the Forestry Commission [page 213] which shoots the majority of the culled deer, approximately 6,000 each year. Wildlife campaigners insist that where culling is deemed necessary the use of professional marksmen with high-powered rifles is preferable to hunting with dogs. In Scotland the hunting of deer with dogs is illegal; shooting is the only permissible form of killing.

FALCONRY

Falconry is a very ancient sport which in the past few years has enjoyed something of a revival in the UK . It involves the training of wild-caught or captive-bred falcons such as the peregrine, or hawks such as the goshawk, to take live prey in its natural habitat. Quarry such as grouse or partridge are flushed from cover, then the falconer releases the hawk which, if successful, catches the bird in mid-air and kills it by the force of its powerful feet and talons.

Game birds may be hunted when in season, although rabbits, rats, grey squirrels and 'pest' birds may be taken at any time. Other species are protected by various laws, such as the Wildlife and Countryside Act 1981 [page 120] which also attempts to protect wild hawks by prohibiting the killing or taking of them (or their eggs or chicks). However, the Secretary of State can issue licences, in certain situations, to permit taking them from the wild or importing them for falconry or breeding. In fact, the Department of the Environment has been issuing licences (sixty-five in 1991) to falconers to kill thousands of protected birds, including sky-larks, meadow pipits, song thrushes, fieldfares and redwings. There are around 500 falconers in the UK, although about twenty times that number of people keep some 13,000 birds of prey as pets (excluding owls and vultures).

Rights and Wrongs

The BFSS [page 212] stresses that falconry is a skilled sport and that the birds receive constant expert attention. It discourages people from taking birds from the wild as this can bring the sport into disrepute. It is also claimed that falconry and its associated captive breeding protect raptors from extinction.

Welfare organizations argue that the keeping of wild birds in captivity, often hooded and tethered on blocks or perches, cannot be justified in the name of sport. Birds of prey are also displayed at schools, country shows and game fairs where they remain tethered all day, often in blazing sun and in close proximity to bustling crowds. A League Against Cruel Sports report (Robinson (1991) [page 140]) claimed that falconry is virtually uncontrolled and conflicts with the principles of conservation and the spirit of bird protection. It alleged that the sport involves cruelty, the theft of eggs and chicks, the smuggling of birds and the killing of otherwise protected birds.

The setting of one species upon another, whether for sport or 'pest' control, is hardly different in principle from other forms of staged animal fighting and hunting, despite the quicker kills.

FOX HUNTING

The hunting of foxes using purpose-bred hounds has been a popular sport since the middle of the eighteenth century and the traditional pageantry surrounding the hunt survives to this day. There are approximately 194 fox-hunting packs in the UK and those registered with the Masters of Foxhounds Association in England and Wales [page 216] have decreased by over 8 per cent in the past twenty years or so. The average number of subscribers to each hunt is less than 100, but fashionable hunts such as the Quorn have over 1,000. Most hunts are also followed on foot and in vehicles.

Before the fox-hunting season proper commences, huntsmen train the young hounds recruited to the pack. This is done via cub hunting which takes place from August to October (inclusive), the fox cubs being born in March/April. The cubs are flushed out of the fox earths early in the morning when the vixen is likely to be away hunting for food, and several older hounds are used to encourage the young ones to hunt and kill the cubs. The fox-hunting season proper starts in November and ends in April, depending on the weather. Before each hunt the known local fox earths, drains and badger setts are temporarily stopped up to prevent the fox from escaping underground. When the hounds catch up with the fox the kill may be far from instantaneous. If the fox does go to ground, terriers are put down the hole to 'bolt' it, or to distract it while terrier men dig down to expose and shoot it.

Foxes are also hunted by individuals using lurcher and terrier dogs. The terriers are used to flush a fox from an earth for the faster lurchers to chase and catch it.

Rights and Wrongs

The BFSS [page 212] sees foxes as pests, an unchecked population of which would cause widespread damage, and wishes to achieve an acceptable balance. However, though acknowledging that there are instances where 'rogue' foxes have been known to take poultry and lambs, anti-hunt groups challenge the mythical view of the fox as a pest. The Ministry of Agriculture considers lamb losses to foxes to be insignificant nationally and most surveys show that only 0.5–2 per cent of lamb mortalities are due to foxes. In such cases expert shooting is a more immediate and more efficient method of destruction than a fox hunt. All the groups agree that many of the alternative methods for fox control, such as snaring, poisoning and gassing, are also inhumane, but do not see this as any justification for hunting foxes with hounds. It is also argued that the fox is useful to the farmer as a natural predator of voles, rabbits and other 'pests'.

Hunting is claimed by its supporters to be an effective and humane way of controlling foxes, but on average each hunt goes out three times per week, giving an average of about 11,000 outings per season nationally, accounting for 12–13,000 foxes per year, which is approximately 2.5 per cent of the total fox population. This low number would seem to refute the argument that fox hunting is necessary as a form of pest control.

Hunting hounds are bred for stamina and are capable of running at slow speeds over long distances, thus encouraging a protracted chase. The fox, in contrast, is more naturally suited to short bursts of speed. Even if there were a case for hunting foxes with dogs, it would be far more humane to use fast breeds such as greyhounds or lurchers which can chase and kill a fox in minutes. A hunt will last several hours.

Other criticisms regarding cruelty are also levelled at hunts, such as the practice of hunting in March and April when many of the vixens are heavily pregnant or lactating; the sending of terriers after a fox that has gone to ground, resulting in injury and/or death to both dogs and foxes; the bolting of a fox from underground in order to prolong the chase; the throwing of the fox to the hounds instead of shooting it; the killing of domestic cats and dogs by rampaging hounds, and the disturbance and distress caused to farm livestock such as pregnant sheep and cows. Other allegations against the hunt include the importation of 'bagged' (previously captured) foxes into areas where there is a shortage, and the breeding of foxes specifically for hunting, with hunts building artificial fox earths.

Again, one of the arguments advanced in favour of fox hunting in recent years is that a valuable contribution towards conservation is being made by preserving coverts which provide wildlife habitat. However, the Report for the Standing Conference on Countryside Sports [page 140] concluded that the least important reason given by farmers for the planting or the retention of cover was the provision of fox coverts. Conservationists and welfarists are also concerned about the damage and disturbance to wildlife and their habitats caused by large numbers of hounds, horses, foot followers and vehicles involved in a hunt crossing the countryside. Naturalists have challenged the practice of stopping up and digging out badger setts to reach foxes, thus adversely affecting the badger and its habitat which are both protected by various Acts of Parliament [pages 128, 129 and 135].

Over the years the League Against Cruel Sports (LACS) [page 196] has taken up in the courts the cause of those people who have unsuccesfully tried to prohibit the hunt from their property. Approximately 120 local councils have banned fox hunts from their land.

HARE COURSING

Hare coursing takes place between 15 September and 10 March, the high point of the season being the Waterloo Cup held at Altcar, Liverpool every February. There are approximately twenty coursing clubs with an estimated 1,000 regular followers in the UK, although around 10,000 are usually attracted to the big event. Coursing involves the flushing out of hares which are then driven by beaters towards the coursing field. Two dogs, usually greyhounds, are then released by the 'slipper' with the aim of giving the hare an 80-metre start. Judges award the dogs marks for their skill and performance in turning, catching and killing the hare. The hare may or may not escape. If the dogs catch the hare, the handlers – if they get there quickly enough – will despatch it by breaking its neck. Or the dogs kill it. An estimated 600–1,000 hares are killed every year by coursing.

In Northern Ireland and Eire the practice of 'closed' or park hare coursing continues. Here the coursing field is enclosed, ensuring that the hare does not escape and capture is inevitable. Bolt-holes are provided in the barriers but escape is into cages so that the hares may be re-used. Cats have been used as coursing prey in the UK.

Rights and Wrongs

The supporters of hare coursing claim that no suffering is involved as the hare (thought of as a pest) is killed quickly, but numerous filmed accounts demonstrate this to be fallacious. If the two dogs get to the hare at the same time, a tug of war can ensue, and prior to death the hare can only be in a state of terror. It is argued that the case for pest control by coursing is bogus as hares are very rare in many areas into which the species is introduced to provide sport.

HARE HUNTING

Hares are hunted from October through to March with beagles, bassetts or harriers, the two former followed out on foot, whilst harriers are followed on horseback. There are approximately eighty packs of beagles, over twenty packs of harriers and a dozen packs of bassetts, with some 7,000 followers, in the UK. An estimated 6,000 hares a year are killed by hunts.

Rights and Wrongs

The BFSS [page 212] claims that most hares escape and that the hunting is selective, the hounds catching and despatching quickly only diseased and older animals. But here again, welfare groups argue that using dogs of great stamina to hunt an animal adapted to short fast sprints is cruel and unnatural. Additionally, the hunting season does not end until after some litters of leverets have been born, thus any does killed may leave orphaned and dependent young.

The hare population is in a serious state of decline, mostly due to habitat destruction and direct slaughter. Hares breed in the centre of fields and so are at risk from farm machinery, agrochemicals and other disturbances. According to the Game Conservancy's [page 214] research, hunting does not have an appreciable effect on the hare population, but with over 100 packs hunting as many as three times a week through the season, plus the thousands of hares shot and others killed by legal and illegal coursing, the hare population has little chance to recover and may become endangered.

MINK HUNTING

Mink hunting takes place from March/April through September/October as a successor to otter hunting which has been illegal since 1978 due to the otter's status as an endangered species. As a result, many of the old otter hunts turned their attentions to mink and there are now sixteen registered packs of mink hounds plus around five unregistered ones. Packs hunt about twice a week with rarely more than a dozen supporters out on any one hunt. An estimated 400 mink a year are killed, though what percentage of the total mink population that represents is unknown. The mink is hunted along its riverbank habitat by hounds followed on foot.

Rights and Wrongs

Mink are not indigenous to the UK but were introduced as farmed animals for fur [page 70]: the wild population is the result of some animals having escaped or been liberated. The mink is now considered a pest, blamed for attacks on chickens and ducks, game birds and fish, and is reckoned to be in need of strict control.

The welfare lobby argues against the use of dogs and the bolting of the mink from trees or other cover when it is exhausted, in order to prolong the hunt. The practice is cruel and pointless. As in the case of the fox, extermination programmes only lead to an influx of neighbouring mink taking over the vacant territories.

Because the mink and otter are riverside creatures, hunting with dogs in these habitats disturbs the latter to such a degree that it prevents them from breeding, as was highlighted by the Nature Conservancy Council (now English Nature [page 213]) in its otter survey at the time of the otter hunting ban (1978). Rioting hounds, out of the control of the master, may kill the wrong quarry species, including the otter.

The Ministry of Agriculture, Fisheries and Food (MAFF) [page 216] recommends cage trapping where mink are seen as a problem and that they should then be shot at point-blank range while captive.

It has also been estimated that hunts in general are responsible for the destruction of around 14,000 hounds per season, consisting of those puppies not good enough to join the pack, and adult hounds having reached the end of their working lives at five to six years of age.

RACING

The racing of animals has long been a favourite British sport, almost certainly due to the emphasis placed on betting on the outcome of the races and to the royal patronage enjoyed by racing. Across the world all sorts of animal species are raced against each other, with the UK specializing in horse, pigeon, and dog racing. Camels are raced in Arab countries, pigs in the USA, and even frogs and snails are raced in some places, though on a less organized scale. Aside from the belief of the animal rights movement that animals have the basic right not to be raced at all, there must always be concern for their welfare in situations where vested financial interests override all else. The use of drugged animals in all forms of racing is one example of this.

HORSES

The racehorse is greatly revered and often treated with great care and specialist knowledge while in training or at stud, but the fate of the unsuccessful lies in seedy auction rings around the country. The thoroughbred is not a hardy breed of horse, and as such can face great suffering when it finds itself in an inexperienced home where its special needs are not met.

There is concern that at some racing events, such as the Grand National, horses are raced over too great a distance, with fences and ditches which are too formidable (though some of these have been modified due to pressure from the welfare lobby). It is not unusual for horses taking part in these events to have to be destroyed as the result of injury (over twenty in Grand Nationals since 1954), and the pursuit of prize money has seen animals driven on to the post, even when lame, by excessive use of the whip.

The Jockey Club [page 215] is the body governing racing in the UK and its Rules of Racing identify improper uses of the whip, including striking the horse anywhere other than on the hindquarters or on the shoulders except in exceptional circumstances (e.g. to stop the horse crossing another's path or to prevent biting). However, while a winning jockey might be suspended for his excesses, the place and prize money often still stand. The League Against Cruel Sports (LACS) [page 196] has suggested that an improvement would be for the Jockey Club to adopt Norwegian rules which allow jockeys to carry whips but insist that they do not take their hands off the reins to use them. Whipping is thus heavily restricted.

That animal-whipping is considered acceptable by the racing fraternity and the general public is another example of how easily institutionalized animal abuse can be wilfully ignored.

DOGS

Recently, dogs have been bred in Ireland (with the aid of EC and Irish government grants) for export to Spanish race tracks where they are allegedly abused. A continuing trade is still suspected despite the Irish greyhound racing board's export ban of October 1991. Some discarded greyhounds have ended their days in laboratories, as exposed in 1989 by British Union for the Abolition of Vivisection (BUAV) [page 180] undercover work.

RODEOS

Rodeos are very popular in the USA and Canada, having evolved from the days when cowboys practised their skills for their own entertainment, to the modern-day mass spectator sport packaged as show business.

Attempts to introduce the rodeo to the UK led to the implementation of the Protection of Animals Act 1934 [page 111], which makes illegal those acts which form the basis of competition in rodeos: steer and bronco riding, steer roping, wrestling and bulldogging. Bucking competitions are especially cruel as they involve the use of spurs and of a cinch, a strap drawn tightly round the animal's sensitive hind belly. In recent years in Cornwall rodeo-style events have been staged involving wild ponies rounded up off the moors.

SHOOTING

There are many different types of shooting, from the single farmer with his gun (and dog) potting a few rabbits, through the vast numbers of 'pest' species shot to protect crops, to the organized business shoot where artificially reared birds are flushed out to fly over waiting guns. The latter sport is an expensive pastime, with much capital invested in bird rearing and release.

Many species of bird are shot for sport: game birds (grouse, ptarmigan, capercaillie, pheasant, black game); wild birds (snipe, woodcock, ducks such as widgeon, tufted duck, teal, mallard, plover, gadwall, pintail, common pochard and shoveller); wild geese (Canada, greylag, pink-footed, white-fronted), and others (coot, moorhen and golden plover). The annual 'bag' in the UK is at least 18 million.

Fallow, Muntjac, red, roe and Sika deer are also shot in Forestry Commission culls in various parts of the UK, and herds and ranges are managed, most notably in the Scottish Highlands, to provide commercial shooting for trophies (antlers) and venison. Some 100,000 deer are thus destroyed annually.

Several Acts of Parliament, some dating from the nineteenth century, govern the shooting of game, with provision made for close seasons, licences, Sunday and Christmas Day prohibition and so on. The EC Bird Directive of 1979 forbids the killing of any wild birds during their nesting seasons to avoid disturbance and to ensure that dependent chicks do not die slowly of starvation in their nests due to their parents being shot. However, the UK government, under threat of EC prosecution, still allows the year-round killing of 'opportunist' birds such as pigeons, crows, magpies, jays and starlings.

Rights and Wrongs

One of the arguments advanced by the groups promoting shooting, such as the BFSS [page 212] and the British Association for Shooting and Conservation (BASC) [page 212], is that it helps to encourage farmers and landowners to provide cover for game and thus aid conservation. This would seem to be true to some extent, although the Report for the Standing Conference on Countryside Sports [page 138] cited it as only the third most important reason for farmers both planting and retaining cover, the most important being its benefit to the landscape. However, the overriding claim made for the continuation of game shooting is its economic value in terms of revenue from business shoots, employment and the hotel trade.

While a clean kill may be the objective of those shooting, this does not always happen, and the consequent suffering cannot be justified. In other countries, such as France, Holland and Germany, there are stringent conditions related to shooting and gun licensing. Applicants have to pass tests in order to prove their proficiency and knowledge of the game laws, quarry recognition and behaviour in the field. Many would like to see these rules enforced in the UK. People who cannot shoot legally in their own country may now be coming to the UK; Scottish shoots in particular are heavily subscribed by Italian, German and Maltese businessmen.

The pressure on gamekeepers to maintain shoots as financially viable businesses has led to them killing many woodland mammals, birds and domestic pets, in order to protect the eggs and chicks of game birds. There are approximately 5,000 gamekeepers in the UK and it has been estimated that they are responsible for the deaths of around 5 million wild birds and animals every year by shooting, snaring, trapping and poisoning, often illegally. Other game bird-rearing practices include brailing (wing-taping), wing-clipping and pinioning to prevent the birds from flying, and de-beaking.

In animal rights terms, the deliberate breeding of birds merely for shooting purposes, and the killing of other species under the guise of herd 'management' or 'pest' control are possibly the most obvious examples of the human arrogance, dishonesty and lack of imagination which lie at the root of animal abuse.

SHOW JUMPING

Show jumping has flourished since the Second World War, and many of the participants have become household names and celebrities. Today, large money prizes and sponsorship have made it big business, with fierce competition at all levels. This has led to concern over the welfare of the horses involved which many people feel are forced to jump too high and too frequently. There used to be a season, finishing around October with the Horse of the Year Show, but with the advent of relatively cheap indoor schools competitions now take place all year round, and top riders are also being able to compete abroad on a regular basis.

Concern has been voiced over the use of the drug Butazolidin ('Bute'), a painkiller which has been administered to lame horses to enable them to carry on jumping. Other problem areas include the excessive use of whips and spurs, and of training practices which cause suffering. In recent years one of Germany's top riders has been at the centre of controversy after being filmed 'rapping'; hitting a horse on its legs with a pole to make it lift them higher as it goes over a fence. More recently, other riders have been suspended for using an astringent under a horse's bandages and for sticking strips of plastic with sharp, protruding points to the inside of a horse's fetlock boots (again designed to make the horse pick its feet up higher over the jump).

Similar concern has been shown over other equestrian sports such as three-day eventing, long-distance riding and polo, especially as these sports are enjoying a new popularity, which may mean that inexperienced riders and animals are involved. An average of twelve horses per year die on cross-country courses; three were destroyed after injuries sustained at Badminton in 1992.

The rights lobby insists that as with horse racing, and indeed with hunting on horseback, any serious concern for animals must at the very least question the right of humans to ride horses at all.

ZOOS

There has been a dramatic increase in the number of zoos (including wildlife parks) in the UK since the end of the Second World War when there were only fourteen. In 1959 there were thirty-one but by 1986 the figure had risen to 223 in England, with eighteen in Wales and thirteen in Scotland. Throughout the 1970s there was great concern over the safety of visitors and staff in many zoos, as well as over the welfare of the animals, which led to the government implementing the Zoo

Licensing Act 1981 [page 122]. Before this, anyone could open a zoo after obtaining planning permission from their Local Authority. While the Local Authorities are still responsible for the inspection of zoos and the issuing of licences, the Secretary of State for the Environment has specified standards of modern zoo practice which include provisions for animal welfare. For instance, the animals should be provided with sufficient space and 'furniture' to allow such exercise as is needed, relevant to the particular species. However, minimum space requirements for individual species have not been laid down.

Worldwide, zoos vary from the larger, better-kept establishments which have attempted to accommodate the needs of some of their animals, to the small private collections that open to the public only for short periods and whose budget does not allow them to do any more than keep the animals in cages. Many foreign zoos, especially, have poorly maintained enclosures and ill-treated animals. In Japan's Aso Park, for instance, where the world's largest collection of bears is held in captivity, some forty bears are kept in an enclosure smaller than a tennis court. Spare bears are incarcerated in underground pens measuring 1 x 2 metres. Certain zoos in the USA and Scandinavia where research into environmental design based on animal behaviour is given a priority, are heralded as progressive. Within Europe the European Commission [page 213] issued the Zoo Directive (1991) which lays down minimum conditions for all of the 1,000 or so zoos within the EC.

Rights and Wrongs
The argument advanced in favour of zoos by bodies such as the National Federation of Zoological Gardens of Great Britain and Ireland [page 216] is that they play an important role in research, conservation and education. Research conducted in zoos has enabled the successful breeding of some animals in captivity for re-introduction to the wild, thus making an important contribution to the conservation of certain species. Given examples are the Hawaiian goose, the Arabian oryx, the scimitar-horned oryx and the pink pigeon of Mauritius. At London Zoo, a preventive medicine database for rare and endangered species is being set up, initially for the Zoo's own species, but it is hoped eventually to collect data for some 19,000 species of mammals, birds and reptiles.

Zoos argue that although wildlife films are important in teaching an understanding of animals and their behaviour, there is no substitute for a properly displayed specimen. However, welfare and rights groups (some calling for the abolition of all zoos) concerned with captive animals have protested at the way in which the animals are managed and kept. Some believe that the answer to the conservation of endangered species does not lie in placing them in zoos as they currently exist, with attempts at reintroduction to the wild. This can only preserve a handful of species, and many are either not suitable for reintroduction, or the reasons why they became endangered in the first place, such as habitat destruction, still exist. Moreover, breeding from a small genetic pool can lead to in-bred deformities, and zoo environments are convenient breeding-grounds for diseases which may be introduced into the wild with the animals.

Captivity of wild species inevitably causes suffering; by the very fact of confinement the animals are prevented from carrying out their natural behaviours. Observed abnormal behaviour indicates the levels of stress and boredom endured by captive animals. Examples include obsessional masturbation and self-mutilation, such as tail gnawing in monkeys; obsessional self-grooming, such as that which causes baldness in parrots and other birds; rhythmic cage-pacing in big cats, foxes and wolves, and head shaking in polar bears. Such stereotyped behaviours are known to be adaptations on the part of the animal to highly stressful environments. Environments which are so barren of stimuli as to cause intense boredom are also extremely stressful.

The majority of wildlife safari parks and zoos in this country have opened up for purely commercial reasons and aim at providing a day out for the public. Some of these places are sited alongside fun fairs and other places of amusement, which again encourages the public to think of animals as a source of entertainment. Some animals are even disposed of for not being enough of an attraction.

Although wildlife parks would seem to be a better environment for animals in terms of space, for most the climate is unsuitable, it is difficult for sick animals to be identified, singled out and isolated for treatment, and inspections may not be as frequent as they should be.

In relation to the total number of zoos worldwide, or even within the UK, those carrying out research of any value are, and can only remain, very few and far between. The flaw in the zoos' arguments is that all zoos and wildlife parks hide behind them, even if they have no education, research or conservation policies. In fact, few zoos have any enlightened education programmes.

Some animals, such as lions, tigers, and certain primates, breed very well in captivity, and thus many become surplus to requirements. Even some of the best and most reputable collections offload superfluous animals on to animal dealers. Some of these animals are bought by people who do not have the necessary expertise to give them adequate care or whose motives are exploitative, such as street photographers on the Continent [page 8]. At one time there was a craze for keeping wild animals such as lions and monkeys as pets, although it is hoped that the Dangerous Wild Animals Act 1976 [page 119] has gone a long way towards limiting this trend.

Animal welfare groups, like the International Primate Protection League (IPPL) [page 193], are outraged by the growing links between zoos and research laboratories. A large number of zoos in the USA dispose of surplus primates via the National Institutes of Health, facilitating the sharing of primates among American laboratories. Experiments on animals have also been conducted by some UK zoos.

Zoo-related wildlife trade encourages the reduction of animal populations, since the capture of one young animal usually involves the killing of the mother and several others of a protective group. The worldwide trade in wildlife is a multi-million dollar industry and encourages widespread poaching; the methods of capture and transport are of additional concern.

Selected Animal Rights and Welfare Organizations
Animal Aid [page 175]
    — all issues.
Animal Liberation Front (ALF) [page 176]
    — Fishing, Hunting, Racing, Shooting.
Animaline [page 178]
    — Street Performers.
Born Free Foundation [page 179]
    — Circuses, Cetacean Displays, Zoos.
Campaign for the Abolition of Angling (CAA) [page 181]
    — Fishing.
Captive Animals Protection Society (CAPS) [page 181]
    — Bullfighting, Circuses.
Care for the Wild [page 191]
    — Circuses, Cetacean Displays, Hunting, Zoos.
Donkey Sanctuary [page 185]
    — Fiestas.
Fight Against Animal Cruelty in Europe [page 188]
    — Fiestas.
Hunt Saboteurs Association (HSA) [page 191]
    — Fishing, Hunting, Shooting.

International Dolphin Watch [page 192]
    — **Cetacean Displays.**
International Fund for Animal Welfare (IFAW) [page 193]
    — **Fiestas, Hunting.**
International Primate Protection League (IPPL) [page 193]
    — **Street Performers, Zoos.**
League Against Cruel Sports (LACS) [page 196]
    — **Fighting, Hunting, Racing, Show Jumping, Shooting.**
Royal Society for the Prevention of Cruelty to Animals (RSPCA) [page 204] — **all issues.**
Whale and Dolphin Conservation Society (WDCS) [page 210]
    — **Cetacean Displays.**
World Society for the Protection of Animals (WSPA) [page 210]
    — **Bullfighting, Fiestas.**
Zoo Check [page 211]
    — **Cetacean Displays, Zoos.**

Chapter Two
ANIMAL EXPERIMENTATION

The subject of animal experimentation provokes highly conflicting views. On the one hand, the anti-vivisection lobby wants all experiments on animals banned immediately or quickly phased out, on the grounds that there is no ethical or scientific justification for them. On the other hand, some scientists involved in animal experimentation defend what they see as their right to conduct any experiment in the search for knowledge. Between the two are those who consider that compromises must be made in order to progress towards radical reduction of the number of animals used in laboratories.

Worldwide, over 100 million animals are used in experiments every year. In the UK, approximately 3 million are currently used annually, with around 17,000 persons holding licences to conduct experiments in some 380 licensed establishments. Figures for the UK are published each year by the Home Office in *Statistics of Scientific Procedures on Living Animals, Great Britain* and by the DHSS in *Statistics of Scientific Procedures on Living Animals, Northern Ireland* [page 142].

The range of experimentation procedures includes burning, scalding, poisoning, shooting, disease inducement, bone-breaking, electric shocks, organ removal/transplant, deprivation and irradiation. Lists of the facilities and people licensed to conduct experiments on animals are no longer widely available.

Legislation Worldwide

Laboratory animal legislation varies from being totally non-existent in some countries like Japan, where atrocious conditions have been reported, to the UK's Animals (Scientific Procedures) Act 1986 which is considered to be part of the most tightly regulated system in the world (see below [and page 123]).

In 1987, the European Community (EC) became signatory to the European Convention for the Protection of Vertebrate Animals Used for Experimental and Other Scientific Purposes, requiring each of the twenty-three Council of Europe member countries [page 213] to pass national laws enforcing its provisions. By UK standards, these are extremely weak and member countries were not obliged to ratify the Convention. However, the EC Directive, On the Approximation of Laws, Regulations and Administrative Provision of the Members States Regarding the Protection of Animals Used for Experimental and Other Scientific Purposes, is enforceable in the twelve EC member states [page 213].

Eurogroup for Animal Welfare [page 186] points out that the Directive, as a regulatory measure, does have several strengths: it allows the infliction of 'only' momentary pain or distress on an unanaesthetized animal (there are certain stringent exceptions); insists that the staff handling the animals should be properly trained; allows the use of primates only in solving serious medical problems, and rules that the care of the animals be in the hands of a named person who has the authority to terminate improperly conducted experiments.

However, the Directive also has certain weaknesses. For example, it still allows pain and suffering to be inflicted as long as the experiment is properly conducted. Eurogroup also insists that each member of the EC be made to institute a proper and effective method of implementation. The Directive not only permits school children to use living animals, but allows experimenters to give only thirty days' notice to the appropriate authority before the start of an experiment. The Directive may, however, afford some benefit to laboratory animals in countries where legislation is minimal, e.g. Greece, Italy and France, and in others where it is non-existent, e.g. Spain and Portugal.

Laboratory animal legislation was not enacted in the USA until 1966 by the Animal Welfare Act which, despite certain amendments and additional control exerted by funding agencies, is poorly enforced and affords little protection, some species being excluded entirely. Instead, the Freedom of Information Act has provided a means of public scrutiny that would be additionally welcomed in the UK. This Act has been used by activists in the USA to obtain information about the work of certain experimenters.

Legislation in the UK

Animal experimentation in the UK was regulated for over a century by the Cruelty to Animals Act 1876 [page 104] which has now been replaced by the Animals (Scientific Procedures) Act 1986 [page 123]. The passage of the 1986 Act through Parliament was accompanied by great controversy. Animal rights organizations formed an alliance to combat the Bill and many others joined in the condemnation of what they saw as the 'Vivisectors' Charter'. They still believe the Act to have been a largely retrograde step, with certain procedures that were previously not permissible now being allowed, such as the re-use of animals under certain circumstances, and the use of rodents for the practice of manual surgical skills.

Furthermore, the Act fails to circumscribe any established experiments despite huge public concern over certain procedures. It fails to encourage the replacement of animals in the long term or to give laboratory animals greater protection, extends no protection to cephalopods (e.g. octopus and squid) and does not demand greater accountability from scientists.

However, bodies like the British Veterinary Association (BVA) [page 212)], the Committee for the Reform of Animal Experimentation (CRAE) [page 183] and the Fund for the Replacement of Animals in Medical Experiments (FRAME) [page 188] worked with the government towards passing the Bill, attempting, with some success, to make it more stringent. While they also have been criticized for doing so, they consider the Act to be the start of a new relationship with the scientific community, aiming at the reduction, refinement and eventual replacement of animals in research.

Rights and Wrongs

Scientists involved in the use of animals in research have their interests represented by such organizations as the Research Defence Society (RDS) [page 216], the British Psychological Society [page 212], the British Association for the Advancement of Science [page 212], and the Royal Society [page 216].

These bodies claim that no scientist enjoys causing suffering to animals but that whilst few or no alternatives exist, animal experimentation is necessary in order to advance knowledge and discover cures for both human and animal diseases. They point to the reduction in the number of animals used over the past fifteen years, from 5.5 million in 1975 to 3.16 million in 1991, as an indication of the scientific community's commitment to minimize the use of animals. They also stress that due to the high cost of animals, researchers are restricted by pure economic necessity.

One of the two main arguments against animal experimentation asserts that it is morally wrong deliberately to cause pain and suffering to sentient creatures. The term 'speciesism', first coined by anti-vivisectionist Richard D. Ryder [page 143], is often used to describe the prejudices, thought to have no logical or moral basis, which humans hold against other animals and which permit all kinds of experiments to be conducted on them. The other argument concerns scientific and medical invalidity.

Animal-based research in medical and veterinary science is a practice that some people still consider to be justified, although the anti-vivisection movement asserts that this is due to the vivisectionist propaganda issued by such bodies as the Research Defence Society, and the lack of public information and education. Some medical researchers continue to claim that, overall, the advantages have far outweighed the disadvantages, with many new drugs and cures for diseases discovered as a result of using animals. However, animals are not good indicators of the effects substances will have on humans; differences between species mean that animal-based research is generally inappropriate, unreliable and in many cases dangerous. After passing their toxicity tests on animals, many drugs have been released on to the market with tragic consequences for humans. The long list includes Chloramphenicol, Eraldin, Opren, Ibufenac, Flosint, Zelmid, Osmosin, Corwin and Clioquinol over all of which lengthy compensation battles have been fought. Moreover, it has been estimated by Social Audit [page 217] that one hospital patient in twenty has been made ill by prescribed (animal-tested) medicines.

Cancer research has been an area of particular controversy, with some experts again expressing the opinion that little relevant knowledge can be obtained from animal studies, since malign animal tumours are not the same as any cancer in humans. The billions of pounds channelled into such research have yielded very few results of any worth and mortalities from cancer continue to rise. In 1991, 46,850 experiments involving the deliberate inducement of cancer in animals were undertaken in the UK. Radiation poisoning is yet another area where inter-species variability makes extrapolation of results almost impossible. Experimental results from animal research vary widely not only between different species but also between different individuals and even between different experimental facilities.

While some drugs do not affect animals adversely as they do humans, others affect animals only. Examples include penicillin, aspirin, streptomycin and chlorpromazine. It has been repeatedly pointed out that if these and other drugs had relied solely on animal tests to gain their validity, they would never have become the major therapeutic agents they are today. Compounding this problem is the countless number of useful drugs lost to humans due to them causing adverse reactions in animal tests. Animal rights scientists believe that tissue culture, clinical trials, post-mortems where possible, and the use of human volunteers lead to more valid and applicable results in medical research than do animal tests. Many also regard the infliction of disease or injury on healthy animals to be immoral as well as unrealistic, especially in cases where there are many people already naturally or accidentally afflicted, e.g. with burns, and on whom clinical observations would be possible.

One of the reasons why so many animals are used for testing is the duplication of experiments resulting from the proliferation of 'me too' products. Rival pharmaceutical companies attempt to fill the same niche in the market with lucrative drugs, thus increasing the number of animal tests (this is also the case in the toiletries and cosmetics industries, see below). Animal experimentation is big business. Wealthy drug companies are in a strong position to influence governments, scientists, doctors and the general public regarding not only the 'need' for more cures and more animal experiments, but also in perpetuating the myth of their success. Welfarists believe that if companies would share their knowledge, for example through a shared databank system, the lives of many animals could be spared.

Many major medical advances did not involve or need animal experiments: the virtual eradication of many diseases, e.g. typhoid, TB, whooping cough, measles, scarlet fever and diphtheria, owed more to social and sanitary reforms than to animal-researched vaccinations. Innovations such as hygienic surgery, the discovery of anaesthetics, and the connections established between heart disease and human lifestyle, are further examples of non-animal-based progress.

It has been argued that the world does not need more, increasingly sophisticated drugs and cures; instead, if all the current knowledge on health and disease was implemented more efficiently, and health education undertaken more effectively, overall world health would improve drastically. An outstanding example of this is smoking.

The connection between cigarette smoking and lung cancer has long been known and recent research also suggests a strong link between passive smoking and cancer. The obvious answer is to take positive steps to encourage and help people to stop smoking, but the tobacco industry still ensures that animal experimentation into this area continues. In recent years it has also promoted the sale of chewing tobacco, using studies conducted on rats to convince the public that this is safer than actual smoking. Implanted wads of the tobacco failed to cause oral cancers in rats, yet this result is the opposite of that predicted in human studies.

AREAS OF PARTICULAR CONCERN

Although all forms of animal experimentation are anathema to the animal rights ethic, several areas of animal experimentation in particular have given rise to major concern among many people.

THE USE OF UNANAESTHETIZED ANIMALS

In the UK, the proportion of experiments involving animals in which no anaesthetic is used, either for part or all of the experiment, is 65–70 per cent (2.2 million in 1991) of the total. In other countries which do not possess laboratory animal protection of any kind the situation is far worse. While many of the animals used in this way will have been subjected to only mild discomfort, others will have been involved in painful and/or stressful experiments.

Even when anaesthetics are used there is further cause for concern as the field of anaesthesia is a highly complex one. Various stages of consciousness are possible in an anaesthetized animal, so that if neuromuscular blocking agents have also been used, it may be sensible to pain and suffering yet unable to respond. Some of the substances used as anaesthetics would not be permissible for use on humans.

THE USE OF ANIMALS IN NON-ESSENTIAL RESEARCH

Non-medical research is seen by most people as non-essential and its use of animals unjustifiable, as in the testing of products such as cosmetics, air fresheners, shampoos, face creams, soaps, pesticides and insecticides. In the case of cosmetics and toiletries especially, many are not only tested on animals but also contain animal ingredients such as whale, civet and musk oil. A central argument here is that there are already hundreds of these products on the market and we do not need any more new ones. All products should in any case be tested by non-animal methods, and an increasing number of companies now produce cosmetics (and other products) without resorting to the use of animals at all (see Farhall, Lucas, Rofe (1991) [page 157]).

Current animal research in this category can be categorized as follows.

PRODUCT TESTING

In the UK, around 250,000 animals are used every year to test the toxicity of non-medical products. In order to put a potentially dangerous product on the market a company has to show that it has passed standard toxicity tests on the basis that it is necessary to know the acute and longer-term effects of the product in the event of accidental ingestion by humans. Anti-vivisectionists have claimed that such testing is performed more to reduce manufacturers' liability than to establish product safety. It is standard practice not to administer painkillers to the test animals during the experiments as these could affect the final results. One toxicity test in particular, the LD50 (see below), has been heavily condemned.

The Lethal Dose 50 per cent Test (LD50)

The LD50 is an *in vivo* test which has been used for over sixty years, although its requirement in the testing of new drugs was dropped in the 1980s. It involves the administering of a single dose of varying strength to several groups of animals, generally fifty to sixty rodents, although a range of species – dogs (usually beagles), rabbits, cats and monkeys – is sometimes chosen. The dose is administered by force-feeding, application to abraded skin or by inhalation.

A dose range is chosen to produce a significant number of deaths in the group receiving the largest dose, with the aim of discovering the dosage at which 50 per cent of the animals die within fourteen days. The results gained from the LD50 are regarded by many as highly irrelevant, given inter-species variability. Other toxicity tests involve the long-term administration of products to observe the chronic toxic effects.

The Draize Eye Irritancy Test

This notorious test involves the instilling of a test substance into the eyes of restrained rabbits. Rabbits are unable to wash away the substance due to their poor tear production, and there have been cases of animals breaking their backs while struggling to escape. The difference between the rabbit's and the human eye, the individual variability of results and the subjective assessment of the damage done to rabbits' eyes, has led to widespread condemnation of this test on scientific grounds alone.

In 1986, following the passing of the Animals (Scientific Procedures) Act [page 123], the Home Office published new guidelines on the use of eye irritancy and corrosion tests, aimed at reducing animal suffering. They include the suggestions that the use of systemic analgesics be considered; that substances which cause severe reactions in skin irritancy tests, or in *in vitro* tests, should not be tested in eyes; and that animals showing severe ocular damage, or severe distress or pain that cannot be alleviated, should be killed by approved methods. The guidelines are not binding, however.

WARFARE EXPERIMENTS

The use of living animals to develop protective measures against attack in human warfare is morally indefensible in the eyes of many people. Such experiments involve the use of nerve gas, radiation, bacterial agents, ultrasonic weapons, and the more conventional ballistic weapons.

In the UK, establishments which conduct such research receive Crown immunity excusing them from compliance with the legislation covering animal experimentation, and so are free from inspection and prosecution under the 1986 Act, although the Ministry of Defence claims to comply with it. About half the establishments are government-owned, the most infamous being at Porton Down in Wiltshire. Between 1974 and 1977, over 800 animals were used in CS gas experiments there, and sheep, pigs, monkeys, mice, guinea-pigs, rats and dogs were involved in over 500 wounding experiments between 1978 and 1984. In 1987, some 9,200 warfare experiments were conducted on animals in the UK.

Anti-vivisectionists suspect that due to the secrecy surrounding such research the actual numbers of animals used could be much higher than those given. Animals are also used in the training of surgeons in manual skills for treating wounds. Doctors specializing in war wounds have questioned the validity of these experiments.

BEHAVIOURAL AND PSYCHOLOGICAL EXPERIMENTS

The range of experiments covered under this heading is wide. Ethologists mainly observe their subjects in their natural environment or living freely, using non-invasive techniques which cause less concern. However, psychology experiments have become infamous due to the various methods psychologists have evolved to create different mental states in animals, such as fear, aggression, apathy and frustration, and also to the negative reinforcement training procedures, using electric shocks. The use of primates in such experiments [page 38] has caused perhaps the most outrage.

Abolitionists believe that these experiments should not be conducted on animals on the grounds that they are either so dissimilar to humans that extrapolations from the results are useless, or so similar to humans that they have the same capacity to suffer and it is therefore immoral to use them as experimental tools. The research is reckoned to be of no medical benefit, and would be better conducted in the light of human example and experience.

In their defence, scientists claim that their animal research has led to the improvement of social conditions for both humans and animals, and the acquisition of valuable information. A cited example here is study of how the loss of a mother early in life causes long-term mental and physical disorders, for which effective therapy has been developed and practised. However, enough humans have suffered the loss of a mother in early life for them to be the subjects of such research instead of the trauma being induced in animals. Moreover, despite the rather predictable findings, animals themselves are still routinely separated from their mothers – in livestock agriculture, for example – which would again seem to render animal experimentation invalid. However, animal research also claims responsibility for improvements in animal housing design in zoos, farms and laboratories; in the assessment of animal health, and in the conservation of wildlife.

AGRICULTURAL EXPERIMENTS

Animal farming is already too intensive, certain (if not all rearing) practices should be abolished, and research on livestock is conducted merely to increase profit. Such strongly held beliefs underpin anti-vivisectionist demands for an end to government funding of research establishments which are considered to be conducting often bizarre research of dubious value, especially that designed to increase productivity. Criticized work in recent years has included embryo transplants, cross-fertilization of species, and the use of hormones to increase yields. [See also pages 59–60]. In the light of the current stock-piling of EC surpluses, such research would seem to be frivolous.

Agricultural research also attempts to increase crop productivity, developing new formulations of pesticides, herbicides, fungicides, hormone regulators, and so on. Under the current legislation these have to be tested for toxicity, thus involving animals in procedures such as the LD50 and irritancy tests [page 35].

SUMMARY

The use of animals in non-essential experiments continues to be a very controversial issue, with even the subject of what is and what is not essential remaining a matter for debate. The Animals (Scientific Procedures) Act 1986 [page 123] makes the Secretary of State for the Home Office responsible for balancing the possible human benefits of all experiments against the adverse effects on the animals involved.

Applications for projects involving cosmetics are examined by the Animal Procedures Committee [page 212]. In February 1992, the European Parliament voted in favour of the proposal to ban cosmetic tests on animals. At the time of writing the proposal still had to be discussed with the European Commission and referred to the Council of Ministers. A ban on such tests could become law by 1994.

THE USE OF PRIMATES

Animals of high intelligence, with complex social behaviour patterns and well-developed sensory systems, non-human primates can endure great suffering when housed under laboratory conditions even before they are subjected to any experimental procedures. Their strong evolutionary link with humans lends strength to the claim that it is morally wrong to experiment upon these animals in particular. As Carl Sagan asks in *The Dragons of Eden*, ' How smart does a chimpanzee have to be before killing him constitutes murder?'

In the UK, the Cruelty to Animals Act 1876 [page 104] originally gave no special protection to primates as at that time very few were used in experiments. However, their laboratory use in the UK increased dramatically during the twentieth century and a condition was latterly attached to licences under that Act requiring special justification of primate use. Only in the past few years has the number used decreased, although approximately 75 per cent of the 2,764 monkeys used (some more than once) in 1991 had been obtained from the wild. Under the Animals (Scientific Procedures) Act 1986 [page 123] primates are afforded the same protection as dogs, cats and horses, i.e. they should be used only when it is considered that no other species is suitable for the intended research.

The use of primates has been especially popular in the field of psychology where concern has been expressed over the use of the restraining chair which disallows any movement of the head or limbs. Some animals have been kept in these devices for many weeks. In 1991, a report by Advocates for Animals [page 174] exposed a wide range of procedures conducted on non-human primates which the organization claimed were not acceptable even under the terms of the 1986 Act; the futility of the experiments could not possibly justify the extreme suffering inflicted.

Another argument against the use of primates is that many species are endangered, with only limited numbers now living wild. Jordan and Ormrod (1978) [page 141] claimed that even at that time seventeen species of primate were threatened with extinction as a result of the trade in laboratory animals.

Chimpanzees

Chimpanzees are much in demand for research into hepatitis and Aids, it being supposed that these diseases can be researched effectively with the species. However, there is a problem with housing both infected and uninfected individuals; they present a hazard to humans, and are also expensive to obtain and keep. Although chimps have a life span in the wild of forty to fifty years, they are slow breeders that do not respond well to captivity, and attempts to speed up breeding by removing nursing babies have been unsuccessful as these hand-reared youngsters then fail to reproduce on reaching puberty. Thus, as is the case with many apes and monkeys, the attempts to establish breeding colonies have largely failed, leading to the taking of animals from the wild, depleting the wild breeding population.

Trade in Primates

As few as two in ten of the monkeys captured in the wild in Indonesia, the Philippines and the rain forests of South East Asia survive to reach their destination, according to the British Union for the Abolition of Vivisection (BUAV) [page 180]. The animals die from disease, are killed during trapping, are slaughtered and eaten having been deemed unsuitable for research, or starve to death in cramped storage and transport cages.

While most species of primate are covered by the Convention on International Trade in Endangered Species (CITES) [page 213], this is often flouted. With large-scale smuggling and poaching, and some countries not signatory to CITES openly trading in the animals, chimpanzees for instance are now threatened with extinction, even though traffic in them has been banned for some fifteen years.

Malaysia banned the export of primates for use in research after discovering that some 12 per cent of the 20,000 primates in the USA were being used for military research. In 1990 the USA banned chimpanzee imports.

THE USE OF PETS

The stealing or other procurement of pet animals for use in animal experimentation has been a cause of concern and distress for many years. In the UK, and especially prior to the 1986 Act, the number of animals bought from casual animal dealers was estimated at 30 per cent of the total of animals used in experiments each year. The original source of such animals has troubled welfarists, who point to the high number of pets that go missing every year as indicating that not all of them were killed in accidents or strayed.

Large commercial concerns wish to protect their public image and so mostly breed their own experimental animals or buy in from accredited breeders. However, universities and colleges especially have been accused of buying stolen pets 'at the back door'. A raid by one of the animal liberation groups on Sheffield University in the 1980s released a pet dog called Blackie, who was later reunited with his owners. The Animal Liberation Front (ALF) [page 176] and others believe that many of the dogs and cats they have released from laboratories have been pets at some time, the dogs often responding to commonplace commands.

Under the 1986 Act, protected animals such as dogs, cats, primates, rabbits, hamsters, guinea pigs, rats and mice, should be purpose-bred and obtained from a licensed breeding/supplying establishment. It was hoped that this would go some way towards stopping the pet stealing trade in the UK, although National Petwatch [page 200] and other organizations believe that there are many other reasons why pets are stolen. In many states of the USA stray pets not claimed from pounds are sold to experimental establishments. On the other hand some states now have similar legislation to the UK's, requiring the use of purpose-bred animals only.

Due to their emotional attachment to humans, pets are even more sensitive to life in a laboratory which entails confinement in cages, limited contact with humans or members of their own species, and often total isolation, in addition to any experimental procedures conducted on them. Some experimenters argue that the use of pets, with their unknown origins, health status and lack of history details, can cause invalid results, whilst others argue for access to as large a mixed genetic pool of random animals as possible. Pet stealing in the USA and in Canada is also rife.

PATENTED ANIMALS

A newer development causing widespread consternation is the genetic engineering of animals to produce strains specifically designed for use in research. In 1988, the first patent for a living mammal was granted in the USA for the onco-mouse, a transgenic animal made susceptible to tumours by inserting an oncogene into it at the embryo stage. In 1991, the European Patent Office also allowed the patent, possibly opening the door for 'brand-name' animals.

More recently, plans have been announced for the breeding of herds of genetically engineered pigs to provide organs for human transplant operations. Scientists involved consider the work to be above criticism as long as ham sandwiches continue to be eaten. The animal rights position is obvious: the existence of one evil does not justify the creation of another. Moreover, the scientists' argument would not seem to be applicable in the case of the onco-mouse.

THE USE OF ANIMALS IN EDUCATION

In the UK the law does not permit any experiment to be conducted in schools which might cause pain, distress or suffering to a live verte-brate, although dissection of dead animals is permitted. However, in the USA and other countries there is no such legislation, and school children are encouraged to experiment on living animals such as rats, frogs, cats and rabbits.

Controversy over animal use in UK education has been fuelled by the National Anti-Vivisection Society's (NAVS) [page 198] Violence-Free Science campaign and more recently by Animal Aid's [page 175] Campaign for Ethical Science. Dissection is no longer required by GCSE and A level examination boards. The campaigns are also aimed at university students in order to encourage them to adopt a charter which protects those science students who refuse to dissect or carry out animal experiments from being penalized academically. Student unions are obliged to act if universities do not give assurances to this effect.

Young people are easily desensitized to the suffering of animals and the use of animals in schools can encourage them to view other species as disposable resources. Anti-vivisectionists also hold that it leads to the waste of animal life. Teaching can be made efficient and humane with the use of aids such as videos and computer simulations.

Other bodies, like the Association for Science Education [page 212], on the other hand, believe that keeping live animals (and using dead ones) in schools is essential to the development of a proper under-standing of animals' needs. They also maintain that while pupils should be encouraged to discuss the moral, educational and scientific issues involved, they should also be advised to consider carefully the career implications involved in not doing dissection.

In postgraduate education, students can be driven by personal am-bition to perform animal experiments. To gain a doctorate a student may be involved in research that has no value other than helping the student obtain that qualification; refusal to participate may also lead to academic failure.

Alternatives to Animal Experimentation

There is a growing awareness within the scientific community of the need to find alternatives to animal experiments to fulfil the three aims – reduction, refinement and replacement – first set by Russell and Burch (1959) [page 143]. Some scientists, disregarding ethical objection, are adamant that there will always be a need for the use of animals and that it will be many years before alternatives can go even a small way towards replacing them. Successive governments have been slow to promote non-animal research, but a number of organizations are actively involved in the development of humane alternatives, such as the Dr Hadwen Trust for Humane Research [page 184], the Humane Research Trust (HRT) [page 190], and the Lord Dowding Fund [page 197].

Alternatives currently available include: mathematical modelling of structure–activity relationships and biochemical and physiological processes; computer graphics; human studies; *in vitro* techniques; improved storage, exchange and use of information; and improved design of experiments. Many of these have already proved to be at least as, if not more, accurate than animal tests and have reduced the number of animals used.

Animal Review Committees

As long as experimenters are working within the law, they seem quite content to leave unanswered the hard ethical questions posed by animal experimentation. Veterinarians especially have been condemned for their refusal to be drawn into the debate on the moral implications of such work. There has been a suggestion that while legislation cannot force this issue, the appointment of animal research review committees can. These have been set up in many countries such as Sweden where they have been mandatory for over five years, and Canada where they are voluntary with the exception of two states where they are mandatory.

There has been interest over their introduction into the UK in order to review animal research protocols, but the response to this suggestion has been negative. The scientific community appears to regard any outside interference with great suspicion, especially when such committees which do exist have the lay public represented. The Home Office also sees no advantage in having these committees. However, they could be used to alleviate some of the burden of the work of the Home Office Inspectors, of whom there are only nineteen to cover almost 400 research establishments in the UK. There have been accusations in the past that due to the large number of applications for licences to conduct experiments on animals there has been a certain amount of 'rubber stamping'. Those who disagree point out that countries like Sweden do not possess the legislative controls that the UK does, which they see as sufficient, and that conflict could occur between the committees and the Home Office Inspectorate.

Selected Animal Rights and Welfare Organizations

Advocates for Animals [page 174]
Animal Aid [page 175]
Animal Concern [page 175]
British Union for the Abolition of Vivisection (BUAV) [page 180]
Dr Hadwen Trust for Humane Research [page 184]
Humane Research Trust (HRT) [page 190]
National Anti-Vivisection Society (NAVS) [page 198]

Chapter Three
ANIMAL PRODUCTION

ANIMALS PRODUCED FOR FOOD

Some 600–700 million farm animals are slaughtered annually for food in the UK. This number includes poultry, sheep, pigs and cattle. The majority are produced under intensive farming conditions which involve keeping large numbers of animals in close confinement, maximizing output in minimum time. These practices have been developing since before the Second World War but it was not until 1964 that they were brought to the attention of the public largely by Ruth Harrison's book, *Animal Machines* [page 146]. Such was the outcry at the time that the government was forced to act by setting up the Brambell Committee [page 145] and the Farm Animal Advisory Council, which later became the Farm Animal Welfare Council (FAWC) [page 214], leading to the preparation of the Codes of Recommendations for the Welfare of Livestock [pages 46 and 147].

Nevertheless, livestock farming systems have continued to become increasingly intensive and the first signs of a return to traditional farming methods have only manifested in the past few years in response to consumer demand for organic farm produce [page xvii]. However, this is not within the mainstream of modern farming.

Rights and Wrongs

The move away from traditional methods of farming into intensive practices has been justified on the basis of providing cheap food for the consumer, many farmers arguing that they have no choice but to compete with farmers in other EC countries [page 213] where the same practices operate. It is claimed that livestock in intensive systems benefit from the provision of shelter, food and water, and do not suffer unnecessary pain or distress. To cause such would be an offence under the Agriculture (Miscellaneous Provisions) Act 1968 [page 117] which, with its various Regulations and the Welfare Codes, is designed to protect farm animals.

However, campaigns against factory farming's maximum-output policy have highlighted the increase in animal disease, lameness, injuries and behavioural abnormalities caused by intensive systems. Farmers have resorted to further practices, e.g. tail-docking in pigs [page 51] and administration of antibiotics, in order to alleviate these symptoms.

Many people still consider livestock farming to be basically natural and acceptable, but the production of animals for human consumption is seen by others as fundamentally immoral and ethically unjustifiable. The livestock industry is the world's single largest cause of avoidable suffering. Becoming vegetarian or vegan, boycotting animal products, is part of the fight to end the production and slaughter of animals for food and other commodities. This is not just a question of animal welfare, rights and human health. Veganic farming, for instance, as promoted by the Vegan Society [page 208], is the growing of food for direct human consumption without any use of animals. Even organic farming retains a dependence on animals and thus involves the use of vast areas of land to rear and feed them which could be used more efficiently. A hectare of land growing soya will feed about 150 people, whilst a hectare sustaining cattle will feed five, and it takes at least 5 kg of grain fed to cattle to produce 0.5 kg of beef. At its most efficient, livestock agriculture can only manage a food conversion rate of around three to one, that is, three units of food in to provide one unit of food out. (And this ignores the other water and energy inputs and polluting outputs). With some seven-eighths of the world's cultivated land used to sustain farm animals, whilst millions of people are starving, the global implications of such figures can hardly be ignored.

Many welfarists accept that there is little likelihood of vegetarianism or veganism becoming dominant in the near future, and such groups as Compassion in World Farming (CIWF) [page 183], while encouraging the move towards the animal rights ethic [page xiii], generally have the shorter-term objective of improving present conditions for livestock. Close confinement is a controversial subject, one that not even scientists and farm animal behaviourists (agricultural ethologists) can agree on. The public reacts strongly to evocative pictures of chickens in cages and sows in stalls, and there is now a small but growing supply of organically produced meat and other products which are free from additives such as antibiotics and growth promoters and, in the case of systems approved by the Soil Association [page 206], produced on pasture with no caging, tethering or penning.

Nevertheless, most people when asked to pay a premium for such 'high welfare' items are unwilling to do so. However, their commitment is poorly tested by inadequate information about which systems lie behind which products.

Codes and Systems

The Codes of Recommendations for the Welfare of Livestock [page 147], as prepared by the FAWC, encourage high standards of husbandry by laying down recommendations on the way that livestock should be kept, and these have aroused much heated debate. Welfare groups argue that the Codes are largely ignored in large intensive systems, and policing of them by the State Veterinary Service [page 216] is ineffective due to the lack of resources.

In 1984/5, CIWF [page 183] brought a test case alleging that veal calves were being kept in contravention of the Codes, in an attempt to establish a precedent in the use of the Codes for bringing prosecutions. (The Highway Codes are used in much the same way for traffic offences). The case was unsuccessful, highlighting the ineffectiveness of the Codes in safeguarding the welfare of animals, and indicating that only mandatory regulations can improve conditions.

As a member of the EC the UK is obliged to bring its legislation into line with directives issued by the Commission. In February 1987, when the European Parliament passed a report on animal welfare by 150 votes to nil (two abstentions), this was seen by welfarists as the start of reform in farming across Europe. The report, compiled by Richard Simmonds MEP, included recommendations to ban veal crates [page 47] and phase out battery cages [page 52] within ten years, a ban on the use of sow stalls and tethers [page 50], a ban on routine mutilations such as tail-docking of piglets [page 51], and a setting down of regulations which would prevent the transport of animals without rest, food or water, for longer than twenty-four hours [page 58]. The European Commission can choose to ignore the Parliament's recommendations and before they become law they must be passed by both the Commission and the Council of Ministers.

In other countries, such as the USA, intensive systems have also been on the increase. However, in 1986 the Swedish government launched a £20-million, five-year plan to eradicate large-scale intensive farming and the spraying of crops with insecticides. Since 1973 Sweden has operated a system whereby all new (or rebuilt) farm buildings, new systems and management methods have had to be approved on the basis of animal health and welfare before they are allowed into general use. A specific research unit employing ethologists and veterinarians has been set up at the Swedish University of Agricultural Sciences at Skara, to evaluate new livestock systems.

Research into farm animal welfare is also carried out in the UK at various research institutes, universities and agricultural colleges.

Funding comes from such bodies as the Ministry of Agriculture, Fisheries and Food (MAFF) [page 216] and the Agriculture and Food Research Council (AFRC) [page 212]. Some of this research is directed at developing alternatives to present intensive systems and then attempting to validate them on economic and welfare grounds. Experience has shown that alternative systems can cause almost as much suffering as intensive ones if badly managed. An example has been the recent increase in free-range laying hens which has resulted in many systems being overstocked, with high levels of disease.

Less objectionable alternative systems are not necessarily extensive, as the indoor group housing of sows has shown, but have taken into consideration the five basic freedoms as outlined in the Brambell Report [page 145]: the freedom to eat, drink, stand and lie down, groom and turn around. Some, such as the Edinburgh Family Pen for pigs, created by a team at Edinburgh University, are designed upon the principle of enabling the animal to carry out its 'natural behaviours', although ethologists often disagree as to the relative importance of behaviours which should be accommodated. Cutting through such research and disagreement, however, the animal rights lobby feels that 'to right the wrong of human treatment of farm animals requires more than making rearing methods "more humane"; it requires the total dissolution of commercial animal agriculture' (Regan (1987) [page 154]).

It may transpire that the consumer demand which led to the development of intensive systems may also result in their demise, but at present, intensive sytems remain commonplace. The following sections describe them in relation to the main species of farm livestock.

CATTLE

Veal Calves

The veal market developed as a method of disposing of unwanted dairy calves and supplying a high-priced luxury product in response to pressure from the catering industry for a supply of white veal. The production of such meat involves taking calves from their mothers when a few days old, and placing them in individual stalls for up to sixteen weeks before slaughter. The stalls are narrow, to prevent the calves from turning round to groom themselves, which can lead to the ingestion of hair, and to keep their droppings over the slatted floor area at the rear, which minimizes mucking out. The calves are often kept in the dark and fed a liquid milk-replacer – a diet deficient in iron and fibre – in order to keep the meat white. For the same reason they are not given bedding, which they might eat. In some systems the calves are kept at relatively high temperatures and without water to encourage them to drink more of the milk replacer. Such calves suffer from clinical anaemia and, as active sociable ruminants, experience high levels of stress from being denied exercise and companionship.

The veal crate was banned in 1990 in the UK where there is little veal production (about 10,000 calves in alternative systems, e.g. in groups on straw). A further 350,000 or so every year are exported live to the Continent where they are reared in crates. Much of the veal produced then finds its way back to Britain.

Other Calves

Many of the calves not used in the veal industry are sent to market. If sickly they will be sold for processed meat, or for rennet to be extracted from their stomachs and used in cheese manufacture, while the healthy ones will be sold to be fattened for beef. The hawking of young calves around markets has aroused much concern, as have their general handling and the practice required by the MAFF [page 216] of tagging their ears when the farmer has received a subsidy. Most of the males are castrates. Young calves transported many miles are often fed large doses of antibiotics to cut down the high mortality rates, but this spreads the threat of multi-resistant diseases into the human population. Welfare groups believe that a better option would be to exclude calves from markets altogether and sell them direct from farm to farm, a practice which is followed to a great extent in the pig industry.

Dairy Cows

Cows are first impregnated (usually by artificial insemination) at about two years of age and for every year thereafter until their milk yield falls to an uneconomic level, when they will be culled, usually after their fourth or fifth calf. Some 25 per cent are culled before they are three and a half years old. After giving birth to the calf – which is taken away usually within twelve to twenty-four hours – the cow is milked for some ten months (and re-impregnated in the second or third) after which she is dried out for about eight weeks before giving birth again, and so the cycle continues. Thus she is simultaneously pregnant and lactating for six to eight months at a time.

There has been a trend towards large dairy herds of up to 500 cows where the milking parlour has become increasingly automated. Use of zero grazing means that many cows spend most, if not all, of the year indoors on wholly or partially slatted concrete floors. Lameness is one of the major causes of culling and is exacerbated in the case of laminitis (swelling of the sensitive laminae of the feet, which can be fatal) by the high-concentrate diet necessary to maintain the high annual yields of around 6,000 or more litres of milk now expected from the modern dairy cow. Organizations such as the Vegan Society [page 208] and CIWF [page 183] claim that the dairy cow has been pushed beyond her physiological limits. Her problems are perhaps the most pressing in the whole of farm animal welfare; her daily energy expenditure has been compared to that of a human jogging for eight hours.

Recent years have seen a trend towards milking three times a day to increase yields, but overproduction in the milk industry has led to government placing quotas on farmers and penalizing excess production. Despite this, certain pharmaceutical companies have been pressurizing governments throughout the world to authorize the use of Bovine Somatotropin (BST), a simulation of a natural hormone, to increase milk yields still further, by up to 20 per cent. BST has been shown to increase the incidence of mastitis – a painful inflammation of the udder which already affects about a third of dairy cows – and is suspected of being mutagenic. The government has admitted that milk produced in secret trials with BST-injected cows is finding its way on to the milk market unlabelled.

As recruited dairy calves make up an estimated 70–80 per cent of the beef industry, dairy cows are often inseminated with semen from beef-type bulls, that is, bulls with a high meat-to-bone ratio. This, and the use of embryo transfer to maximize reproduction from genetically superior cows, can lead to calving difficulties and the need for repeated caesarian deliveries.

Mutilations of dairy cows have included the crude amputation of a large part of the tail to prevent it from getting in the way during preparation for milking.

Beef Cattle

The increase in the number of cattle kept permanently indoors in intensive housing systems has, as previously mentioned, given rise to a high incidence of lameness associated with the use of fully slatted floors. In the USA the beef lots are outdoors, but with no grazing and huge numbers of cattle per square mile they are no improvement. In the UK, roofless intensive housing has been developed which has also been criticized for its totally barren environment. Extensive farming of suckler cows and calves has caused concern too; exposure and low energy intakes are major causes of suffering, especially in autumn calves.

Mutilations of beef cattle include the punching of holes in the ears and the sawing off of horns, although the calves are usually disbudded at an early age before proper horn growth has commenced. For many years this was done with caustic potash, which can be very painful, or with a hot iron. There are now more sophisticated variations on the latter, such as the hot-air blower, but whatever instrument is used a local anaesthetic is essential, as the nerve running up to the horn bud lies just beneath the skin. Most males are castrated by rubber ring, knife or emasculator methods, in order to make them more docile. Beef cattle are slaughtered at any age from ten months (intensive bull beef) to two years (autumn-born calves finished on grass).

PIGS

Breeding Sows

Around 600,000 breeding sows are kept in close confinement in the UK. This entails the sow being kept in a stall in which she cannot turn round or groom herself and can only stand up and lie down with difficulty. In some systems the sows have tethers around either the neck or the girth; all systems have partially slatted floors for dung to pass through to the slurry channels below. Water is often restricted as the sows will play with it and dilute the slurry too much. The sow stays in the stall until her sixteen-week pregnancy is nearly over when she will be transferred to a farrowing crate to give birth.

The farrowing crate has evolved in an effort to prevent the sow from crushing her piglets, but it creates as many problems as it solves. While it prevents the sow from savaging the piglets, the difficulty she encounters in lying down and standing up may contribute to her crushing them. The crate is constructed of metal bars to restrict the sow's freedom in the same way that the stall does and is often positioned over a perforated, slatted or woven wire mesh floor, without bedding, and with a creep heater to keep the piglets warm placed to one side. After the piglets are removed at weaning, the sow returns to the stall where she will be served by the boar (or impregnated by artificial insemination) as soon as possible. This breeding cycle will continue until the sow's production decreases, when she will be culled, usually after her fourth or fifth litter.

Norwegian studies have found that the main reasons for culling sows are leg defects, which account for around 20 per cent. Other researchers have found that an increase in lameness and posterior paralysis in sows appears to be associated with intensification of management systems. Sow confinement does not allow for certain behaviours, and frustration of these, together with the boredom of such barren environments, leads to the development of stereotypies. These highly repetitive actions have no function and are an indication of chronic stress and suffering. In 1986, the Athene Trust [page 178] published an independent report by the Scottish Farm Buildings Investigation Unit (now the Centre for Rural Building) [page 213] which concluded that close confinement causes sows severe distress. The way they adapt to confinement resembles the development of chronic psychiatric disorders in humans.

In 1991, after much lobbying from welfare groups, the Welfare of Pigs Regulations 1991 were passed, prohibiting new installations of sow stalls and tethers, and requiring all existing systems to be phased out by the end of 1998. However, although the European Parliament voted in 1987 and 1990 for a phase-out of stalls and tethers, in 1991 EC Agriculture Ministers decided not to prohibit the former and ruled that a ban on the latter should not be effective across Europe for another fifteen years, although no new tether systems may be put in from 1996.

Piglets

Although the average number of piglets born is twelve per litter, only some 80 per cent survive to weaning. While still with the sow the piglets have their sharp eye teeth removed by crushing them with pliers, the justification being that their removal prevents damage to the sow's teats. Their tails are cut off to prevent later outbreaks of tail-biting (see below), and the males are castrated to prevent 'boar taint' in the meat, although this practice is becoming less common.

Welfare groups claim that such mutilations are unnecessary and cause suffering. They argue that teeth removal has only become necessary because the sow in the crate cannot escape the demands of the piglets. Tail-biting is a sign of poor management, bad ventilation and stress due to boredom. There is evidence, too, that the public cannot detect any taint in meat from uncastrated males, which in any case are slaughtered nowadays at too young an age for the 'taint' to apply.

Pigs have a natural weaning age of twelve weeks, but commercial practice is to wean at three to four weeks. Some farms even practise two-week weaning to enable the sow to be put back into the breeding cycle as soon as possible. At such a young age piglets are vulnerable to disease and are kept in a relatively sterile environment in flat decks or occasionally in cages stacked three layers high. The unbedded wire floors enable the dung to pass through and the pigs are kept in these cages until they are moved into the growing and finishing pens, at ten to twelve weeks.

Fattening Pigs

Fattening pigs are produced for pork or bacon, being slaughtered at around five months and seven months respectively. Groups of pigs are kept in concrete pens with fully or partially slatted floors, with access to feed hoppers and drinkers; sometimes chains or tyres are suspended above the pens to give added interest. Very little or no straw is provided as it blocks up the slurry channels, and lighting is kept low to prevent aggression.

Fattening conditions for pigs are generally barren, causing chronic boredom and stress which may lead to outbreaks of fighting and tail-biting. The space allocations are defined in the Welfare Codes [page 147] but many pens are overstocked. Routine administration of antibiotics via feed is common as the pigs' environment is an ideal breeding-ground for disease. One system which has caused sudden high mortalities is the 'sweat box', which involves large numbers of pigs being kept in a small pen at a high humidity level to stimulate their growth rate.

POULTRY

While the domestic chicken is still the major source of poultry meat and eggs, production of ducks, turkeys, geese, partridges and quail for food has been increasingly intensified. For example, around 33 million turkeys are reared annually in the UK in deep-litter systems. Some of these are de-snooded (the fleshy snood on the turkey's head is removed) to minimize damage during fighting, de-toed and de-beaked. Ducks are kept on wire mesh to facilitate dung removal and many have their beaks trimmed (due to be made illegal except when carried out by a vet for specific purposes) and wings clipped.

Battery Egg System

Of all the issues involving livestock, one that has caused great concern among welfarists and public alike has been the production of eggs by the battery cage system.

Around 90 per cent of the 35 million laying birds in the UK are kept at any one time in battery cages, with approximately 5 per cent of the egg-producing companies responsible for 75 per cent of the eggs. The wire cages usually measure 50 x 45 cm and contain four or five birds, with food supply and often dung removal automated, and controlled lighting to minimize activity and aggression. The birds are kept in the cages for between one and two years before being taken to slaughter, after which they will be used in products such as chicken soup and baby food.

Those involved in the industry, such as the British Poultry Federation [page 212], claim that the battery cage evolved as a welfare response to the problems of egg production. The chicken is free of predators, inaccurate feeding, poor weather and infected pastures.

However, such a deprived environment where birds cannot stretch their wings (a chicken's wing span is around 80 cm), build a nest, dust-bathe or exercise, causes stress and boredom, which lead to aggression, feather-pecking of other birds, and eventually cannibalism. The industry's answer to this – to de-beak the birds, burning off a third of the upper beak – results in acute and chronic pain. Some 40 per cent of battery hens are de-beaked, although the Welfare Codes recommend that it is only carried out as a last resort. Birds are very like mammals in sensory perception and if it is accepted that other animals feel pain there is no reason to deny that chickens feel it too.

Birds brought out of cages for slaughter can hardly stand due to deformed limbs and broken bones (affecting some 30 per cent), and suffer from sores and abscesses and raw skin with few feathers. It has been estimated that 95 per cent of feather loss is due to pecking by other birds although the industry suggests it is due to abrasion from the cages or natural moult. The average annual mortality of the national flock is 6 per cent and although some diseases, such as coccidiosis and parasitic infections, are now controlled, there are still other problems like infectious bronchitis, cage layer fatigue, prolapses and egg peritonitis. Non-therapeutic antibiotics are routinely administered in feed to minimize outbreaks, a practice which has alarmed consumers and scientists alike.

Welfare societies and many other bodies, including the House of Commons Select Committee on Agriculture [page 214], have condemned the battery system. If the EC [page 213] acts on the report of the European Parliament [page 213] of 1987, the battery cage may well be phased out over the next ten years (although it would seem that protracted discussion on cage sizes will continue for a longer period). This would involve over 200 million laying hens in battery cages in the EC. This number has fluctuated in recent years due to public concern about cholesterol, residual drugs found in eggs, and outbreaks of salmonella poisoning. Also individual birds are producing more eggs as the genetic manipulation of strains becomes more effective.

At one time forced moulting was popular, which involved the with-holding of food, water and light for twenty-four hours and a gradual restoration of them over two weeks, inducing the birds to pass through their unproductive moult period quickly and to carry on laying for another year. Forced moulting was banned in Britain by the Welfare of Battery Hens Regulations 1987 but welfarists claim that the practice continues. On some farms abroad, the birds are fed high concentrations of zinc to stop them laying in certain periods. The zinc poisons the birds sufficiently to stop them eating and therefore laying.

Some of the problems of the battery unit are intrinsic to the system. The keeping of large numbers of birds in cages stacked on top of one another means that thorough inspection of each bird is impossible. Injured or even dead birds are left in cages with live ones for a number of days. Most stockpersons find battery cages objectionable. High levels of ammonia occur, especially in battery houses which have a deep-pit system for the collection of chicken dung.

Removal of the live chickens is undoubtedly traumatic. They are difficult to manoeuvre out of the high cages, the handlers may be in a hurry, causing injury to the frightened birds, and the way they are packed into travelling crates can be brutal. Ex-battery hens usually travel long distances to a specialist slaughterhouse, stacked in crates on open lorries, and once they are on a lorry it is impossible to feed, water or even see them properly.

Alternative Systems
Alternative systems exist although some are in the early stages of testing and development.

Getaway Cage System. This houses groups of up to twenty birds, with each bird allocated about double the amount of space given in a battery cage. The getaway cage provides perching, dust-bathing and nesting areas, giving the hens space to carry out certain behaviours and to enable them to escape the more dominant hens.

Free-range System. The birds are kept in houses and allowed access to pasture, although there has been condemnation of over-large flocks kept on small areas of land, and the use of fixed houses. The use of the latter means that the land around them becomes stale and sick, increasing the risks of infection and internal parasites and rendering it useless for much else afterwards. Movable houses are recommended, including the plastic tunnel type.

Straw Yard System. The straw yard is totally or partially covered and sometimes provides nest boxes. This system gives the birds larger amounts of space in low-cost housing, although there are problems with dirty eggs and disease.

Aviary and Perchery Systems. The birds are still housed in large numbers indoors, but in flocks where they have access to perches and individual nest boxes. In the aviary there is one or a series of platforms connected by a ladder and in the perchery there is a series of individual perches in steps. In both systems the floor may be partially or fully wired when there is a deep pit for dung collection or a scraper to clear it. Shavings or dust for dust-bathing are often provided. Problems here include cannibalism, floor-laid eggs and a high incidence of disease, although these are more connected with high densities of birds (twenty-five birds per square metre).

Deep-litter Systems. In deep-litter systems the birds are kept in big sheds on a floor covered with straw or shavings, with access to nest boxes, and the same problems as in the aviary and perchery systems have been found at high densities of eleven birds per square metre. Some of the semi-intensive systems, such as deep litter, may include access to the outside via poopholes, although in practice the number of these may be totally inadequate for the number of birds in the shed.

The EC now directs that all except battery eggs should be described according to the system of production used. Welfarists are demanding that all eggs be labelled so that people know exactly what they are buying, and that misleading terms like 'Farm Fresh' should be banned: eggs sold as such are usually battery eggs.

Disposal of Male Chicks

Often overlooked is the disposal of unwanted male chicks. After the eggs from the breeding stock have been incubated and the chicks sexed, around 35 million males are destroyed annually at one to three days old because they are not suitable for meat production. Destruction methods vary: suffocation, when large numbers are packed into containers; homogenization in a mincing machine; decompression; drowning; neck-breaking, or gassing. The Welfare Codes on the destruction of ducklings and chickens recommend gassing the chicks with 100 per cent carbon dioxide, although in small numbers (unspecified) they may be decapitated.

Broiler Chicken Production

Some 600 million broiler chickens are slaughtered annually for the table in the UK. They are reared loose-housed in large sheds which vary in size and can hold up to 100,000 birds, sometimes more. The birds are kept in light during the first two weeks to stimulate growth, then the lights are turned down to moonlight level to keep aggression to a minimum. Nevertheless, at high stocking densities feather-pecking and cannibalism can arise, so some de-beaking [page 53] is carried out. Other mutilations include de-toeing the males used for breeding, to prevent injury to the females during mounting (though most become too obese to perform this function), and dubbing, i.e. the chopping off of the bird's comb which is thought to prevent damage during fighting (this is also carried out on show stock for cosmetic reasons and as a prelude to cock fighting [page 10]). These practices probably cause the same trauma to the bird as de-beaking. The birds are slaughtered at six to seven weeks old when they have reached approximately 2 kg weight, by which time they will each have been living on a floor space of about half a square foot.

Welfare groups claim that unacceptable suffering results from the stimulation of growth by breeding techniques and a high-protein diet which causes the birds to increase weight by a multiple of fifty times in the same number of days. The unnatural growth rate leads to leg weaknesses, fragile bones, leg deformities (affecting up to 90 per cent), hock sores and breast burns. Intensive conditions lead also to trampling and suffocation as the birds compete for food, water and space. At the end of the six to seven weeks the dirty litter (which has been there since day one), high levels of ammonia and the number of dead and injured birds that the farm workers have been unable to retrieve and cull, cause an environment in which diseases such as botulism and campylobacter can run riot. Salmonella is present in up to 80 per cent of the birds, and new strains of antibiotic-resistant bugs always threaten to develop.

Sudden disturbances in a flock due to handling and other treatment of broilers can lead to mobbing behaviour during which birds are again trampled and suffocated. Transportation can also be traumatic, though many broilers are now produced in integrated sytems where they are slaughtered near to the point of production.

SHEEP

With over 16 million breeding ewes the UK is the EC's [page 213] largest producer of sheep meat, supplying some 40 per cent of the total. (It is also the fifth biggest exporter of sheep meat in the world). Many of these animals are kept on hill and upland grazing land which, it is claimed, is unsuitable for other farming purposes. It is a harsh environment, especially in the winter months. The recent development of intensively rearing large numbers of housed sheep has been accompanied by a rise in the incidence of disease.

Most sheep meat consumed is from lambs slaughtered at various ages, although a small market for home-produced ewe mutton persists. Depending on the climate and grazing, ewes can produce two lambs at a time, although the average on lowland farms is 150 lambs per 100 ewes. Some research has been carried out in the use of embryo transplantation to make one ewe give birth to four lambs, and ovulation stimulation can produce three lambs per ewe.

Tooth-grinding

Tooth-grinding was supposed to reduce the number of ewes culled prematurely due to bad teeth, known as 'broken mouth'. Two methods were used. One, the 'Caldow' method, imported from Australia, involved the use of a rotary-stone cutting machine at 11,000 rpm to slice off the ewe's front teeth through the pulp and down almost to the gum. This was done by stockmen, without an anaesthetic. The British form of bite correction was less severe, involving the shortening of the front teeth without cutting through sensitive tissue, and was defended on the grounds that it increased longevity in the ewes and reduced the incidence of tooth disease. The government banned both methods (the Agriculture [Miscellaneous Provisions] Act 1968) after a recommendation by the Farm Animal Welfare Council (FAWC) [page 214], but they are still practised in Australia.

Other Mutilations

Short-tail-docking of sheep was banned in 1983, but sheep with illegally docked tails are still seen at markets and shows. The Welfare of Livestock (Prohibited Operations) 1982 demands that sufficient tail be left to cover the vulva of female sheep and the anus of male sheep, although this does not take into consideration the breed of sheep, location and type of grassland. Tail-docking is carried out by the use of an elasticated ring, and castration of male lambs by the use of a knife, or by pincers known as bloodless emasculators. Ear-tagging is routine for identification purposes at markets, and EC directives may increase the practice.

Sheep in Australia

Australian sheep industry practices in management and in the export trade have been highlighted by Townend (1985) [page 147]. There are an estimated 135 million sheep in Australia, mainly Merinos for the wool industry, and the high numbers of sheep kept per farm worker contribute heavily to high mortality rates; an estimated 8 million sheep die on-farm annually. Welfare groups claim that shearing is carried out with little regard for welfare; cuts and tears are commonplace as the workers are paid according to the number shorn, and many sheep die afterwards from exposure and infection.

Not only is tooth-grinding, as mentioned above, a routine operation for older sheep, but an estimated 100 million sheep are 'mulesed' every year. 'Mulesing' involves the removal of folds of skin, without an anaesthetic, from under the sheep's tail, to form a wool-free scar which discourages breech strike (blow-flies deposit their eggs in the moist wool and on hatching the maggots eat into the sheep, causing intense suffering). Welfare groups argue that mulesing is an unnecessary form of cruelty which has several humane alternatives, e.g. regular crutching, removing just the wool from the tail area, the use of oviposition suppressants to dip the sheep in and disorientate the blow-fly, or even the use of a local anaesthetic to prevent immediate suffering.

MARKETS AND TRANSPORT

Most cattle and sheep, and many other animals, pass through markets, and welfare groups monitoring them have found, among other things: un/loading ramps too steep, unstrawed and slippery; major commotion and force used; misuse of goads and sticks; lack of protection from heat, cold and rain; ailing animals; insufficient straw and water.

Apart from the points made under specific species above, the transport of animals in general is a problem area, especially when large numbers are herded into multiple-decked lorries, the top deck being exposed to the weather. At the best of times, transportation over short or long distances can be traumatic for animals and while many are shifted to and from markets and farms (and slaughterhouses) within the UK, many others (over 1 million, plus 21 million poultry, in 1991) are exported abroad. UK law states that animals being transported must be given food and water every twelve hours (unless the journey can be completed in fifteen), while EC law allows twenty-four. Welfarists have been campaigning for a limit of eight. Many animals are fasted for sixteen to twenty-four hours before departure.

The Royal Society for the Prevention of Cruelty to Animals (RSPCA) [page 204] has trailed consignments of animals from Dover to other countries such as Spain and Italy, finding that export dealers break many regulations, causing great suffering to the animals, many of which die before reaching their destination. The most common infringement is transporting animals for long periods (up to sixty hours) without stopping to feed, water or rest them, and papers have been falsified to show that animals have been rested at an approved lairage for the legally required ten hours before leaving the UK.

Welfare groups have also been campaigning for an end to the live export of animals, proposing slaughter as near as possible to the farm of production and the export of fresh meat instead. The system of export licences in the UK is inadequate to protect animals being transported across the Continent. Under the EC Directive on the Protection of Animals during Transit 1992, a licence or lairage is no longer required. The Ministry of Agriculture leaves officials in the other countries to ensure that the welfare of the animals is protected, often with disastrous results. Attacks on lorry-loads of British sheep during 1990–1 by disgruntled French farmers focused even more attention on the plight of animals in transit.

Export of Australian and New Zealand sheep to the Middle East sees the animals travel hundreds of miles on ships, in cramped conditions, with contaminated food and water. Many die from heat exhaustion, injuries, infections and disease in the feedlots where they may stay for up to six weeks. At their destination the survivors are cruelly handled, and slaughtered by the Halal method [page 66].

GENE TECHNOLOGY

As mentioned on page 37, experiments are conducted on farm animals in order to find ways of increasing productivity, and for other purposes as well. For instance, human genes have been injected into pig embryos which are then transplanted into surrogate pigs to produce transgenic sows whose milk will contain an anti-blood clotting chemical for pharmaceutical use. (See also Dairy Cows and BST [page 49]).

Similar kinds of work, representing a huge technological extension of selective breeding, have also given rise to the geep (half-sheep, half-goat); cloning which has led to the production of freak giant lambs and calves; and the Beltsville pig which, treated with human growth hormone, developed poor vision, arthritis, impotency and a heightened sensitivity to stress. An EC draft Directive, opposed by welfare and rights groups, intends to allow the patenting of new forms of life produced via gene transfer; the onco-mouse [page 40] has already been granted the first patent, bestowing 'ownership' on the creators.

MISCELLANEOUS

Different countries regard different animals as suitable for eating. In South East Asia, dogs and cats are eaten [page 82], a custom that horrifies most British people. Worldwide there exists a trade in exotic wildlife such as leopards, bears, and crocodiles for culinary purposes [page 89]. The French are very fond of frogs' legs [page 92] which have now become popular in many Western countries; whale meat [page 89] is considered a delicacy in countries such as Japan, Norway and Iceland; the demand for turtle soup in Western countries has led to turtle farming [page 93]; and in Hong Hong live monkey brain [page 90] has been considered a gourmet dish. In the UK, swans have been taken from the wild to be eaten.

There is cause for concern over the welfare of several other species in the UK, although the numbers involved are relatively small.

Deer

In the 1970s a boom in the production and sale of farmed deer was predicted, research having been carried out on management systems at the Rowett Research Institute in Scotland. This has now closed its deer farm due to the demand for deer meat failing to reach expectations. None the less, there are now some 300 deer farms in the UK, farming approximately 45,000 deer, most of which are red deer.

Possibly the main concern regarding deer is the method of their slaughter. The FAWC's report on *The Welfare of Farmed Deer* (1985) [page 146] recommended that deer be slaughtered in licensed slaughterhouses, despite its findings that deer are nervous, highly strung and easily frightened animals. Four members of the Council added a note to the report to show their dissention at this recommendation.

Deer going to slaughterhouses must first be restrained in a crush and have their antlers sawn off (this is not allowed if they are in velvet), which causes them severe stress. They are then transported, handled into the abattoir, and restrained while stunned, although the captive-bolt stunner may not be properly effective. There has also been some interest shown in ritually slaughtered deer [page 66].

The alternative of shooting deer on-farm is conducted while the animals are feeding, which is considered by many to be the most humane way. Or the deer may be placed in a handling crush and stunned with a captive bolt prior to being stuck and bled [page 64].

One of the reasons given by some supermarkets for not accepting farm-killed animals is lack of hygiene, although the animals are bled and hung immediately they are shot. This is not the case for game venison shot in the wild [page 22], which has attracted no such criticism and is accepted by supermarkets. Approximately 3,000 tonnes of game venison are produced per year, in comparison with the 500 tonnes or so produced on-farm.

Horses

The trade in horsemeat for human consumption has never established itself in the UK, presumably because of the special British affection for the horse [page 83]. However, the UK still exports a certain number of equines which comply with the conditions laid down in the Animal Health Act 1981 [page 137], and it is estimated that about 50,000 horses per year are slaughtered by the five EC licensed abattoirs in the UK for carcase export [page 85].

Geese

The production of *foie gras* from distended goose liver has become big business in recent years, the process being increasingly automated for speed. It involves the bird being held in a restraining brace which stretches the neck; a funnel tube is then inserted into the throat, with a clip holding the bird's head in place. The operator uses an augur and foot-pedal to pump cooked maize down the bird's throat, and can feed up to sixty birds per hour. The birds are fed from about four months old for about four weeks during which time they will reach a consumption of up to 3,000 g (6.5lb) of maize per day, and increase in weight by 60 per cent, with a nearly four-fold increase in the weight of their livers. While such practices are illegal in the UK, this country none the less imports *foie gras* and *pâté de foie gras* from France. CIWF [page 183] has been prominent in the campaign to have the UK government ban the import of these products and for the EC to ban the practice altogether.

SLAUGHTER

Whatever the method of production, the slaughter of livestock in the UK is subject to regulations and laws regarding hygiene. The law related to the welfare of the animals requires them to be instantaneously rendered insensible to pain until death supervenes (Slaughterhouses Act 1974 [page 135], Slaughter of Poultry Act 1967 [page 134]). However, there are four exceptions: Jewish slaughter; Muslim slaughter; decapitation in poultry, and neck dislocation in poultry. The first two are known as religious slaughter, sometimes referred to as ritual slaughter, and these are dealt with on pages 66–68, while the slaughter of poultry is dealt with on pages 65–66.

Licensing

There are about 800 licensed abattoirs in the UK, and many more unlicensed ones for poultry. Licences to permit slaughtering of animals are issued by local authorities, who also issue licences for the slaughtering premises. Initially, a trainee licence is issued, which permits slaughtering under the supervision of a licensed slaughterman, until sufficient experience is gained to permit issuing a full licence. For this a minimum age of eighteen years is required, and a full licence can be issued in as little as three months.

This system of licensing has been criticized due to the lack of formal training involved; bad habits and a poor attitude to animal welfare can easily be perpetuated within abattoirs. By way of comparison, in Denmark trainees must pass a course at an approved institute before being granted a licence. Although insensitivity in abattoirs may lie in part with the slaughtermen concerned, insufficient emphasis on animal welfare by management is also a contributing factor.

Slaughtering Practices

Concern over the slaughter of farm animals has led to FAWC [page 146] research and the publication of three reports: *The Welfare of Poultry at the Time of Slaughter* (1982); *The Welfare of Livestock (Red Meat Animals) at the Time of Slaughter* (1984), and *The Welfare of Livestock when Slaughtered by Religious Methods* (1985). Only a few of the hundreds of recommendations in these reports have been implemented by the Ministry of Agriculture, Fisheries and Food (MAFF) [page 216].

Before reaching the slaughter-point in an abattoir, an animal will have experienced the stress of transportation and handling, and will frequently be mixed with groups of strange animals in the holding pens. This can lead to outbreaks of fighting, particularly in the case of pigs, resulting in lacerations, torn hides and bruising. Another area of concern relating to slaughter has been the transportation of casualty animals to slaughterhouses; some of the animals are so lame or injured that they have to be winched on to the lorries. Calls have been made for an effective system for these animals to be slaughtered on-farm, since the carcases are still acceptable for human consumption as long as they are accompanied by a certificate issued under the Slaughter-house Hygiene Regulations.

While awaiting slaughter, animals are often fasted in order to save on the cost of feeding and to facilitate the removal of offal. This fasting can be quite prolonged, particularly for battery chickens.

Many abattoirs operate on a piece-rate basis, paying the work force according to the number of animals slaughtered per day. This encourages as fast a work rate as possible, and the emphasis on speed can have a deleterious effect on handling and stunning practices.

Another possible source of welfare problems in abattoirs is that no one is clearly responsible for ensuring that proper practices are enforced. The management is responsible for hygiene but not welfare. The FAWC [page 146] recommended that when a vet was present, he or she should have the duty of ensuring the welfare of the animals, and the Welfare of Animals at Slaughter Act 1991 [page 136] now gives the government new regulatory powers to enable it to implement this and other FAWC recommendations.

Mobile slaughterhouses, as approved by the Ministry of Agriculture in 1992, could fulfil a need for local slaughter facilities in remote areas not serviced by an abattoir. British abattoir numbers are dwindling and may fall from 750–800 to around 300 by 1993 due to the prohibitive expense of complying with new EC hygiene regulations.

Stunning Methods

The aim of research into pre-slaughter stunning methods is to evaluate the effectiveness of present ones, and to investigate alternatives which may result in improvements in animal welfare. Due to differences in sizes and handling methods, each species requires its own stunning practices.

Cattle

Approximately 3.5 million cattle are slaughtered annually for food in the UK. They are stunned by the captive-bolt method, which consists of placing a hand-held pistol at a specific point on the animal's forehead and firing a retracting bolt into the brain, using a blank cartridge. Unconsciousness results from the impact of the bolt on the animal's head and the tissue damage to the brain by the bolt's penetration. A variation on this method is percussion stunning, involving a mushroom-shaped tip on the bolt which does not penetrate the skull. This method of stunning has been accepted by certain Muslim authorities for religious slaughter purposes [page 66].

After stunning, the animal is shackled, hoisted and stuck (i.e. the throat is cut). Cutting the large vessels of the neck stops blood circulating to the brain, and death should follow while the animal is still unconscious.

The two principal problems arising from captive-bolt stunning are inaccurate shooting, and poor maintenance of the stunning pistol. Few stunning pens have the facility to restrain the animal's head, and therefore movement at the moment of firing can lead to misplaced shots. Hopefully, this is to be rectified by the Slaughter of Animals (Humane Conditions) Regulations 1990. Also, the power of the pistol can be substantially reduced if residues are allowed to develop within the breach, which can lead to ineffective stunning.

Pigs

Approximately 14.5 million pigs are slaughtered annually for food in the UK. The captive-bolt method is rarely used as the ensuing convulsions make the animal difficult to handle and reduce meat quality. Electrical stunning is therefore the principal method used with this species.

Most pigs in the UK are stunned by low-voltage electricity, which consists of passing 70–90 volts through the animal's head using hand-held tongs. With conventional low-voltage stunning a minimum application of the current of seven seconds is required. The animal is then shackled, hoisted and conveyed out of sight of the animals remaining in the pen, before being bled out.

In order to stun by electrical means, an epileptic-type fit must be induced to render the animal unconscious. CIWF [page 183] has claimed that low-voltage stunning does not invariably lead to epilepsy-induced unconsciousness, particularly if the tongs are not applied for the required duration. This can result in immobilization or paralysis of the animal without loss of consciousness.

The higher the voltage used during the electrical stunning, the greater the certainty of inducing unconsciousness, and high-voltage stunning systems are available. Manually operated high-voltage stunners employ 350 volts, but these have been associated with meat-quality problems and so are resisted to some extent by the industry. Even higher voltage (600–1,000) systems are also available, but these must be automated by the use of restraining conveyors to avoid risks to the operator. While a conveyor can minimize meat-quality problems, cost precludes its use in most British abattoirs.

A feature of the stunning systems described above (where the current is passed through the head only) is that the animals will, in due course, recover fully from the effects of the stun. This means that sticking must be prompt and carried out effectively in order to prevent recovery of the animal before death occurs by exsanguination. An alternative to these head-only stunning methods is the head-to-back method. This involves the passage of current not only through the head to produce unconsciousness, but also through the heart to produce cardiac arrest, thus preventing recovery. But unless the stun is instantaneous and fully effective, the animal may be fully conscious during cardiac arrest. Some form of restraint is required for head-to-back stunning. The frequently cited concern of the industry that a beating heart is necessary to ensure complete bleeding out of the carcase has been shown to be unfounded.

Sheep

Approximately 20 million sheep are slaughtered annually for food in the UK. About 12 per cent are stunned by the captive-bolt method [page 63], and the remainder by electrical stunning, usually of the low-voltage variety [page 64]. Captive-bolt stunning has been shown to be effective in sheep as long as the accuracy of shooting is maintained. However, percussion stunning has been found to be unsuitable in this species and should not be employed.

The wool on the head of sheep can provide an additional resistance to the passage of the current, but most evidence suggests that the voltage needed to stun sheep is rather lower than that for pigs, particularly if electrical contact is improved by the use of wet electrodes. However, Norway has banned the use of low-voltage stunning for sheep altogether.

Poultry

Approximately 600 million chickens, 33 million turkeys and 10 million ducks are slaughtered annually for the table in the UK. Chickens and turkeys are shackled upside-down when they enter the abattoir, and pass along a conveyor belt for at least three minutes (turkeys for six minutes) before being stunned. Most poultry are stunned using a water bath as one electrode and the shackle as the other, the current passing through the brain and body. Alternatively, the dry stunner uses a metal grid as an electrode; hand-operated electrical stunners also exist.

Following stunning the animals are stuck [page 64], often with the use of an automated neck-cutter. Several different cuts can be made according to the positioning of the blades. Some cut the back of the neck, severing one or both the vertebral arteries. Some cut an external carotid artery, although by this system the spinal cord is also usually cut and so death can result from asphyxiation. A proper cut to the neck is not used due to the industry's insistence on keeping the windpipe intact to facilitate automated evisceration. After sticking and bleeding out the birds are dipped into a scalding tank to loosen the feathers which are then removed by automated plucking devices.

The slaughter of poultry is the cause of considerable suffering, due to poor transportation, handling and stunning practices. In particular, research into poultry stunning has found that up to 23 per cent of birds have a positive corneal reflex at the time of scalding. Research has also shown that stunning is influenced by differences in the electrical resistance of the skull of birds, and recommends that higher voltages, which would stun and cause cardiac arrest, should be employed. Also, the automated neck cutters cannot account for variations in the size of birds, many of which enter the scalding tanks still alive. The currently permitted method of poultry slaughter by decapitation has been shown to result in apparently normal responses in the brain for up to thirty seconds afterwards.

Religious Slaughter

In the UK, approximately 3 million cattle and sheep and 12 million poultry are slaughtered each year by religious slaughtering methods, for either Jewish or Muslim consumption.

Religious slaughter consists of cutting the throat while the animal is conscious, and in this way causes unconsciousness and eventually death by preventing the flow of blood to the brain. The use of pre-slaughter stunning is not acceptable to either Judaism or Islam, on the grounds that an animal must be in perfect health, alive and without injury at the time of slaughter. Stunning is considered to be injurious to the animal and so renders it unfit for consumption.

Cattle killed by religious slaughter are restrained in an upright pen prior to slaughter. Until it was banned in 1992, a rotating crate (such as the Weinberg, Dyne or North British) was used to place the cow on its back so as to expose the neck. In the case of sheep, the animal is usually slaughtered on its back on a cradle, although it can also be either restrained on its feet or hoisted off the ground by its back legs before the cut is made. By the Jewish method (Shechita), a trained rabbi (shochet) must carry out the slaughtering, using a knife kept to a prescribed standard of sharpness. A proportion of the meat produced by Shechita is sold to the general public and to the Muslim trade. This meat is usually the hindquarters of animals sold off due to the high labour cost associated with the removal of large blood vessels (porging) found in this area of the carcase.

By the Muslim method (Halal), the slaughterer does not have to be trained and any adult male may do the slaughtering, although some countries require a special licence.

Rights and Wrongs

Those of the Jewish and Islamic faiths feel that their slaughtering methods are humane, claiming that the use of an extremely sharp knife prevents the animal from experiencing pain, and that the dramatic drop in blood pressure and cessation of blood circulation to the brain following the cut result in almost immediate loss of consciousness.

One argument sometimes offered in favour of religious slaughter is that a conscious animal bleeds out better than a stunned one, an important issue in both Judaism and Islam, which consider the consumption of blood to be unacceptable. The Humane Slaughter Association (HSA) [page 191] has demonstrated to representatives of the Union of Muslim Organizations that, after stunning, the animal is still alive at the time of sticking and that bleeding out is still effective. Also, percussion stunners, because they do not penetrate the brain and so produce less injury to the animal, can sometimes be accepted as a method of pre-slaughter stunning in a religious context.

When deciding whether religious slaughtering methods are 'humane' or not there are three issues to consider: is the animal duly distressed by restraint? Is the cut painful? Does the animal experience pain/distress after the cut before it dies? There is as yet no conclusive evidence either way as to whether the cut is painful or not. Although it does seem to be the case that the animals show little response to the cut, the RSPCA [page 204] points out that the animal is unable to vocalize or escape, its natural responses to painful sensations. Regarding distress after the cut is made, most of the scientific evidence suggests that loss of consciousness is not immediate and thus there can be no doubt that suffering exists. Research has shown that whilst the captive bolt, when used effectively, instantly and irreversibly abolished electrical responses to visual and tactile stimuli, cattle slaughtered by a shochet showed variable responses which could be measured up to 126 seconds after the cut had been made.

Summary

The scientific evidence clearly indicates that religious slaughter causes suffering. The 1985 FAWC [page 146] report on *The Welfare of Livestock When Slaughtered by Religious Methods* argued that religious slaughtering methods were a matter of tradition rather than religious obligation and so recommended that exemption to permit slaughter without prior stunning should be discontinued. However, the religious groups in question have taken strong exception to this argument, pointing to past and present use of the issue of religious slaughter as a racially motivated attack on their communities. Thus the MAFF [page 216] has failed to carry out the FAWC recommendations, and the matter has now entered the political arena.

To the growing number of vegetarians and vegans, however, the concept of 'humane' slaughter is untenable. The often brutal killing of a healthy animal, by whatever method, to provide a kind of food (meat) which no human needs is condemned as immoral.

FISHERIES

While fish farming (see below) and angling [page 12] have generated much debate in animal rights and welfare contexts, the taking of fish from the sea has excited public interest mainly in terms of *over*fishing and incidental dolphin slaughter.

However, both the Vegan and Vegetarian Societies consider the catching of half a million or so tonnes of fish per year by UK vessels (and the 70–95 million tonnes worldwide) as yet another form of animal abuse, whereby sentient creatures are taken from their natural habitat to die of asphyxiation, shock or crushing on board ship. By netting, hooking, dredging and potting, all manner of fish and shellfish are landed (some, like lobster, to be boiled alive and others gutted while still alive) for human and livestock consumption.

Up to 60 per cent of a catch may be 'trash' fish, non-target species and sizes caught by mistake and later dumped overboard, thus depleting future breeding stocks. In addition to concern over the tens of thousands of chemicals which now pollute the oceans and concentrate in fish flesh, environmentalists fear that cod and haddock may disappear from the North Sea within five years unless steps are taken to cut the EC fishing fleet (about 45,000 vessels) by half.

Worldwide, over 25 per cent of fish species are endangered, which means that an already fragile food chain for birds, seals, other fish and cetaceans is threatened. These creatures are already killed indiscriminately as a consequence of sea fishing, most noticeable being the deaths of hundreds of thousands of dolphins and millions of sea birds caught up in drift-nets in the Eastern Pacific and other areas.

FISH FARMING

The intensive production of fish (mainly salmon and trout but also carp, eels, crayfish and others) takes place on over 1,000 fish farms in and around Britain; about 70,000 tonnes (over 50 million fish) per year are produced.

Salmon are kept in crowded underwater (sea or loch) cages and fed pelleted food which contains a dye additive to compensate for the lack of colour in their flesh, plus antibiotics to control the diseases inherent in intensive culture (furunculosis features strongly in a 20 per cent mortality rate). Salmon are also treated with the pesticide Aquaguard to rid them of parasitic sea lice. The fish are starved for up to three weeks prior to slaughter, which is by asphyxiation, blow to the head, electric shock or placement in a carbon dioxide tank before being bled out by cutting the gills. No regulations govern fish slaughter.

Aside from the welfare of the fish, which wear down their dorsal fins in efforts to escape the nets, and whose migratory instincts are frustrated, protest has been made over the estimated 3–5,000 seals (plus diving birds and otters) killed annually to protect the captive stock. Escaping salmon are thought to contaminate the wild genetic pool and the waste matter from such farms is an ecological threat.

Trout farms are mainly land-based ponds, tanks and raceways with similar feeding methods, disease problems and slaughter (though the fish may be ice-packed and left to die in transit), and involving similar killing of wild predatory species. In both salmon and trout farming, breeding is by mixing eggs and milt extracted from females and males, and genetically manipulated sex-reversal enables the production of all-female fish.

Selected Animal Rights and Welfare Organizations

Royal Society for the Prevention of Cruelty to Animals (RSPCA) [page 204]
Universities Federation for Animal Welfare (UFAW) [page 208]
Vegan Society [page 208]
Vegetarian Society [page 209]

FUR PRODUCTION

The decline in the popularity of fur in the UK – fur sales have declined by 50 per cent in the past six years – has seen the closure of many fur shops and departments in big stores. In 1989 the Hudson's Bay Company departed for Helsinki after trading in London for over 300 years, in the course of which it auctioned millions of animal skins.

There are two main types of fur production: farming and trapping, which together account for some 80 million animals killed worldwide each year.

Rights and Wrongs

Those involved in fur farming promote it as being in no way different to other forms of livestock production, claiming that there is no cruelty involved in the farming of animals for their skins, and that every attempt is made to ensure that standards are maintained in the keeping of caged fur-bearers. Those involved in the trapping of fur-bearing animals view them as a natural renewable resource which, they maintain, needs controlling.

Many people believe that with the wealth of synthetic materials now available, there can no longer be an argument for the use of animal fur, and that the suffering involved for the animals, whether farmed or trapped, can never be justified by the production of a luxury product such as a mink coat. Over and above such considerations, the rights view is opposed to the animals-as-resources attitude which lies at the root of fur production.

FARMING

In the late 1970s approximately 27 million wild animals per year were farmed for their fur worldwide. That number increased in the 1980s, with Scandinavia alone in 1986 estimated to produce around 25 million animals from 11,000 fur farms; by 1990 the world figure stood at approximately 40 million. The most popular animal is the mink; other farmed fur-bearers include the silver fox, the blue fox, the chinchilla, the sable, the nutria and the fitch. Attempts to raise captive ocelot, otter, lynx, beaver, coyote, racoon and marten have been largely unsuccessful. In the UK there are around twenty-seven mink farms, producing about 200,000 pelts per year, licensed under the Destructive Imported Animals Act 1932, and by the Mink (Keeping) Order 1987 which was scheduled for government review by 1993.

The animals are usually kept two to a wire cage (about 2 cubic feet) with mesh flooring to facilitate dung removal. Breeding females have access to a nest box. Breeding mink are killed at about four to five years old, whilst other mink are killed before one year old as they produce their best pelt in the winter of their first year. Many different shades of pelt are produced by cross-breeding. Slaughter is usually by lethal injection, although other methods such as neck dislocation and gassing with engine exhaust have been used. On at least two farms in the UK, Arctic foxes are kept in larger cages and killed by the use of mouth (clamp or rod) and anus (rod) electrodes. Methods of slaughter in other countries include the use of chloroform and strychnine. Thirty-five to sixty-five mink or ten foxes are required to make one fur coat.

In the wild, the active semi-aquatic mink is a solitary predator covering 2–3 miles of riverbank or 22 acres of marshland, and Arctic foxes range territories of up to 15,000 acres. The confinement of these animals in barren cage environments leads to the development of stereotypic behaviours symptomatic of stress and boredom. The breeding of mutants for colours, especially in the case of mink, has led to genetic abnormalities.

Specific welfare legislation covering the farming of fur is non-existent: there are no required standards for cage sizes, and no Welfare Code [page 147] is issued by the MAFF [page 216], even though the breeders are classified as farmers.

Domestic Animals

Domestic animals are also farmed for their fur, although the rabbit, which is produced in different varieties such as the Angora, Dutch and Silver Grey, is reared chiefly for its meat, its fur being used in smaller, low-value goods. In Afghanistan, Russia and South West and South Africa the Karakul sheep are farmed to produce 'Persian Lamb' (known as Swakara in Africa). Karakul lambs are born with tight, shiny, black curls which last only five days before straightening out, which means that they are slaughtered before then, by cutting of the throat. These countries produce some 33 million Karakul skins per year; twenty-five are needed to make one coat. Another type of sheep fur, the broadtail, is the skin of a premature lamb. As abortions rarely occur naturally in sheep, even in the harsh environs of Central Asia, the practice is to slaughter old pregnant ewes and remove and skin the foetus.

Other domestic animals used for fur include unborn calves from cows that are pregnant at slaughter, and ponies, the skins of which come mainly from Poland, Russia, the Baltic States and China. Dog and cat skins come from Russia, Mongolia, Korea and China although the UK welfare organization National Petwatch [page 200] has evidence of a growing trade in pet skins within the UK. Whilst many of these come from companies who provide a disposal service for veterinary practitioners and rescue shelters by collecting the bodies of dead pets, many come from stolen pets.

TRAPPING

Worldwide around 40 million animals are trapped for fur each year, the USA accounting for over half. Trapping has increased greatly since the 1970s as the fashion for racoon, bobcat, lynx, coyote and wolf fur has boomed.

Most of the animals trapped are caught in various forms of the steel-jaw leghold trap in which the jaws slam shut on any part of an animal that applies pressure to the base plate. Animals may be caught by a paw, leg or jaw or, in the case of small animals, by the pelvis, and suffer from hunger, thirst, shock, panic and traumatic injury. Many animals try to escape by chewing off the caught paw or limb and when they are successful, the paw remaining in the trap is known in the trade as a 'wring off'. Extensive injuries to teeth and jaws have been found in such animals. The trapper is supposed to check his 'trap line' at regular intervals to ensure that no animal is left suffering, and to kill any such animal. In the USA and other countries, however, there are no regulated methods for killing animals found alive in traps, and practices such as beating, strangulation or stomping are used.

The leghold trap is extremely cruel; it has been likened to a car door slamming upon human fingers. Animals are often left alive in the traps for many days as a trapper may have a line of 100 miles and cannot cover it all within a day. Animals have remained trapped for many weeks while members of their families brought them food.

The trap is also indiscriminating, an estimated 75 per cent of the total number of animals trapped being discarded as 'trash' animals. These include domestic pets, farm animals, deer and rare endangered species like the lyrebird in Australia.

There are several variations on the leghold trap. The pole trap swings the caught animal in the air on the end of the trap and prevents it from escaping or being eaten by other animals. 'Humane' traps, which include the padded offset trap in which padding reduces the injury inflicted, and the cage trap in which the animal is captured uninjured, or the use of tranquillizer tabs with the leghold trap, have never been taken up by trappers due to the extra cost involved.

Use of the leghold trap has been illegal in the UK since 1958, but the government still allows the manufacture and export of the trap and the import of the products of its use. In 1990 the European Parliament [page 213] voted to ban, from 1995, the import of fur from fourteen species of animal which are usually caught in the leghold trap, including the badger, otter, squirrel and wolf.

One of the arguments used by trappers is that fur is a renewable resource in comparison with fake furs and synthetic materials in the manufacture of which petrochemicals are used. However, a study by G. H. Smith of Ford Motor Company's Scientific Research Laboratory found that it took at least three times the number of energy units to make a real fur coat than to make a fake one (see Nilsson (1980) [page 147]).

Many species, like the North American sea mink, the Falkland Island fox, the Rufous gazelle and the snow leopard, are now endangered due to the fur trade. Several of the species commonly hunted for their fur are now protected by the Convention on International Trade in Endangered Species (CITES) [page 213], but trade in illegal pelts, such as tiger skins, continues. Many countries do not enforce CITES and major discrepancies have been found between Customs reports and the number of animals reported to be imported–exported as declared under CITES. Other countries do not belong to CITES, or have joined only on paper.

Not all furriers refuse to deal in endangered species' skins. In the UK it is legal to sell the fur of an animal provided that it is accompanied by the correct licence which, in the case of restricted animals such as leopards, must state that the skins are old stock of pre-1970 when the protective legislation was first enforced. However, there have been cases of these licences being either non-existent or falsified. This has been found to be especially the case with furs bought in Greece where an enormous fur trade is operated as the result of low taxes, low labour costs and a long tourist season. Similarly, a great assortment of fur coats, made from the world's most endangered wild cats, which have been killed by poisoned spear, bamboo-staked traps, or by gunshot, are sold in Nepal. Welfare groups argue that the blatant trade in endangered species such as the cheetah calls into question the *bona fide* intentions of the International Fur Trade Association which has proposed a voluntary ban on the trade in leopard and cheetah skins and financed a survey of these animals by the International Union for the Conservation of Nature and Natural Resources (IUCN) [page 214].

Selected Animal Rights and Welfare Organizations

Animal Liberation Front (ALF) [page 176]
Animal Protection Foundation [page 177]
Campaign Against Leather and Fur (CALF) [page 181]
Compassion in World Farming (CIWF) [page 183]
International Fund for Animal Welfare (IFAW) [page 193]
International Wildlife Coalition [page 194]
Lynx [page 198]
Royal Society for the Prevention of Cruelty to Animals (RSPCA) [page 204]

Chapter Four
COMPANION ANIMALS

General

Britain has always prided itself on being a nation of animal-lovers, and on having the world's first animal welfare society. It also has a tradition of sentimentalism about pets, and other European countries have always regarded the British as being rather foolish over their companion animals, especially dogs, cats and horses.

However, the reality of pet ownership in the UK is very different, as demonstrated by the annual statistics released by the Royal Society for the Prevention of Cruelty to Animals (RSPCA) [page 204]. In 1986 the RSPCA reported a record number of cruelty cases, up nearly a third on the previous year, and each year since has reported a further increase. In 1991 it secured 2,718 convictions. The grim catalogue is an indictment of just how callous humans can be, with intentional acts of cruelty including smashing puppies against walls; skinning cats alive; stabbings; airgun and crossbow shootings; stamping on animals, *ad nauseam*.

Unintentional cruelty is often the result of ignorance, and many pets have been found to be at the point of starvation or suffering from gross neglect. In addition, dumping of unwanted animals on to motorways and into rivers is commonplace and especially prevalent at holiday times, after Christmas and during the puppy and kitten seasons. Most people do not realize that such acts are illegal under the Abandonment of Animals Act 1960 [page 116]. Many organizations and societies, large and small, are involved in the rescuing of such animals, large numbers of which are subsequently destroyed – around 100,000 by the RSPCA alone each year.

The disadvantages of pet ownership, both to the owner and the general public, are very tangible. Zoonose diseases, pollution from excreta and noise, and the nuisance of behavioural disorders such as biting, are well documented. The advantages, such as companionship, responsibility, care and love, are much less obvious. Some researchers have promoted a recognition of the benefits of animal contact for a variety of mentally and physically handicapped people as well as for the old, the lonely and the imprisoned. Serpell (1986) [page 149] deals favourably with the potential of such therapy work in his history of pet–human relationships, exploring our ambivalent attitudes towards pets and other animals used for human purposes, whilst a severe critique of pet-keeping is offered by Bryant (1990) [page151] from an animal-rights perspective. The reader is strongly advised to consult these publications.

A craze for keeping more exotic pets such as lions, monkeys and tigers declined after the implementation of the Dangerous Wild Animals Act 1976 [page 119] but a boom in 'designer' pets like pythons, tarantulas and pot-bellied pigs has created new problems. Such animals are bought as status symbols and then neglected as victims of a throwaway culture. In recent years there has also been a fashion for keeping the more aggressive breeds of dog, such as German Shepherds, Doberman pinschers, Rottweilers and Pit Bull terriers. The government hurriedly brought in the Dangerous Dogs Act 1991 [page 127] as a result of public outrage after an allegedly growing number of attacks on humans.

The sale of animals in pet shops is regulated by the Pet Animals Act 1951 [page 113], though this is largely ineffective: the ease with which people can buy pets at such establishments leads to a careless attitude towards animals. Boarding establishments are covered by the Animal Boarding Establishments Act 1963 [page 132], but a weakness of the Act is that it does not deal with livery stables for horses, although riding establishments for tuition/hiring are covered by the Riding Establishments Act 1964 [page 133]. The breeding of pet animals, especially dogs at 'puppy farms', has generated much suspicion (see Puppy Watch [page 202]), especially as the Breeding of Dogs Act 1973 [page 135] is also inadequate to protects dogs' welfare.

One of the main areas of concern with cats and dogs, and horses to a certain extent, has been not only deliberate cruelty and neglect, but also the disappearance of these animals. It is estimated that over 250,000 cats and dogs go missing every year. Some are run over, caught in snares, find new homes or otherwise, but there is evidence to suggest that many are stolen for a variety of purposes. Before the Animals (Scientific Procedures) Act 1986 [page 123] there was no control on the supply of such animals to laboratories for animal experimentation [page 39] and it was suspected that up to 30 per cent of laboratory animals had been family pets. Stolen dogs of the larger, fiercer breeds such as German Shepherd or Doberman, have been shipped abroad to be used as guard dogs in African and Middle

Eastern countries. Conditions in these countries are so poor that the dogs do not survive the hot climate for long. Dogs and cats have been stolen to supply the demand for furs and fur goods from Eastern European countries and others (including the UK); skinned corpses have been found in some areas. Stolen cats have been used as bait for fighting dogs and for coursing lurchers [page 18], while dogs of the bull terrier type are rumoured to have been stolen to train for dog fighting [page 10] and badger baiting [page 9]. Horses, ponies, donkeys and mules are known to have been stolen and sold at markets in other parts of the country where they may be bought for the meat trade [page 84].

Animals are also offered as prizes, a practice welfare societies oppose on the grounds that whatever the conditions a prize-giver tries to impose on the winner, these are inadequate to ensure the well-being of the animal. It has not been uncommon to see ponies offered in newspapers as competition prizes, pigs as prizes at agricultural fairs, and goldfish as trophies in plastic bags at fun fairs and amusement arcades. Welfarists have tried to stop the giving of goldfish by urging local councils to ban the practice when they rent land to fairs.

While these are some of the general concerns relating to pets, several major issues regarding particular species are outlined below.

DOGS

There are about twelve dogs per 100 people in the UK which, although greater than the number for Austria, Germany and Switzerland, which all have approximately four per 100, is less than France with fifteen and the USA with twenty-five dogs per 100 people respectively. The dog is the most popular pet in the UK; there are around 7.3 million dogs in 5.9 million homes. It is also, according to the RSPCA [page 204], the most abused animal.

Legislation

Various pieces of legislation refer specifically to dogs, such as the Dogs Act 1906 [page 132], the Dogs (Protection of Livestock) Act 1953 and the Breeding of Dogs Act 1973 [page 135], which was amended in 1991 [page 130]. Dog licensing in the UK has long been a matter of debate. The licence fee was kept extremely low for many years and welfarists lobbied for its increase to enable the funding of a National Dog Warden scheme, but in 1986 dog licences were abolished as not being cost-effective.

Stray Dogs

The stray dog problem is increasing. In London alone some 2,000 strays are picked up from the streets every day and nationwide the stray population is around half a million. Only about 15 per cent are claimed by their owners, the others being either rehomed or destroyed. The RSPCA estimates that about 1,000 strays per day are destroyed in the UK.

The problem may be aggravated by the Environment Protection Act 1991 which came into force in April 1991, making councils responsible for appointing dog wardens to round up and impound stray dogs; owners are liable for a £25 fine plus any expenses incurred. Animal charities suggest that many owners simply will not bother to claim their dogs as it is cheaper to buy a new puppy and, due to the lack of a national registration scheme, owners abandoning dogs are difficult or impossible to trace.

Associated with stray dogs are the problems of attacks on the public and on property, the fouling of public footpaths and parks, road accidents, and in the countryside the worrying and killing of livestock. Many seemingly stray dogs do have homes but are put out each day while their owners are out at work. In 1990, the RSPCA proposed a dog registration scheme, similar to the one which operates in Ulster, to encourage responsible dog ownership and to make people accountable for their pets. Dogs would be identified either by tattoo or by a microchip placed in the loose skin at the top of the neck. However, the scheme has not been taken up by the government, despite support from the National Farmers Union (NFU) [page 216], the British Veterinary Association (BVA) [page 212] and the Police Federation.

Dog Breeding

The RSPCA partly blames irresponsible and uncontrolled private and commercial breeding for the great numbers of stray and unwanted dogs, puppy farming being the main source of the problem. Although it is probably impossible to give an exact definition of puppy farms, and hence difficult to encourage legislation against them, in general they are establishments where dogs of several breeds are intensively bred purely for commercial purposes. The breeders are not concerned with protecting the interests of individual breeds and possess little if any knowledge of genetic factors, which results in the breeding of unwelcome characteristics. Many of these establishments have little consideration for the welfare of the dogs in their care. Breeding bitches have been found kept in deplorable conditions in barns, huts, etc., and are bred when too young or too old, and too often. Cases have been highlighted in the media of large numbers of sickly, undernourished puppies being sold to the unsuspecting public.

The Breeding of Dogs Act 1973 [page 135] made Local Authorities responsible for granting licences to anyone owning more than two breeding bitches and breeding puppies for sale. However, until 1991 councils had no powers of entry to a property suspected of being used for breeding dogs. Now a Local Authority can apply for a magistrate's warrant to search a property if it has reasonable cause to suspect that unlicensed dog breeding is being conducted there. However, for a successful prosecution to take place, proof of sale of three or more puppies from different bitches must be obtained within six months of sale. Documentation of this sort is difficult to obtain and the only solution is to be able to trace the puppies back to their breeders. Due to a large dealer network this is presently often impossible and once more highlights the need for an effective dog identification scheme.

Another type of establishment has also come to light, where the dealer keeps only male stud dogs, hence requiring no breeder's licence. The services of the dogs are given free to owners of bitches provided they sell the resulting puppies to the dealer at an agreed price, thus removing from the breeder the worry of selling the puppies elsewhere. In return, the dealer has neither to feed nor care for the bitches and pups, and the resulting profit on both sides is rarely declared.

Once the puppies have been sold from puppy farms to animal dealers they are often transported unaccompanied over long distances as rail freight. Their documentation has been false in some cases and the fate of the unsold puppies is largely unknown. Many of them go abroad to countries like Japan where little animal protection law exists but where pedigree dogs are often seen as status symbols, fetching large prices even though they are often substandard and sickly. Although the number of dogs exported from Europe has fallen since their ill treatment came to light, dogs are exported to the USA which in turn still exports a large number, especially to Japan. Australia and the UK have been exporting Chows to Singapore and Hong Kong where they have been used for illegal human consumption. In other parts of South East Asia dogs are routinely killed for the table [page 82].

The UK government has been lobbied to tighten up the laws controlling the export of dogs, especially the sale of greyhounds to Spain. In 1986, *The Sunday Times* reported finding atrocious conditions at racing tracks run for tourists in Spain, where 95 per cent of the dogs had come from England and Ireland [page 21].

The most popular breeds of dog kept as pets in the UK are German Shepherds, Labradors, Yorkshire Terriers and Jack Russells, but the breeding of certain fashionable dogs is causing growing concern amongst the veterinary profession which sees many of the worse cases. Such breeds include the Shar-pei, the Pekinese, the Bulldog and the St Bernard, which can all have congenital faults due to in-breeding for characteristic features, like the drooping eyes of the Bloodhound. Some breeds, such as the Boston Terrier and the Bulldog, are now in the position where it is likely that there has to be professional intervention at birth in order for the bitches to whelp; the puppies are simply too large for them.

Mutilations

Tail-docking dates back to ancient Rome. In the first week of life the dog's tail (or part thereof) is cut off with scissors or bone cutters, or an elasticated band is applied for a few weeks, after which the tail rots away and drops off. Breeds such as boxers, Old English sheepdogs, spaniels, rottweilers, terriers, and poodles are commonly docked for mainly aesthetic reasons although the argument for docking sporting dogs is that they then sustain fewer injuries. However, in the main it is only the breeder's prejudice that has prevented the abolition of the practice as there are no benefits for the dog. A survey carried out at the Edinburgh Veterinary School found that observed docked dogs sustained as many injuries to the tail region as undocked ones.

Tail-docking not only causes suffering to the puppy but the dog may suffer adverse consequences in later life, such as a perineal hernia resulting from a weakening of the side of the bowels caused by a lack of tail muscles. The British Veterinary Association (BVA) [page 212], the British Small Animal Veterinary Association [page 212] and the Royal College of Veterinary Surgeons (RCVS) [page 216] consider tail-docking an unnecessary mutilation unless carried out for a therapeutic reason. Many vets now refuse to carry out this operation, although some believe that it is better for a very young puppy to be docked, with what they see as momentary discomfort, than for the dog to be exported abroad and then docked under dubious conditions as an adult. As from 1 July 1993, under an amendment to the Veterinary Surgeons Act 1966 [page 134], only vets will be permitted to dock tails.

Other mutilations of dogs include ear-cropping, for reasons of fashion or fighting, which is illegal in the UK, and de-barking, a practice resorted to in cases of social disturbance.

Training Aids

These range from the metal choke chain to electrified dog collars and walking sticks. The choke chain has long been a favourite among the likes of the late Barbara Woodhouse in teaching a dog obedience. However, the chain is often misused, for few people appreciate the suffering and injuries it can inflict. The 'Halti' headcollar is designed to be a more humane method of control.

The electric collar, imported from Japan, was designed to give the dog a shock every time it barked. It failed to become popular after being declared cruel by the RSPCA which threatened to prosecute anybody found using one. The electrified walking stick was also condemned by the RSPCA and the Kennel Club, although some interest had been shown in this country as to its use to protect postmen and the elderly from attacks by dogs.

Selected Animal Rights and Welfare Organizations

National Canine Defence League (NDCL) [page 199]
National Petwatch [page 200]
Pro-Dogs [page 202]
Puppy Watch [page 202]
Wood Green Animal Shelters [page 210]

CATS

The cat is second in pet popularity to the dog in the UK; approximately 6.9 million cats live in 4.7 million households. Apart from the general cruelty mentioned earlier, one of the major areas of concern here is the welfare of the feral cat.

Feral Cats

The feral is distinct from the stray domestic cat which has either got lost or been abandoned. Feral cats are born in the wild and adults are extremely difficult if not impossible to tame. Stray cats often gravitate towards feral colonies and one of the methods of controlling them is the eradication of indiscriminate breeding. Thousands of pet cats and kittens are abandoned every year and the major animal welfare societies all promote neutering programmes.

Large populations of feral cats exist in the grounds of hospitals, factories, warehouses, docks, and around slums and disused buildings, suffering a high mortality due to disease and malnutrition, especially in kittens. The fighting, noise and the risk of flea and worm infestation mean that such colonies are not popular with the authorities whose answer to the problem in the past has been mass extermination using pest destruction firms. This has led to accusations of cruelty, wounded cats fleeing the area, inhumane techniques being used, and so on.

A more humane approach has been proposed by the Universities Federation for Animal Welfare (UFAW) [page 208]. Research by UFAW has shown that a more successful method of control is to trap, neuter and release the healthy adult cats which are then fed by volunteers, the kittens being taken, tamed and found homes where possible. Mass extermination appears to lead to the immigration of cats from adjacent territories. Large colonies may require a certain amount of culling in order to bring the population down to manageable proportions, but maintaining small neutered colonies is cheaper than repeated mass extermination.

Legislation
Cats are not afforded the same protection in law as dogs and farm livestock. They are not included in the Road Traffic Act 1972, which means that the police or owners do not have to be notified if a vehicle runs over a cat, though under the Protection of Animals Act 1911 [page 105] it should not be left to suffer. Breeding establishments are not covered by law, but boarding establishments [page 132] are, and under the Animals (Scientific Procedures) Act 1986 [page 123] the use of cats in experiments requires special notification. (Four thousand, five hundred and forty cats were used in experiments in Britain in 1991. See Chapter 2: Animal Experimentation [page 29]).

Human Consumption
Human consumption of cats (and dogs) in countries such as South Korea led to considerable outcry in the UK when it was found that the animals were being cruelly treated in the markets: the cats were being boiled alive and the dogs slowly hanged. Welfare organizations have been trying (successfully in the Philippines) to ban such atrocities. There have also been allegations – strongly denied – that certain ethnic communities in the East End of London have been involved in stealing pets for human consumption.

Selected Animal Rights and Welfare Organizations
Cats' Protection League (CPL) [page 182]
International Fund for Animal Welfare (IFAW) [page 193]
World Society for the Protection of Animals (WSPA) [page 210]

HORSES

The past twenty years have seen an enormous increase in the number of people riding and/or owning a horse, pony, donkey or mule in the UK. There are now over 2,500 riding establishments licensed under the Riding Establishments Act 1964 [page 133] involving an estimated 50,000 horses and ponies, plus approximately 600,000 more in private ownership. The British Horse Society [page 212] tries to monitor all the establishments and operates a welfare inspection system to deal with complaints.

The rise in popularity of the horse does not appear to have been associated with a rise in the standard of care, however, and many family ponies are kept in appalling conditions. Horses are held in garden sheds and back gardens, a Shetland pony was found kept on the balcony of a high rise block of flats, and others are endlessly galloped over the treacherous cobblestones of Dublin streets.

Veterinarians have reported many family ponies being fed unsuitable diets, such as cornflakes and tinned rice pudding, and the lack of knowledge has led to overgrown hooves, illnesses such as laminitis, and parasitic infestation.

Tethered Horses

Without the necessary facilities many owners resort to tethering animals on common land and verges, which leads to considerable suffering, as the animals have no shelter from hot or cold weather, little to eat, no water, and are prey to attacks by vandals.

Horses have been found tethered with barbed wire, chains and old tyres and in some cases have died from strangulation. The situation became so bad that the government implemented the Protection Against Cruel Tethering Act in 1988 [page 127] with the aim of stopping these practices, which have not yet ceased, however.

Welfare of Native Ponies

The welfare of native moorland ponies such as those grazed on Dartmoor, Exmoor and in the New Forest has caused concern for many years, especially during the harsh winters when some die from starvation and exposure. The Dartmoor Commons Act 1986 aims to promote the welfare of the stock on Dartmoor and action is still being taken by welfare groups in order that standards might improve there.

'Commoners' (local inhabitants with a right to graze animals on the moorlands) have been putting too many animals on the land and in some cases have been failing to give any supplementary feed in winter, a negligence that is especially hard on the mares, which may often be in foal and with a foal at foot. The true native stock is being diluted with other breeds, creating a problem of too many ponies of 'inferior' type which are less hardy and less likely to find suitable homes. The fate of these ponies at the annual 'drifts' when the ponies are stampeded and rounded up by people on horseback and in vehicles, continues to cause outrage.

Horse Sales

Poor conditions and bad handling are regularly witnessed at horse auctions throughout the country, and annual sales of moorland ponies such as the New Forest and the Dartmoor are possibly the worst of all. At most horse and pony sales of a low standard it is estimated that around 85 per cent of the animals are bought by/for the meat trade, which suggests much indiscriminate breeding.

Stolen horses are often put into sales, sometimes at considerable distance from where they were originally stolen. Trailer-loads of horses have been known to disappear out of the same area in one night, though an attempt to stop this has been introduced by owners having their horses freeze-branded.

Horse-meat Trade

The trade in horse meat both for the pet industry in this country and for human consumption abroad has long been a problematic area due to the horse not enjoying the same protection as conventional farm livestock. Conditions for transporting the animals are often very poor, with mares, foals and stallions of all ages and sizes, some of them shod, often crammed in together. In these circumstances fighting can easily break out. If an animal slips and goes down it is impossible to rescue it and it may be trampled by the others, with ensuing injuries and deaths. The codes and laws which do exist to protect horses are openly flouted and there are too few officials to oversee loading and unloading at markets.

In some cases, such as ponies travelling by boat from the Shetland Isles, the animals will have already travelled many miles before the sale, often without food, water or bedding. Some dealers ('guinea hunters') have been discovered putting animals in one sale after another in order to get a few pounds more. Others have been known to put a sickly foal out on to the side of a motorway in order to make space in their horsebox for another, healthier animal at the next sale.

The Minimum Values Order 1969 (later expanded by the Animal Health Act 1981) ensures that animals under a certain value are not exported live for slaughter and to a great extent this has stopped the once considerable trade in live horses. However, the opening of the free European market in 1992/3 threatened this piece of legislation and 1991 was a year of tremendous campaigning by welfare organizations as they lobbied the EC [page 213] to continue the exemption for horses. In October 1991, it was announced that no resumption of the export of live horses would be made for the time being. Horses destined for human consumption abroad must therefore continue to be slaughtered in the UK and in an EC-licensed abattoir: there are only five of these in the UK, which means that the animals still have to travel many miles before being slaughtered.

Welfare Abroad

Russia and other Eastern bloc countries export large numbers of horses by train to Europe for the meat trade. The conditions are so bad in the trains that in freezing weather many of the animals die before reaching their destination. The same occurs in the transportation of animals by sea between Greece and Italy where few animal protection laws are enforced.

In countries where the horse and donkey are still beasts of burden their welfare often suffers as a result of ignorance as well as deliberate cruelty. Many of the organizations listed below have been actively involved in the education of the owners in provision of care for their animals. They also highlight such practices as the donkey safaris in places like Tenerife, and horse-drawn caravan holidays in the UK, as needing proper control if not prohibition.

Mutilations

Tail-docking of horses has been illegal since 1949 but a number of other practices still continue in the UK. These include firing and blistering which are carried out in an attempt to strengthen otherwise weak tendons in the legs. The idea is that the application of a 'blister' or firing iron to a horse's leg creates scar tissue which adds support to the weak muscles. These age-old practices have the support of the racing [page 20] and hunting [page 14] fraternities, although opinion amongst many vets is that they cause unnecessary pain and distress.

Selected Animal Rights and Welfare Organizations
Brooke Hospital for Animals [page 180]

Horses and Ponies Protection Association [page 190]
International Donkey Protection Trust [page 193]
International League for the Protection of Horses [page 193]
World Society for the Protection of Animals (WSPA) [page 210]

REPTILES

The tortoise trade dates back to the 1890s. A Royal Society for the Prevention of Cruelty to Animals (RSPCA) [page 204] study of this trade, starting in 1977, found that 80–90 per cent of tortoises imported were dying in their first year of captivity. The conditions of capture, washing and transportation from mainly Mediterranean countries were very poor, and many animals still die in transit. The tortoise population in the wild was being depleted at a great rate; it is estimated that over ten years 5 million tortoises were exported from Morocco alone. In 1984, the trade in the Mediterranean species of tortoise was banned by the Convention on the International Trade in Endangered Species (CITES) [page 213] but tropical tortoises were not included. Thus unscrupulous pet traders began to import other species which are more closely related to terrapins, such as the hingeback from Western Africa and the box tortoise which originates from America and Mexico. These are not suitable as pets.

Red-eared terrapins are the world's most commonly traded pet reptile, with 4–7 million exported annually from terrapin ranches in the USA which have been taking up to 300,000 from the wild each year to maintain breeding stocks. The UK imports around 200,000 annually (a figure boosted by the Teenage Mutant Ninja Turtle craze), yet within their first year of captivity 75–99 per cent die, mainly from unnatural causes. Unwanted pet terrapins are flushed down toilets or released into local rivers and ponds where they are unlikely to survive our cold climate. In warmer countries such release can threaten ecosystems. Also, terrapins frequently carry salmonella bacteria and for these reasons several countries have now banned their import, but around thirty (including the UK) still participate in the trade.

Selected Animal Rights and Welfare Organizations
Reptile Protection Trust [page 204]

CAGED PETS

Small mammals such as hamsters, guinea pigs and gerbils are too readily available at pet shops to people who have little knowledge of their needs. Prior to being sold the animals may have suffered during breeding, transportation and being held for sale. For animals taken from the wild such ordeals are intensified and might be best illustrated by the trade in wild birds (see below). The animal rights movement holds that the keeping of animals in cages, hutches and other forms of captivity, leading lives of desperation with all natural instincts frustrated, is not only unacceptable in itself, but perpetuates a general lack of respect for animals.

Selected Animal Rights and Welfare Organizations
Royal Society for the Prevention of Cruelty to Animals (RSPCA) [page 204]

WILD BIRDS

More than 5 million birds of 2,500 species are traded every year after being trapped in Indonesia, Guyana, Argentina and African countries (the largest exporter being Senegal). The largest importers are the EC (1.5 million per year, with the UK accounting for around 184,000), USA and Japan. For every bird that reaches a home as a pet three are estimated to have died due to the stress of capture, handling, cramped transportation, starvation, dehydration and captivity. Unlicensed trapping, trade in protected species and under-declaration of numbers are commonplace.

Over seventy airlines, including all the major US, European and Japanese ones, have voluntarily banned the carriage of wild-caught birds, and campaigners continue to call for a worldwide ban on the trade, lobbying the British government and European Commission to prohibit imports. The public are being asked not to buy such birds as the trade causes great suffering and the numbers living in the wild are extremely low.

In many European countries, such as Spain and France, annual large-scale netting of migratory birds is routine. Some will be caged and sold as pets and many others killed for human consumption, crop protection reasons, taxidermy, and for sport. There have been campaigns to stop such capture and slaughter.

Selected Animal Rights and Welfare Organizations
Environmental Investigation Agency (EIA) [page 186]

Chapter Five
WILDLIFE SLAUGHTER

Wildlife is slaughtered worldwide on a large scale due to certain animals' status as pests, as sources of food, providers of fur, skin, horns, oils, and so on, and as trophies. Some of the slaughter is legal, such as the snaring of foxes in the UK, but much of it is not, for example the poaching of rhinoceros in Africa.

For much of what follows, the reader is advised to bear in mind the differences of approach and philosophy between conservation, welfare and animal rights as outlined in the Introduction [page xi].

Slaughter of Wildlife in the UK

In many instances wide-scale slaughters have been justified by economic factors or by the prevention of disease. For example, great controversy has surrounded the slaughter of badgers by the Ministry of Agriculture, Fisheries and Food (MAFF) [page 216]. This has been defended on the grounds that badgers are thought to spread bovine tuberculosis and infect dairy cattle, although a 1986 report by the independent Dunnet Committee suggested that such a justification for this blanket slaughter was tenuous. The report recommended trapping only around infected farms as a more humane and effective policy. A new blood test developed by government scientists in 1992, which shows whether badgers are carrying TB, could lead to the end of the indiscriminate killing, but welfarists are demanding a full moratorium on culling badgers until better cattle blood tests are available. To date, badger-culling strategies have not reduced herd breakdowns. The badger, a protected species [page 128], also suffers from the rise in popularity of badger baiting [page 9].

Other native species such as rats, mice, grey squirrels, foxes, weasels, stoats, etc., are considered as 'pests' and it is permissible by law to kill them. Although the Wildlife and Countryside Act 1981 [page 120] and various Acts dealing with poisons lay down certain prohibited methods of killing, they are difficult to impose and still allow the use of the snare, for instance. The snare – a noose of wire tied to a stake

in the undergrowth – can catch the victim by the neck to kill by strangulation. If a limb or other part of the body is caught, the animal dies
of its injuries or of starvation. It is an indiscriminate method of slaughter; many domesticated pets, especially cats, and protected species
such as badgers, have been found in snares. A Royal Society for the
Prevention of Cruelty to Animals (RSPCA) [page 204] survey in
1983–4 found that the regulations governing the use of snares were
being flouted in every case it investigated. It also found that although
the use of self-locking snares is illegal under the 1981 Act [page 120]
they were still being widely used. It is estimated that around 100,000
foxes are snared every winter for their pelts, snaring being preferred
to shooting as it is more discreet and causes less damage to the pelt.

The status of wild animals under UK law is still problematic in
relation to cruelty. As recently as 1992 the RSPCA was still unable to
secure a conviction for cruelty to a hedgehog, as the animal was not
deemed to be captive at the time. The RSPCA and the League Against
Cruel Sports (LACS) [page 196] continue to call for changes to the law
to protect all wild animals (not just those considered to be endangered) whilst they are still in the wild. A step in this direction was
attempted with the narrowly defeated Wild Mammals (Protection)
Bill 1992 which would have banned the hunting of wild animals with
dogs.

Some of the 5,000 or so gamekeepers in the UK are also responsible
for the slaughter of large numbers of wild animals to protect game-
bird chicks from predators [page 23]. The slaughter of wildlife for
sport accounts for a considerable number of animals and is dealt with
in detail in Chapter 1: Sports and Entertainment; Hunting [page 14].

Slaughter of Wildlife Worldwide

Elsewhere in the world the slaughter of wild fur-bearing animals takes
place on a huge scale, especially in Canada, the USA and Russia. This
is dealt with in detail in Chapter 3: Animal Production [page 70].

Worldwide there exists a trade in exotic wildlife for the table; many
rare species are considered delicacies by different nationalities. It is
well known that the French like frogs' legs (see below), but other
countries' exotic tastes are not so well publicized. In West Germany,
butchers sell elephant, tiger, leopard, lion, springbok, python, tapir,
puma, bear and crocodile meat. Japan, Norway and Iceland consider
whale meat a gourmet treat, and in Hong Kong huge prices are paid
for illegally smuggled clouded leopards from China. These are
drowned, boiled and served – as are bear cubs in Asia – to enable rich

people to impress their gourmet friends. For the same reason, again in Hong Kong, monkey's brains have been served by strapping a live monkey in a cage below a table through the centre of which the monkey's head protrudes for the diners to eat the brains.

While many wild animals are slaughtered for food and fur, various parts of animals' bodies are sought for other purposes. Examples include the rhinoceros, poached almost to extinction due to the Asian demand for rhino horn as an aphrodisiac; the musk deer, poached for the pod of musk oil in its abdomen which is worth four times its weight in gold; Canadian and Siberian beavers, hunted for their castorium which is used as a scent fixative; crocodiles, hunted for their skins for handbags, shoes and trinkets; dolphins, hunted for their eyeballs which are thought to have mystical powers; elephants, poached for their ivory and hides which are used to make chess sets, piano keys, trinkets, and luggage (see below); and the trade in bear parts such as gall bladders has resulted in the slaughter of thousands of the animals in China since 1989. In many countries exotic birds are trapped for the pet trade [page 87], or slaughtered in large numbers for their beautiful plumage to be used in the clothing industry.

Other animals are regarded as pests because they compete for the same resources with humans or livestock. The Canadian government has pursued a massive wolf extermination programme aimed at eradicating the wolf population from selected areas of the country where big game ranches are being stocked with mountain sheep and elk for hunting purposes. The largest herd of free-roaming buffalo, whose population on the great plains of North America was reduced from 200 million in 1800 to just 800 in 1889, is under threat of slaughter in Alberta due to cattle-ranching interests.

In Australia, ranchers claim that the wild horses (brumbies) eat too much of the grass, and shoot them from helicopters and light planes. The animals are terrified into running, many are wounded by poor shots, and youngsters left orphaned by the indiscriminate slaughter die later from starvation. The horses are also rounded up and taken to slaughterhouses to be killed for pet food or exported to Europe and Japan for human consumption. Also in Australia the aerial baiting of dingos leaves many animals suffering from the poisoned bait.

Whether or not there is justification for some or all of the wildlife slaughters, in many cases the methods are undoubtedly questionable. Poachers in particular appear to have little concern for animal welfare, and the sheer logistics of wildlife slaughters make it impossible to ensure a humane end for every animal. The International Union for the Conservation of Nature and Natural Resources (IUCN) [page 214] specifies guidelines for what it considers to be justifiable wildlife slaughter, but groups such as the International Wildlife Coalition [page 194] claim that very few large-scale slaughters actually meet these criteria.

In the past few years a number of specific slaughters have been widely publicized due to their scale, alleged cruelty or lack of justification, or all three.

ELEPHANTS

Native poaching of African elephants has always taken place in some small way, but in the last twenty years or so poaching has become big business. Elephant herds have been reduced from a world population of 1.3 million in 1979 to just over 600,000 today. In 1986 the tusks from 89,000 elephants were illegally traded. Professional, well-organized gangs of poachers from adjoining countries raid wildlife parks with sophisticated weapons, making the job of protecting the remaining elephants very difficult. With hundreds of square miles to police, the rangers are outnumbered and outarmed.

Not only do the animals targeted for their tusks suffer from poor marksmanship and brutal tusk removal, but many of the orphaned calves are then taken and sold to animal dealers for uncertain futures in circuses or zoos [pages 7 and 24].

Another problem arising from the poaching of the older animals carrying the largest tusks is that the herd will then consist predominantly of young elephants. Elephants normally maintain close family relationships, the young effectively disciplined by the older ones. In a young herd behavioural problems arise from the lack of leadership.

Estimates that 100 elephants were being slaughtered for every ton of ivory obtained, and that if the slaughter continued the African elephant would become extinct by the end of this century, led to the elephant gaining Appendix 1 (endangered) status in 1989 at the Convention on International Trade in Endangered Species (CITES) [page 213]. In the same year the European Parliament banned the import into the European Community of ivory from the African elephant. Though challenged by some of the Southern African countries, the Appendix 1 listing was upheld in 1992 (next meeting 1994).

Selected Animal Rights and Welfare Organizations
Beauty Without Cruelty (BWC) [page 179]
Elefriends [page 186]

Environmental Investigation Agency (EIA) [page 186]
International Wildlife Coalition (IWC) [page 194]
World Society for the Protection of Animals (WSPA) [page 210]

KANGAROOS

Around 5 million kangaroos are slaughtered annually in Australia –
the largest land-based slaughter of an animal species in the world.
However, some groups estimate that if the numbers of nursing and
unborn babies are included, as many as 12–15 million kangaroos and
wallabies die every year. The Kangaroo Advisory Committee, which
has no representative from welfare or conservation groups, meets
annually to decide a quota for the numbers killed as 'pests' to the
ranching industry. In 1991 this was 4.2 million. The animals are shot
anywhere to bring them down, then they are skinned – sometimes
alive – and the babies smashed against the ground or left to starve.
Acts of cruelty are commonplace, with roos having their heads chopped
off to see how far they will run, wounded roos thrown on to fires, and
so on. The skins are worth most and are sold for cowboy boots,
running shoes, football boots and coats (mostly unlabelled), while
trinkets for the tourists are made out of the heads, paws and feet. The
meat goes for pet food though some, allegedly, finds its way into
hamburgers and other junk foods, posing a high salmonella infection
risk. Groups in Australia fighting against the trade have boycotted
kangaroo goods, but powerful business interests are involved and law
enforcement is minimal.

Selected Animal Rights and Welfare Organizations
Beauty Without Cruelty [page 179]
International Fund for Animal Welfare (IFAW) [page 193]
International Wildlife Coalition [page 194]

FROGS

The trade in frogs' legs has been growing steadily. Once favoured as
a rare delicacy, they are now to be found in UK wine bars, pubs and
take-aways. The legs have been traditionally exported from India and
Bangladesh, but Indonesia, Thailand, the Philippines, Brazil and Mexico also export them. Europe and the USA are the main consumers, the
latter importing the equivalent of 50 million frogs per year.

The wild frogs are hunted at night and taken to very basic process-
ing plants, where they are severed in half while fully conscious, the top

half being discarded. Some are dipped in salt solution first which is supposed to anaesthetize them, and some are skinned alive for small leather goods. Because the frogs eat many waterborne agricultural and household pests, the decline in their number has been accompanied by a dramatic rise in the pest population. This has led to an increased use of expensive imported pesticides, such as DDT, an increase in malaria and encephalitis in humans, and an increase in cattle diseases. India banned the commercial killing and export of frogs' legs in 1987 but the other countries have increased their trade. The processed legs are associated with high incidences of salmonella poisoning.

Selected Animal Rights and Welfare Organizations
Compassion in World Farming (CIWF) [page 183]

TURTLES

The increasing demand in Western countries for turtle delicacies such as soup, and trinkets made from turtle shells, has led to the turtle becoming an endangered species. Turtle farming has become big business and farms operate in the Seychelles, France, Surinam and the Cayman Islands (thus UK interests are involved). After capture the turtles are left on their backs for long periods of time to keep them fresh, and have their flippers pierced, with a leather strap passed through the holes to tie them up. They are then thrown into a shallow pool to await the journey to market. Once there they may be left for many hours in the sun until taken to the slaughterhouse where they are literally hacked from their shells alive. The welfare groups concerned suggest that, while it is very difficult to kill a turtle humanely, the best way, if it is to be done at all, is to use a stunner [page 63] followed by decapitation.

Selected Animal Rights and Welfare Organizations
People's Trust for Endangered Species [page 201]
Reptile Protection Trust [page 204]
Sea Turtle Survival [page 205]

WHALES AND DOLPHINS

In 1961 the number of whales killed worldwide peaked at 66,000, although since then there has been a considerable decrease due to campaigning, public pressure and the fact that many countries such as the UK, the USA and Australia have stopped whaling. The International Whaling Commission (IWC) [page 215] was set up in 1946 to regulate the world catch, and in 1982 the member countries agreed to a ban on commercial whaling, to run from 1986 to 1990. This moratorium has since been extended to 1993. However, Japan and Norway have continued whaling under the pretext that the whales are caught for scientific research. Iceland left the IWC in 1992 and Norway announced that it will resume commercial whaling in 1993.

The methods of killing whales are inhumane. Boats may chase a whale for up to an hour before closing in for the kill, when either an explosive or a cold grenade harpoon is fired from the deck into the whale, aimed at the heart or the brain. Whales have highly developed nervous systems and, depending on the accuracy of the harpoonist, a whale may take up to fifty minutes to die a very painful death. Over 50 per cent of the time more than one harpoon is needed to do the job and if a harpoon fails to explode within the whale's body, it is left with severe internal injuries from the barbs on the harpoon head. Other methods have been tried with little success.

Apart from the cruelty aspects, there has been a steep decline in numbers, especially of the blue, the sei, the fin and the minke whales. Welfare groups and conservationists want the IWC to consider also the smaller whales, dolphins, porpoises, orcas and pilot whales (an estimated 1 million are killed every year) which are now in danger from the whalers since the bigger whales have become rarer.

Principal whale products are oil and whale bone, although whale meat is now used by the pet trade and in certain countries, e.g. Japan, for human consumption. The oil is used in cosmetics such as lipstick and cold cream, in machine lubrication, margarine and cooking oil. Ambergris, a substance coughed up by the sperm whale, or removed from the whale's stomach after slaughter, is used as a fixative for perfume. Whale teeth are used as trinkets and piano keys. Vegetable or synthetic alternatives to all these products now exist.

The Faroe Islands' Slaughter of Pilot Whales

The Faroe Islands lie midway between North Scotland and Iceland, and belong to Denmark. The slaughter, which has taken place annually for over 400 years, begins when the lead male of a group of whales is stabbed with a lance and its thrashings attract the others which are then driven by boats up towards the beach, gaffed and pulled ashore to be hacked to death. In 1991, some 658 pilot whales and sixty-two bottlenose dolphins were slaughtered in eleven separate 'grinds' (kills). Although the Faroese claim that population numbers are not impaired, no substantiating survey has been conducted. The Faroese also claim that the whale meat constitutes more than a quarter of their meat consumption and that the tools used are designed to kill with minimum suffering. However, the gaff harpoon, the lance and the knives are available to anyone who wants to join in, and both adults and children hack indiscriminately at the whales as they lie on the beach or in shallow water.

The high standard of living enjoyed by the Faroese makes the killing of whales for consumption unnecessary, and much of the whale meat and blubber is wasted, surplus carcases being left to be washed away by the tide. Boycotts of the Faroes fishing industry have been organized in order to bring pressure on the Faroese government to ban the slaughter.

Dolphin Slaughter

Similar slaughters of dolphins have taken place in recent years around the coast of Japan. These started as a result of the decline in the fishing industry, partly caused by overfishing but also, in the case of the buri fish, because they have been farmed intensively and stocks of young fry are taken from the wild. The fish are also highly susceptible to disease and contamination from the pollutants which are prevalent along the Japanese coastline.

Japanese fishermen claim that there are not enough fish for them and the dolphins and at regular intervals herd several hundred dolphins at a time into bays where the animals are dragged on to the beaches and speared to death. The government perpetuates the slaughter by offering bounties for each dolphin killed, promoting the consumption of the meat, and by providing machines which grind the bodies up for pig feed and fertilizer. Over 160,000 Dall's porpoises have been killed by Japanese fishermen since 1985 and in 1991, in defiance of an agreed maximum quota of 10,000 set by the International Whaling Commission, Japan slaughtered 17,000. These slaughters are on the increase and have occurred in other parts of the world.

Tens of thousands of dolphins are slaughtered each year when they are caught in the drift-nets of tuna fishermen operating off the coast of the USA and other countries. Some of these nets measure up to 90 km long and are invisible to fish, mammals, birds and reptiles. The United Nations has now banned the use of drift-nets over 2.5 km long and the European fishing industry can use drift-nets of the same maximum length until the end of 1993 when the effects will be reassessed. Tuna fishermen, especially in the Eastern Pacific Ocean, also deliberately set nets on dolphins near the surface to locate shoals of tuna beneath them. Powerful speedboats then chase and herd the dolphins into massive purse seine nets which are closed around both tuna and dolphin. Every year, over 100,000 dolphins die from drowning in these circumstances.

Selected Animal Rights and Welfare Organizations
Environmental Investigation Agency (EIA) [page 186]
Greenpeace [page 214]
International Fund for Animal Welfare (IFAW) [page 193]
International Wildlife Coalition [page 194]
Whale and Dolphin Conservation Society [page 210]

SEALS

The campaign against the commercial Canadian and Norwegian slaughter of baby harp and hooded seals in the North West Atlantic saw the birth of various welfare groups, such as the International Fund for Animal Welfare (IFAW) [page 193]. These argued that the hunt was unnecessary, that little research had been done at that time on the effect of seal numbers on the fishing industry, and that the method of killing the seals by clubbing their heads to crush the skull was inhumane, as was the common practice of skinning the pups alive. Clubbing is used because shooting lowers the price of the valuable seal pelts which were bought mostly by European furriers.

The campaign received great media coverage due to the appeal of the fluffy-faced pups, the efforts of the welfare groups and celebrities, and also the support of the public of whom 2.25 million signed a petition calling for a ban on the slaughter.

In 1982 the EC [page 213] voted to ban the import of products derived from harp and hooded seal pups which, with the EC as the world's largest single market, had the effect of drastically reducing the number of pups killed. In 1989 the European Parliament extended the ban indefinitely, and in 1984 the Canadian government appointed a Royal Commission to investigate seals and the seal cull in Canada, and the Commission's report recommended that the commercial slaughter should be halted, stating that clubbing was less humane than authorized slaughterhouse practices.

However, Canada still has the largest seal hunt in the world, totalling over 60,000 in 1991. The IFAW has drawn attention to a net fishery for seals off the East Coast of Canada which catches an estimated 6,000 annually: the seals are caught in the nets and take thirty minutes or more to die from 'dry drowning'. The Royal Commission report condemned this practice as inhumane and called for the Canadian government to ban it.

Other seal culls continue around the world, most notably by Norway and Russia (some 59,000 harp and hooded seals are taken annually from the Greenland and White Seas). Moreover, there is a constant threat of halted hunts reopening. Some killing is carried out illegally by fishermen who claim that seals steal fish, transmit codworm to fish and damage valuable fish farms. At present there is a ban on the culling of grey seals in the UK but future culling policies will depend on the results of research conducted on seal populations in the past few years. Animal Concern [page 175] has highlighted the plight of seals in Scotland where an estimated 5,000 per year are killed by salmon farmers.

Welfare groups are now working towards the closure of all the world's markets for seal products.

Selected Animal Rights and Welfare Organizations
Animal Concern [page 175]
International Fund for Animal Welfare (IFAW) [page 193]
Sea Shepherd UK [page 205]

PART TWO

Chapter Six
ANIMAL WELFARE AND THE LAW

This chapter is intended as a concise review of the major pieces of UK legislation relating to animals and their welfare. As with all laws there are conditions, exclusions and prerequisites which demand expert interpretation by a qualified lawyer. This account therefore introduces the reader to the laws and their main purposes, and, in order to provide some context, a brief overview of the circumstances which gave rise to some of them is given. Where necessary, specific details are appended to some of the major statutes, and summaries only are given for the others. The reader is advised that although the UK boasts a plethora of animal welfare Acts, these are viewed generally by welfarists and rightists as disparate, incoherent, inadequate and confusingly administered. A number of publications offer a more detailed account of animal-related law, and the legislation-minded reader is advised to consult the titles listed on page 151.

The Legal System in the UK

Apart from Euro-legislation in the form of Regulations (which apply directly to all EC member states) new UK legislation can be brought about in three main ways: by statute, by subsidiary regulations made under a statute, or by case law established in a sufficiently senior court, which comprises the setting of a legal precedent during the proceedings of an individual case. In the field of animal welfare law this usually establishes a particular interpretation of a statute which, unless disputed by later appeal, can be referred to in future cases. Case law is an intricate and highly specialized area and will not be dealt with in any great detail here, although the most important examples of precedents which have been established are outlined at relevant stages in the text.

A new statute is brought about by the passing of an Act of Parliament. An Act starts its long and sometimes tortuous route through Parliament in one of three ways: (1) by being introduced by a Member of Parliament as a Private Member's Bill; (2) by being proposed by the Opposition on a Supply Day (twenty-eight Supply Days are granted in each session, on which new legislation can be proposed); or (3) by being proposed by the Government. After a Bill has been introduced, it will be read in the House of Commons, then in the House of Lords and then return to the Commons, passing through various committees, and at each stage it may well be amended. If the Bill successfully completes its journey it becomes an Act of Parliament, given Royal Assent by the Queen. Some laws come into force immediately while others may be phased in to allow people time to bring their systems into line with the new law, as was the case with the Zoo Licensing Act 1981 [page 122].

Many statutes permit Ministers to make regulations which have effect in the same manner as the principal statute itself once simple parliamentary procedures have been complied with. These types of regulations are preferred when the subject matter is complicated by technicalities. The Agriculture (Miscellaneous Provisions) Act 1972, for example, deals with the overall and general care of livestock whereas regulations made under the Act deal with the more specific and technical matters, such as the welfare of battery hens, calves, deer and so on.

As already mentioned, the UK is also bound by the minimum standards set by European Community (EC) legislation, which has been formulated as directives by the European Commission and given unanimous approval by the Council of Ministers [page 213].

The statutes discussed in this chapter are applicable to England and Wales, although in many cases a section of an Act will refer to Scotland and/or Northern Ireland, or a corresponding piece of legislation will exist, as in the case of the Protection of Animals Act 1911 [page 105] which became the 1912 Act of the same name in Scotland.

The Early Days

In the middle of the nineteenth century the public became increasingly outraged at stories of atrocities being committed against animals, mostly by scientists and veterinarians throughout continental Europe. Claude Bernard, for example, became notorious for vivisecting conscious animals in his physiological research in France. In that age of moral enlightenment, which saw the abolition of slavery and the reform of prison and factory conditions, an animal protection movement emerged. (For an overview of these developments see Turner (1980) [page 155] and Ryder (1989) [page 155]). In 1875 a Royal Commission was appointed to review the practice of subjecting live animals to experimentation. Concluding, among other things, that Bernard's type of experiment was 'inhumane', the Royal Commission's report resulted in the Cruelty to Animals Act 1876 which, until replaced by the Animals (Scientific Procedures) Act 1986 [page 123], was one of the oldest pieces of animal welfare legislation in operation.

Some legislation prior to the 1876 Act related to animals but is of interest here mainly because it reveals the legislators' ulterior motives rather than their concern for animal protection. For instance, the Black Act of 1722 made it illegal for anyone to kill, wound or maim cattle or horses but it was necessary to prove malicious intent against the owner, making this a law concerned with protection of human property rather than the *bona fide* protection of animals. In 1800 Sir William Pulteney introduced a bill to ban the then popular sport of bull baiting. Although the bill failed to become law, it is interesting to note that Pulteney's intentions appeared to be to stop poor and disorderly people being distracted from their work, collecting as spectators and causing breaches of the peace .

In 1822 Royal Assent was granted to a Bill which prevented cruelty to cattle and horses, with the intention of stopping bull baiting. However, in a test case the judge ruled that a bull was a superior animal to 'cattle' and as such was not included in the terms of the Act. Bull baiting, bear baiting, dog fighting and cock fighting were all eventually outlawed in 1835, while the 1822 Act was extended to include dogs and protect animals impounded without food. In 1854 protection was again extended to cover all domestic animals of any kind or species, whether quadruped or not. This Act also prohibited the use of dogs as draught animals, pulling barrows, and so on.

The motives behind the passing of the Seabird Protection Act 1869 were also concerned primarily with the protection of human interests. The close seasons enforced through the Act ensured that there were plenty of seabirds crying from the clifftops to warn seamen of the impending dangers of the rocks below.

Even the 1876 Act stemmed from selfish human motives. A common notion in morality at that time was that the ill-treatment of animals was a source of moral degeneracy which would lead to immoral conduct towards fellow humans. Animal protection was therefore a way of preventing human immorality, but in an entirely different way from that proposed by the animal rights philosophy which emerged in the 1970s [see Introduction, page xiii]. However, the 1876 Act afforded some protection to experimental animals for the first time in the UK .

Cruelty to Animals Act 1876

The history of the passing of this Act is well documented in Moss (1961) [page 155], Hollands (1980) [page 155], Turner (1980) [page 156] and Ryder (1989) [page 155]. If it is considered that 'only' some 350 experiments were carried out on living animals annually at the time (compared with today's 3 million), then it is a great tribute to those such as Lord Carnarvon who were responsible for the legislation's enactment. The recommendations of the 1875 Royal Commission were not heeded, however, and the Bill put before Parliament by Lord Carnarvon was weakened by the Home Secretary, who was responding to pressure exerted by the medical and scientific community. This powerful lobby's continuing influence largely explains why it took 110 years for the 1876 Act to be replaced.

Lord Carnarvon's original Bill would have had all animals anaesthetized from the beginning to the end of all experiments, whatever the circumstances, and anti-vivisectionists suspect that had this become law, the scale of vivisection would not have increased from 350 experiments in 1876 to some 5 million in 1976. In the latter half of the twentieth century it became increasingly obvious that the Act was inadequate to protect animals in the way it was intended to do. Not only had the number of animals greatly increased but the nature of the experiments had also changed considerably from the simple anatomical and physiological experiments of the nineteenth century to the sophisticated experiments [page 000] in a multitude of disciplines in the twentieth, plus the growing number of safety and toxicity tests such as the notorious LD 50 and Draize [page 35].

The 1876 Act worked on the same principle as the new Act; that no one may carry out painful experiments on any living vertebrate animal unless they have been issued with a licence from the Home Secretary, and that the experiments must be carried out at licensed premises. One of the criticisms of the 1876 Act was that the policing of it was undertaken by Home Office Inspectors who were, in the main, ex-licencees, and there were only three, fairly undistinguished cases brought to court under this Act in its 110 years of existence. Even the most ardent supporter of animal experimentation must consider that it is unlikely that in all those years more researchers would not have contravened the regulations. However, the 1986 Act is subject to similarly inadequate policing.

Protection of Animals Act 1911

In the following few years several other animal-related Acts were passed, but the one which made the most impact on animal welfare was the Protection of Animals Act 1911 (1912 in Scotland). This still stands as 'the sheet anchor of animal welfare' (Moss (1961) [page 155]). It was introduced as a Bill by Sir George Greenwood, drafted by himself and a Reverend Bowen, a hunting man. Greenwood compromised by making no mention of hunting other than a reference which ensures that hunting is an activity not covered by the Act.

The 1911 Act covers various topics such as police powers, inspection of traps and use of poisons. But by far the most important body of this Act concerns cruelty to animals in general. Section 1 of the Act makes it an offence to: inflict physical cruelty, for example by kicking, beating, overloading, torturing; inflict mental cruelty, for example by terrifying or infuriating an animal; cause unnecessary suffering during transportation of animals; permit operations to be performed without due care and humanity; administer poisons or injurious substances without good reason. In addition to these specific causes of cruelty, a person was guilty of an offence of cruelty if s/he maliciously or unreasonably carried out, or caused to be carried out, an act which resulted in an animal suffering unnecessarily. This involved for the first time the omission of an act being regarded as an offence if that failure to act caused unnecessary suffering.

Most importantly, the concept of 'unnecessary suffering' had been introduced. This automatically acknowledged the existence of 'necessary suffering', a concept many people find unacceptable. It also lays open to debate the interpretation of the word 'necessary', although the law interprets it as 'the balancing of the interests of man in the benefits of a particular course of action against the interests of the animal in freedom from suffering' (Hollands 1980 [page 155]). Thus the courts have to decide whether an act of cruelty was 'necessary' on a sliding scale on which human interests are weighed against an animal's and, if the act was 'necessary', whether an acceptable degree of suffering was inflicted on the animal to obtain the object of the act.

This balancing of interests was already tipped in humans' favour by the Act exempting: anything made legal by the 1876 Act (and thus the later 1986 Act, that is, experiments permitted by Home Office Licences); the slaughter of animals for food for humans (unless it is accompanied by unnecessary suffering); and the hunting and coursing of captive animals (excluding birds) unless they have been released in an injured, mutilated or exhausted state, or if the animal is under control, has been recaptured or is in an enclosure from which it cannot reasonably escape. From the definition of 'animals' used [page 107], it can be seen that the Act does not protect wild animals unless they are more than temporarily restrained in some way – with man exercising his 'dominion' over them – when they fall into the category of captive animals. The courts have not been helpful in their interpretation of the level of captivity required before a wild animal is granted protection under the Act.

Therefore, under this Act limitless suffering could be inflicted on a wild animal to attain a 'necessary' objective. The Act considers hunting and coursing to be necessary, which means that there was, and in many cases still is, no protection for a hunted or coursed wild animal. It can be seen also that it is legal to hunt 'bagged' animals [page 18], that is, animals which have been captured then released in the proximity of a hunt for the purposes of being hunted. Later legislation in the Wildlife and Countryside Act 1981 [page 120] and its Amendment 1991 [page 131], was to provide protection for some specially selected wild animals; the target of this legislation being environmental protection rather than the welfare of animals. Consequently, some species, particularly the most common animals, are still to this day completely unprotected unless they are held captive, such as the grey squirrel and the fox. Domestic animals are protected by the 1911 Act whether they are living in domesticity or in the wild.

The Act also introduced the concept of the accused being guilty of an act of cruelty without it having to be proved that that it was his or her intention to be cruel. The only fact that has to be proved is whether pain or suffering was inflicted and if so whether it was necessary or not. The Act now made it an offence not to kill an animal that was in pain if it was in the power of, and if it was reasonable to expect of, a person to destroy that animal. It is not an offence to kill an animal using a humane method, although if the animal belongs to someone else then that may constitute an offence under the Criminal Damage Act 1971 (the law still regarding animals as 'chattels'). Thus, subject to the provisions of the Wildlife and Countryside Act affecting certain species, it is perfectly legal for a person to kill his/her own animal even if there is no reason for doing so as long as no more suffering is inflicted on the animal than is necessary to kill it.

The 1911 Act has many shortcomings, among the most important being that it does not provide powers of entry to private premises to inspect animals. Thus animals which are at risk on property that is not overseen or within earshot of the public, cannot be inspected. This includes farm animals which were to be better protected later by the Agriculture (Miscellaneous Provisions) Act 1968 [page 117]. Another area of concern are the soft penalties imposed for breaking the law, which bear no relation to the offences committed and do not represent an effective deterrent. Although the Act provides power to the courts enabling them to confiscate animals which are the subject of prosecution, and the power to prohibit owners from keeping animals, these powers are exercised in an inconsistent manner and certainly not used often enough. Thus, many offenders go on to create further suffering.

The 1911 Act is undoubtedly the one most used in prosecutions for cruelty, the majority being secured by animal charities' inspectorates after investigating complaints by the public. The inspectorates have no special powers other than those granted to any member of the public, but the public in general prefers to leave formal matters to organizations such as the Royal Society for the Prevention of Cruelty to Animals (RSPCA) [pages ix and 204] which have greater knowledge of the workings of the judiciary system. The RSPCA is the most prominent in bringing prosecutions for cruelty, securing 2,718 convictions in 1991, mostly using the 1911 Act.

The original 1911 Act still stands as the principal piece of legislation relating to cruelty though it has been amended on several occasions and its scope has been widened by other Acts. All of these are therefore referred to as the Protection of Animals Acts 1911–1988.

Summary

The Act deals with the prohibition of cruelty and unnecessary suffering whether by a malicious act or an act of omission, or whether the act was intended to be cruel or not. It prohibits:

(a) anyone (or being the owner permits anyone) from cruelly beating, kicking, ill-treating, over-riding, torturing, infuriating or terrifying any animal or causing unnecessary suffering;

(b) anyone to transport any animal in such a way as to cause unnecessary suffering;

(c) anyone to cause or assist in the fighting or baiting of any animal;

(d) anyone to permit an operation to be carried out on an animal without due care and humanity;

(e) anyone to administer poisonous or injurious substances to an animal without reasonable cause;

(f) anyone to use a dog to to pull carts, etc. on the public highway;

(g) anyone to sell or give away or place poisonous grain or seed (except that for *bona fide* agricultural use), though there is a defence that the poison was placed for destroying rats and mice, etc. and all reasonable precautions were taken to prevent other animals taking it. This defence was amended by the Animals (Cruel Poisons) Act 1962 [page 117].

Exemptions from (a) to (e) inclusive are: anything done lawfully under the Animals (Scientific Procedures) Act 1986 [page 123], i.e. all procedures licensed by the Secretary of State under this Act; slaughtering of animals for food, except where unnecessary suffering is caused; coursing and hunting of any captive animal unless it is liberated in an injured or exhausted condition, though it shall not be considered to be coursed or hunted before it is liberated for the purpose of such, or after it has been recaptured, or if it is under control, or if it is coursed or hunted in an enclosed space from which there is no reasonable chance of escape.

Powers are given to order the destruction of an animal if a court is satisfied that it would be cruel to keep it alive (vet's evidence required if the owner protests); and to deprive the owner of the ownership of the animal. The police are given powers to: slaughter an animal on the evidence of a registered vet; have animals removed without the owner's consent (the definition of *animal* for these purposes only is taken to be any horse, mule, ass, bull, goat, sheep or pig); apprehend anyone on suspicion of cruelty; and take into possession any animals or vehicles that belong to anyone apprehended under this Act.

Animals kept in pounds (enclosures for confining animals) must be given sufficient wholesome and suitable food and water.

Any spring-traps for catching rabbits or hares must be inspected at reasonable intervals of time and at least once every day between sunrise and sunset.

Definitions
Animal – any domestic or captive animal.

Domestic animal – any animal such as any horse, bull, mule, ass, sheep, pig, goat, dog, cat, fowl or any other animal that is tame or has been tamed or is being sufficiently tamed as to serve some purpose for use by man. The terms horse, bull, mule, etc. include all ages and sexes of those animals.

Captive animals – any animal (not being a domestic animal) of any species, including any bird, fish or reptile, which is in captivity or confinement, or which is maimed, pinioned or subjected to any appliance or contrivance for the purpose of hindering or preventing its escape from captivity or confinement. However, if an animal is temporarily unable to escape then this is taken as not being in a state of captivity.

Wild animals are not included in this Act unless restrained as described above. Protection is offered to some wild animals by other legislation such as the Wildlife and Countryside Act 1981 [page 120] and the Badgers Acts 1973 and 1991 (Protection of Badgers Act 1992) [pages 135 and 128].

The Performing Animals (Regulation) Act 1925

In 1921 a Select Committee of the House of Lords was appointed to investigate the training of performing animals. (For an overview, including extracts from the evidence given before the Select Committee, see Westacott (1962) [page 140]). Public concern was growing over the treatment of animals in circuses [page 7], some of the methods of training allegedly involving beating with crowbars and burning with hot irons.

Only a few of the Committee's eight recommendations were incorporated into the final Act which restricts the training of animals for performances, and the actual exhibition of such animals, to those holding Certificates of Registration. The Local Authority responsible for issuing licences keeps a register of trainers which can be inspected at all reasonable times, on payment of a fee. Trainers can be struck off the register and disqualified either permanently or for a specified time if they are convicted of an offence against this Act or the Protection of Animals Act 1911 [page 105]. On the licence, the description of the animals and the performances for which they are to be trained does not have to reveal any professional secrets. Thus, while apparatus used in the actual performances has to be described, that which might be used in the taming and training of the animal does not. To ensure that the conditions of a licence are not being contravened the Local Authority can appoint inspectors who, along with the police, can inspect the animals 'at any reasonable time' at the place where the animals are exhibited or quartered.

The Act is not without its faults. It does not stop anyone obtaining a certificate; the Local Authority is bound by law to grant certificates unless applicants are under disqualification at the time. The Act contains no specific safeguards for the animals (no cage sizes specified), nor regulations on the conditions of transport. The later Zoo Licensing Act 1981 [page 122] regulates conditions in zoos [page 24], but circuses are exempt from these regulations and from those contained in the Dangerous Wild Animals Act 1976 [page 119]. Thus anyone can register as a trainer, own a circus and move animals around the country as they wish. Local Authorities have limited resources and also vary in how they regard their responsibilities, leading to difficulties in attaining any continuity in this Act as performers travel all over the country and abroad, and circuses in Britain may in return accommodate many foreign acts although very few circuses now bring animals into Britain due to quarantine regulations.

Anyone training animals for agricultural or sporting purposes, or for the exhibition of such, needs no licence. Neither do the police nor the military.

Summary

The Act prohibits the training or exhibition of a performing animal unless by a registered person who has been issued with a certificate, on payment of a fee, from a Local Authority. Every Local Authority keeps a register of all the animal trainers living in its area and this register can be inspected at all reasonable times, on payment of a fee. If an animal trainer has no fixed address in Britain then s/he must choose a district and register with its Local Authority.

The application for registration must contain a description of the animals and of the performances for which they are to be trained, with mention of any apparatus which is to be used for the purpose of the performance. This description need not give away any professional secrets, and the definition excludes any apparatus which might be used in the training of the animals.

A person cannot hold a certificate if s/he has committed an offence under this Act or under the Protection of Animals Act 1911 [page 105], and the courts have the power to disqualify a person from holding a certificate either permanently or for a specified length of time. Thus, if a police officer or Local Authority official makes a complaint against a trainer, the trainer can be struck off the register permanently.

The Local Authority has the power to appoint officers to inspect the animals at their quarters, or at the place where they are exhibited, at any reasonable time. However, this does not include during a public performance, when the police and the Local Authority inspectors are not allowed to go behind the stage.

The police and inspectors may also ask the trainer to produce his/her certificate of registration; failure to produce such is an offence, as is obstructing the police or inspectors, or hiding any animal from such inspectors. It is also an offence to apply for registration while still disqualified.

Definitions

Animal – vertebrates; invertebrates are not protected under this Act.

Trainer – someone who trains animals for exhibition to the public.
Exhibition – any entertainment to which the public is admitted whether free of charge or not.

The Protection of Animals Act 1934

In 1924 an attempt was made to introduce the American rodeo to the UK. The RSPCA [page 204] unsuccessfully took proceedings against the organizers of the event, which took place at Wembley and resulted in several cattle being badly injured. However, the RSPCA was later successful in prosecutions of similar offences of cruelty to cattle while being ridden by 'cowboys'. Public opinion was such that when another attempt was made to organize a rodeo in Britain in 1934 a Bill was rushed through Parliament in record time.

The essence of this Act was to forbid the public performance of throwing with ropes untrained horses and bulls, wrestling with untrained bulls, and the stimulation of bucking by the appliance of the cinch-rope round the tender hind regions of the animals. This in effect prohibits rodeos in this country as these acts are the basis for the sports of steer and bronco riding, steer roping/wrestling, and bulldogging. Nevertheless, the public performance of riding or attempting to ride a horse or bull is not illegal as long as the above-mentioned practices are not involved. The definition of performance does not include a film shown to the public, although it may be considered that this is covered by the next piece of relevant legislation, the Cinematograph Films (Animals) Act 1937 [see page 122]. However, although the law has considered the rodeo to cause suffering in its practices, films and television programmes featuring rodeos are still common.

Summary
The Act prohibits rodeos in the UK, by banning the public performance of: casting or throwing with ropes, etc. any unbroken horse or untrained bull; wrestling, fighting, etc. with any untrained bull; riding any horse or bull which is being made to buck by the use of cruel means; the public participating in such rodeo riding.

The onus is on the accused, in any proceedings taken under this Act, to prove that the horse or bull used was broken or trained.

Definitions
Horse and *bull* – includes all ages and sexes of these animals.
Public performance – does not include public showing of films of rodeos.

The Cinematograph Films (Animals) Act 1937

As early as 1913 the RSPCA [page 204] was making representations to the Film Censor regarding the suffering of animals in the film industry. In 1935 a Film Consultation Panel was established, on which the RSPCA was represented, to review films in which animals had been used, and two years later the Society was successful in bringing about legislation with the aim of protecting such animals. The Cinematograph Films (Animals) Act 1937 made it an offence for a person to supply or exhibit a film (which does not have to have been made in the UK) to the public if any of the scenes were directed to involve pain or terror in any animal or if the animal had been goaded to fury. Thus there is a defence that the scenes were not directed with the deliberate intention of being cruel, and the film director could also make a film of persons outside his direction carrying out acts of cruelty, as in the case of filming bullfights and so on.

The definition of animal used here is the same as for the 1911 Act and so excludes wild animals, except those in captivity. A film depicting suffering in wild animals is not covered by this law. Also the British Board of Film Classification has the power to cut scenes which involve animal suffering from films though this comes too late for the particular animals involved. In consideration of the films that have been released in the UK it would seem that this piece of legislation is of limited value and is not enforced [see page 11].

The Docking and Nicking of Horses Act 1949

Prior to this Act it had long been the practice among horsemen to amputate or 'dock' about two-thirds of a horse's tail if the horse was used in harness. The reason for doing this was to prevent the tail from becoming caught up in the harness as the horse swished its tail about, though fashion played a part too at one time. Old paintings of horses show them with stubby fan-shaped tails which would have been of little use in keeping flies away. Not only was the actual removal of the tail an act of cruelty but the horse was left without protection from flies which are a considerable nuisance to horses in summer. The 'nicking' of a horse's tail, cutting some of the tail muscles or tendons, was carried out to give the horse an exaggerated high tail carriage. This practice was carried out on riding horses purely for fashion and some breeds of horse in the USA are still subjected to it.

In 1949 an Act was implemented which prohibited both the docking and the nicking of horses' tails. The exemption is when the tail is diseased or injured and the operation is necessary for the health of the horse, in which case a member of the Royal College of Veterinary Surgeons [page 216] must certify this fact in writing. The Act also prohibits the landing of imported docked horses, with the exceptions that they must be re-exported as soon as possible, or that they are licensed by the Ministry of Agriculture, Food and Fisheries (MAFF) [page 216].

The sight of a horse without a flowing tail is unusual these days, although two men were convicted at Kilmarnock District Court of docking nine Clydesdale horses in 1986.

Definitions

Docking – intentional removal of a bone, or part of a bone, from a horse's tail.

Nicking – intentional severing of any tendon or muscle in a horse's tail.

Horse – all ages and sexes of horse and pony, including mule and hinny.

The Pet Animals Act 1951 and 1983

After the Second World War an upsurge in the opening of new pet shops and the practice of selling pets at street markets led to the RSPCA [page 204] drafting regulatory legislation. The Bill was introduced to Parliament by a Mr Russell MP, and eventually became the Pet Animals Act 1951 which made it an offence to run a pet shop without a licence. Local Authorities were made responsible for the licensing of pet shops and it was they who had to consider the applicant's suitability.

After years of demonstration by welfare groups at London's notorious Club Row market, this Act was amended in 1983 when the selling of pets in the street or any public place was made illegal. Included in the exemptions to this Act is anyone who breeds and sells pedigree pets, although dog breeders must be licensed under the Breeding of Dogs Act 1973 [page 135].

Summary

The Act deals with the licensing of pet shops and prohibits: keeping a pet shop without a licence, or in contravention of the conditions laid down in a licence; selling pets to children under the age of twelve years; selling pets in the streets or any public place; obstructing an inspector or vet authorized to inspect a pet shop by the Local Authority, in order to ascertain that the Act is not being contravened.

The Local Authority has the responsibility of issuing licences and must try to ensure that the animals will be properly cared for, accommodated in suitable containers with the correct conditions with regard to temperature, lighting, etc., are fed suitable food and visited at suitable intervals. In the case of mammals they must not be sold at too young an age and precautions must be taken to ensure disease is not easily spread, and that in the case of an emergency such as fire, the appropriate steps could be taken. Other conditions may also be included in the licence.

The Local Authority can authorize an inspector or a veterinarian to inspect the premises to ensure that the conditions of the licence are not being or have not been contravened. A court can withdraw a licence and disqualify anybody from holding one for as long a time as it feels fit if it is convinced of offences committed under this Act or the Protection of Animals Act 1911 [page 105].

Definitions
Pet shop – any premises, including private dwellings, where anyone sells pets or keeps animals that will be sold as pets (whether to be sold by the person keeping them or by someone else). There are two exceptions. A person is not keeping a pet shop if s/he is keeping or selling pedigree animals which s/he has bred or offspring from a pet of his/hers. Any person who is in the business of breeding pedigree animals and is at the same time selling animals as pets is deemed not to be keeping a pet shop as long as the Local Authority is satisfied that the animals being sold were acquired with a view to using them for breeding or showing purposes and were later found to be unsuitable. However, while exempt from this Act, breeders of dogs are not exempt from having to obtain a licence under the Breeding of Dogs Act 1973 [page 135]. There is no offence under this Act of selling unfit animals but the Local Authority may impose such a condition on the licence.
Animal – includes any vertebrate.
Pedigree animal – any animal which, due to its breeding, is eligible for registration in a register kept by any recognized club or society.
Pets – for cats and dogs this includes those sold or kept for wholly or mainly domestic purposes, and for any animal this includes those sold or kept for ornamental purposes.

The Protection of Animals (Anaesthetics) Act 1954

Whilst the Protection of Animals Act 1911 made it an offence to perform an operation on an animal without due care and humanity, the 1954 Act (and the Protection of Animals [Anaesthetics] Act 1964) further protected animals from the infliction of unnecessary suffering during operations. They made illegal any operations conducted (with or without instruments) on sensitive tissue or bone structure without the animal being sufficiently anaesthetized to prevent it feeling any pain. These Acts do not cover birds, fish or reptiles which, during operations, are thus only covered by the 1911 Act.

Summary

Under this Act it is an offence to operate on sensitive tissue or bone structure without the animal being sufficiently anaesthetized to prevent it feeling any pain. It prohibits the dehorning of cattle and the castration of a male animal, unless as stated under the exemptions.

Exemptions: injections or extractions using a hollow needle; experiments licensed under the Animals (Scientific Procedures) Act 1986 [page 123]; emergency first aid for the purpose of saving life or relieving pain; amputation of dew claws of a puppy before it opens its eyes; minor operations performed by a vet that are quick and painless, and those that are performed by a vet or other person, that are lacking in complexity; the following castrations of livestock at the specified ages – bull before two months, ram before three months, goat before two months, pig before two months of age; castration by the application of a rubber ring (or similar device) which constricts the flow of blood to the scrotum in the first week of life; docking of lambs' tails by rubber rings that constrict the blood flowing to the tail, in the first week of life; docking of pigs' tails in the first week of life; disbudding of calves by chemical cauterization in the first week of life.

In addition to these, further limitations have been added by the Removal of Antlers in Velvet (Anaesthetics) Order 1980 which regulates the removal of any part of deers' antlers while in velvet, and the Welfare of Livestock (Prohibited Operations) Regulations 1982.

Definitions

Animal – does not include fowl, bird, reptile or fish.
Cattle – any sex or age of cattle.

The Pests Act 1954

The abolition of the gin trap (or leghold trap [page 72]) only came about after a long and strenuous battle, fought in the main part by the Universities Federation for Animal Welfare (UFAW) [page 206]. In 1935 a Gin Traps (Prohibition) Bill, promoted by Viscount Tredegar, had only narrowly been defeated. At this time the University of London Animal Welfare Society estimated that huge numbers of birds, cats and rabbits were being caught each year in gin traps.

Later, the 1951 Scott-Henderson Committee on cruelty to wild animals (which, incidentally, recommended that wild animals be included in the protection afforded by the 1911 Act [see above]), was to describe the trap as 'a diabolical instrument which causes an incalculable amount of suffering'. Yet its recommendation to prohibit the use of the gin trap was not followed until five years later, and even then the prohibition was not to come into force until August 1958. This did not include Northern Ireland and Scotland, and it took until 1969 and 1973 respectively to prohibit the use of the gin trap in these countries.

Although the use of gin traps is illegal in the UK, it is still legal to manufacture and export them for use in other countries, and it is also legal to import the furs of animals that have been caught in such traps abroad [page 72]. However, with effect from 1995, an EC Regulation will ban the use of leghold traps in the Community and prohibit the importation of furs and fur products from countries continuing to use such traps. The free-running snare is still in use in the UK [page 88] and both the RSPCA [page 204] and the League Against Cruel Sports (LACS) [page 196] have mounted campaigns in recent years to try to put an end to its use.

Summary

The Act prohibits: the sale, possession or use of spring-traps to kill or take animals, unless the trap is of an approved type and is used in approved circumstances; open trapping of hares or rabbits with a spring-trap; use of a rabbit infected with myxomatosis to spread disease among uninfected rabbits. Provisions are made for the making of Orders specifying approved traps, etc.

Exemptions are made for any experiments conducted lawfully under the Animals (Scientific Procedures) Act 1986 [page 123] and action taken under licence from the MAFF [page 216].

The Abandonment of Animals Act 1960

The Act prohibits the abandonment of animals, either permanently or temporarily, in circumstances likely to cause unnecessary suffering, unless there is a reasonable excuse. This applies to the owner or any person having control of the animal, or anyone who causes an animal to be abandoned, or any owner who permits his/her animal to be abandoned. Ostensibly wild animals which are released back into the wild may be the subject-matter of an offence under this provision if the release is improperly carried out in circumstances where the animals would suffer.

Definition

Animal – as for the Protection of Animals Act 1911 [page 105].

The Animals (Cruel Poisons) Act 1962

Whilst the 1911 Act covered the administering of poisons, laying of poisoned grain, and so on, this only applied to those animals protected by the Act. Thus it was perfectly legal to use all sorts of poisons to kill wild animals. The 1962 Act and its subsequent amendments made it an offence to kill any mammal by cruel poisons which have been defined in later regulations and include red squill, strychnine (exemption for killing moles) and yellow phosphorus. The Act made it clear that a defendant cannot rely, in his/her defence, on the fact that s/he laid such poisons for vermin even where reasonable precautions are taken to prevent domestic animals having access to them.

The Agriculture (Miscellaneous Provisions) Act 1968

In 1964 Ruth Harrison's book, *Animal Machines* was published [page 146], detailing modern factory farming practices. The subsequent public outcry led to the Minister for Agriculture appointing a Technical Committee to Enquire into the Welfare of Animals Kept under Intensive Livestock Husbandry Systems. Chaired by Professor Brambell it gave rise to the now famous Brambell Report [page 145], submitted to government in 1965.

The Committee recommended that 'the existing animal welfare legislation does not adequately safeguard farm animals and a new Act is needed incorporating a fuller definition of suffering and enabling Ministers to make regulations requiring conditions for particular animals. The Act and regulations should be enforced by the State Veterinary Service, and a Statutory Farm Animal Welfare Standing Advisory Committee should be set up to advise ministers.' In 1967 the government established the Farm Animal Welfare Advisory Committee which was replaced by the Farm Animal Welfare Council (FAWC) [page 214] in 1979.

Some of the Committee's recommendations were incorporated into the Agriculture (Miscellaneous) Provisions Act 1968. This was a mixed bag of legislation regarding agriculture, but the section relating to animal welfare states that a person is guilty of an offence if s/he causes unneccessary pain or distress to any livestock on agricultural land under his/her control. Also if he knows of, or may reasonably be expected to know of, any such pain or distress caused to livestock and fails to act, he is guilty of an offence. This Act (and the Welfare of Animals Act [Northern Ireland] 1972) gives the Agricultural Ministers the power to make regulations in the interest of the welfare of farm animals kept on agricultural land, and to prepare Codes that contain recommendations for the keeping of such animals. The difference between the two is that regulations are mandatory, thus contravening a regulation is an offence, while the Codes are not. Though these Codes [pages 46 and 147] are not binding in law, if a person is accused of causing unnecessary pain or unnecessary distress to livestock, then failure to observe the Welfare Codes may be relied upon (in theory) by the prosecution as tending to establish guilt.

Government's thinking on the Codes is that with a lack of established experience and sound scientific knowledge it is impossible to keep up with all the innovations and advances of new technology and know what their consequences are for the welfare of livestock. It also considers that the Codes are a most useful way of providing advice and guidance to farmers on how best to ensure the well-being of livestock. To reinforce their impact, members of the State Veterinary Service carry out visits to farms specifically to check that Code provisions are being followed. The opportunity is taken to discuss with the farmer any necessary steps to improve conditions. However, not everyone agreees with this advisory approach and there has been considerable condemnation of the Codes for their lack of 'teeth', and for the vagueness in which their recommendations are couched. Some welfare organizations are adamant that little headway will be made in ensuring the basic welfare of livestock until the Codes are made mandatory.

The first Welfare Codes were approved by Parliament in 1969 and a year later the State Veterinary Service submitted a report on how they were working in practice on farms. It generally considered that the welfare of animals was not in any danger even where the recommendations in the Codes were not being followed, and observed that stockmanship was 'sound' on most intensive farms. Their suggestions, along with those of the Farm Animal Welfare Advisory Committee, were debated in Parliament and from this a new set of revised Codes for cattle, pigs, domestic fowl and turkeys was issued in 1971. Sheep Codes followed in 1977 and another set was issued in 1983. Later Codes cover farmed deer, ducks, goats and rabbits.

The Regulations which have been made under this Act include the Welfare of Livestock (Intensive Units) Regulations 1978, the Welfare of Livestock (Prohibited Operations) Regulations 1982, the Welfare of Calves Regulations 1987, the Welfare of Battery Hens Regulations 1987, the Welfare of Livestock Regulations 1990 and the Welfare of Pigs Regulations 1991. These require the inspection of equipment and stock by a stockperson at least once a day. They also make a long list of operations illegal, including tail-docking of cattle, tongue-amputation of calves, hot branding of cattle, surgical castration of male birds, teeth grinding in sheep, etc. Certain operations are permitted but only up to specified ages. For example, piglets can only be tail-docked if less than eight days of age. However, there are exceptions to these prohibitions: anything made legal by the Animals (Scientific Procedures) Act 1986 [page 123]; first aid in an emergency; and an operation performed by a veterinarian in whose opinion the operation was necessary to treat a disease or injury.

Definitions
Livestock – any creature kept for the production of food, skin, wool or for use in the farming of the land, including the farming of deer for antlers in velvet.

Agricultural land – land used for agriculture for the purpose of a trade or business. The definition is not clear in a number of areas (fish farming and mixed-use deer parks, for example).

The Dangerous Wild Animals Act 1976

Prior to the Dangerous Wild Animals Act 1976 there was a craze for the keeping of exotic pets by private owners in the UK. A proliferation of pet lions, monkeys, pumas and other animals were being held in the most deplorable conditions. Regulation of this practice was needed in order to protect both public and animals.

The Act made the keeping of exotic pets an expensive pastime. To the cost of buying an unusual pet was added the burden of providing suitable accommodation, compulsory insurance, and the Local Authority's considerable discretion in deciding the licence fee.

Summary
The Act prohibits the keeping of dangerous wild animals without a licence issued by the Local Authority (LA); and the holding of such licence if disqualified under this Act, the Protection of Animals Acts 1911–1988 [pages 105 and 126], the Pet Animals Act 1951 [page 113], the Animal Boarding Establishments Act 1963 [page 133], the Riding Establishments Act 1964 [page 133] or the Breeding of Dogs Act 1973 [page 135]. A licence has to stipulate the species and number of animals kept and the premises at which they are kept. The LA has to

ensure that public safety is not at risk and that the applicant holds a suitable liability insurance policy against damages caused by the animals. The LA also has to ensure that the animals will not cause a public nuisance. A meagre attempt is made to safeguard the welfare of the animals by the provision that the LA shall not grant a licence unless it is satisfied that the animals will be properly accommodated, cared for, exercised, precautions taken against the spread of infections and against emergencies like fire. Licences are not granted to persons under the age of eighteen years.

Before a licence is issued a registered veterinarian must have inspected the premises and submitted a report to the LA. The LA can also ask other suitably qualified persons, such as a fire prevention officer, to inspect the premises. The licence lasts for one year during which time the LA can give written consent to a vet or someone it considers competent to inspect the animals to ensure that the conditions of the licence are being fulfilled. In the case of an offence against the Act, animals may be taken away and the LA has the power to dispose of them.

Exemptions: circuses, pet shops, zoos (all governed, to a greater or lesser extent, by other legislation [pages 109, 113, 122]; premises licensed under the Animals (Scientific Procedures) Act 1986 [page 123]. In certain cases a person is exempt from needing a licence if s/he only has possession of a dangerous wild animal for the purpose of preventing its escape, restoring it to its owner, transporting it for its owner, or for it to undergo veterinary treatment.

Definitions

Keeper – person who has the animal in his possession or is the last person to have possession of the animal. The keeper must hold the licence, and while it is not uncommon for the keeper and the owner to be two different people, the Act discourages the practice by only granting licences under these circumstances in exceptional cases.

Dangerous wild animals – the obvious species and others on a list far too long to be included here. The Secretary of State has the power to change the list at any time.

The Wildlife and Countryside Act 1981

The Wildlife and Countryside Act 1981, which replaced various Protection of Birds Acts, covers many areas of relevance to the protection and conservation of both land and the wild animals living on it. There are sixteen schedules to the Act, covering the protection of birds, animals, plants, land and footpaths. The Act contains long lists specifying the prohibited methods of taking, killing, injuring or disturbing certain animals and birds, some of the methods being applicable to all wild animals (such as self-locking snares, crossbows, explosives, live animal decoys), whilst others are only applicable to listed animals.

There are numerous offences created by the Act and even more numerous specified exemptions and defences. Thus, there are various exemptions that can be used in defence against a charge brought under this Act such as the setting of the following articles: any trap or snare; any electrical device for killing or stunning; any poisonous, poisoned or stupefying substance. These methods are permissible for killing wild animals (though subject to their own relevant legislation, such as the Pests Act 1954 [page115] for traps, and the Animals [Cruel Poisons] Act 1962 [page 117]), except certain protected ones such as the badger, wild cat and red squirrel. If one of these species is caught in one of the aforementioned devices, and it was set to protect public health, agriculture, forestry, fisheries or nature conservation, and all reasonable precautions were taken to ensure that none of the protected species was injured, then this may be proffered as a defence.

Another exemption is if the methods are used in accordance with, and under a licence issued to, the defendant. Licences under this Act are issued by the Nature Conservancy Council [as was; see page 216] for those related to such topics as ringing, photographing, conserving or re-introducing wild animals. The Minister of Agriculture, Fisheries and Food (MAFF) [page 216], the Secretary of State for Wales, and the Secretary of State for Scotland, are responsible for issuing licences related to activities protecting agricultural or forestry interests.

The habitats of specially protected species are also covered. It is an offence to damage or obstruct access to any structure or place that they use as shelter or protection, unless that place is in a dwelling house. It is also prohibited to disturb these animals while they are in such a place. These animals include several species of bats, butterflies, moths, snails, otters, and the red squirrel. The sale of these animals, whether they are alive or dead, intact or in part, is prohibited, as is the advertisement of such a sale.

One particularly useful provision in the Act affects the way in which prosecutions may proceed. Normally, prosecutions of offences (of the type contemplated in the Act) must be commenced within six months of the date of the offence. However, for some offences under this Act, evidence-gathering is assisted because prosecution may be commenced within two years of the date of the offence, provided that it is commenced within six months of evidence coming to light. For many wild animal-related offences, where the deeds are committed in remote places, this provision is of great assistance to the prosecutor.

Under this Act birds in captivity must in general have sufficient space to stretch their wings freely. Significantly, and conveniently for the factory farmer, this does not apply to poultry [page 52].

The Zoo Licensing Act 1981

The Zoo Licensing Act was designed to protect the public and zoo animals by ensuring that the standard of accommodation is high enough to guarantee the safety of the visitors and the welfare of the animals. The Act came about after the enormous increase in the number of zoos and wildlife parks [see page 24] in the 1960s. The term 'zoo' covers wildlife parks as the definition is taken to be the exhibition of wild animals to the public other than for the purposes of a circus or pet shop, and applies to any zoo to which the public have entry (free or otherwise) for seven days in any twelve months.

It is unlawful to operate such a zoo without a licence issued by the Local Authority (LA). Licences are granted initially for four years and then for six-year periods during which time the licence can be revoked, varied or have additional conditions attached. Licences can be refused on the basis of the LA inspector's report with regard to public safety and animal welfare, or if the applicant has been convicted of an offence under this Act or any of the Protection of Animals Acts 1911–1988, and others. The Secretary of State has issued Standards of Modern Zoo Practice with the aim of improving conditions.

Several criticisms have been voiced by welfare organizations regarding this Act. Apart from the licensing procedure being too complicated, the LAs are not bound by their inspectors' advice when considering an application for a licence. An inspector's report is not made public and so the LA can ignore it if it so wishes. Concern has also been expressed over the fact that some of the inspectors are zoo staff and as such could not be expected to be unbiased when inspecting other zoos. Regarding the granting of dispensations by the Secretary of State in the case of small or specialized zoos, the fear is that a small zoo may be granted a full dispensation and thus not be subject to any inspections. The zoo could then obtain more animals, even dangerous ones, and yet still be exempt from the provisions of the Act. While dispensations are revocable, it can take a long time for a LA to become aware of such a situation.

Summary

The Act prohibits the keeping of wild animals in a zoo unless a licence has been obtained from the Local Authority (LA) within which the whole/major part of the zoo is situated.

The applicant has to notify the LA, in writing, of his/her intentions two months before applying and has to publish such intentions in one local and one national newspaper. S/he also has to display a copy of the notice at the intended site of the zoo. The notice to the LA is kept available for public inspection free of charge at reasonable hours, at the LA offices, until the application has been dealt with. The notice must include detail of the situation of the zoo; the type and number of animals to be kept and the arrangements for their living accommodation, maintenance and well-being; the approximate numbers and categories of staff employed or to be employed in the zoo.

Before it can grant or refuse a licence the LA must consider inspectors' reports made after inspection of the zoo, or if no inspection has taken place it shall consult persons specifically nominated by the Secretary of State. The LA must also take into consideration any representations made by: the applicant; the local fire services; the local chief of police; the governing body of any national institution concerned with the operation of zoos; a planning authority if the site is not in a LA with the power to grant a licence; any persons who allege that the zoo would injuriously affect the health or safety of persons living in the neighbourhood of the zoo, or seriously affect the preservation of law and order; or any other person whose representations might show grounds on which the authority has a power or duty to refuse to grant a licence.

The LA is responsible for carrying out periodical inspections and must give a zoo at least twenty-eight days' notice of the date of an inspection. No licence may be revoked on grounds involving the care and treatment of animals unless the LA first consults such persons named on a list held by the Secretary of State for this purpose.

The Animals (Scientific Procedures) Act 1986

As can be seen from the historical overview [page 102], the Cruelty to Animals Act 1876 was designed to regulate very few experiments of only a limited nature and could never cope with the vast array of sophisticated experiments developed in the last thirty years or so.

It would seem that history repeats itself in this area. In 1963 the government appointed a Departmental Committee on Experiments on Animals, chaired by the late Sir Sydney Littlewood. The report of the Committee's findings was published in 1965 and gave eighty-five recommendations, forty-eight of which required new legislation, along with fifteen general comments. The report met the fate of the earlier Royal Commission of 1875; its recommendations were ignored by the government and it took another twenty-three years for it to enact a new law dealing with animal experimentation.

The Animals (Scientific Procedures) Act 1986 has been the source of a great deal of controversy which is dealt with in Chapter 2: Animal Experimentation [page 29] and came about largely as a result of pressure exerted on government by the anti-vivisection lobby, and also because of concern among sections of the scientific community over the use of animals in 'non-essential' research, as in the LD 50 test [page 35].

The basic principle of the Act is the same as for its predecessor; that is, no one may carry out an experiment on a protected animal unless he/she holds a personal licence granted by the Secretary of State, and the experiment is carried out on licensed premises. The definition of 'protected animals' is any living vertebrate other than humans, which excludes invertebrates, thus giving no protection to the octopus and the squid, for instance.

The new Act goes further than the old one in controlling all 'regulated procedures', which increases the scope of the Act beyond that of experiments. These procedures must be specified in the personal licence along with a specification of the animal(s) to be used. The definition of regulated procedures covers any experimental or scientific procedure applied to a protected animal which may cause pain, suffering, distress or lasting harm.

Another new concept is that procedures must be part of a specified programme of work which is authorized by a *project* licence issued to the person who has overall responsibility for the project. Each *personal* licence must be sponsored by a senior licensee who is required to assess and testify as to the applicant's qualifications, training, experience and character. A licence will not be granted to a person under the age of eighteen.

For the first time the Secretary of State is required to consider the likely adverse effects on the animals in relation to the possible likely benefits to humans. The project licence balances the 'severity' (mild, moderate, substantial) of the procedure against such 'benefit'. Also, the licence applicant must have given adequate consideration to the use of alternatives to animals, and in the case of a dog, cat, primate or equine, there must be no other animal suitable for use in the procedure, and if there is it must be shown to be impracticable to obtain it.

The licence granted to a scientific establishment must be issued to a person of authority there and specify a person who is responsible for the day-to-day care of the experimental animals, plus a veterinary surgeon or other suitably qualified person, to provide advice on the animals' health and welfare. The same conditions apply to breeding and supplying establishments. These must be licensed if they are breeding or supplying certain protected animals (dogs, cats, primates, rabbits, hamsters, guinea pigs, rats or mice).

One of the conditions of the personal licence is that the animals mentioned above have to be purpose-bred for use in experiments and the supplier of purpose-bred dogs and cats must be identified. This is an attempt to eradicate the practice of stolen pets being used in laboratories [page 39]. Another condition is that an animal which is in severe pain or distress which cannot be alleviated must immediately and painlessly be killed by one of the methods specified by the Act.

An area of contention in the Act has been the re-use of protected animals clause which allows the re-use of animals in certain situations. While this may be one way of reducing the number of animals used, it can lead to one animal undergoing several painful procedures before being killed. Another area of concern has been the repeal of the previous total ban on the use of urari or curare (a muscle-relaxant) as an anaesthetic. The new Act also allows the use of neuromuscular blocking agents where this is specified in the personal and project licences. The use of rodents for the practice of manual skills is also newly permitted. The rodents should be humanely killed at the end of the procedure.

Secrecy was increased by the inclusion of a clause prohibiting the disclosure of any information a person may have obtained in the carrying out of any functions under this Act and who knows, or has reasonable grounds to believe, that the information was given to him/her in confidence. An important source of public information has thus been lost, especially to the anti-vivisection movement.

The Animal Procedures Committee has been established to advise the Secretary of State, and it has a similar remit to that of the Farm Animal Welfare Council (FAWC) [page 46]. It can instigate research relevant to its functions and must submit a report every year to the Secretary on its activities. The Committee has to take into consideration both the interests of science and industry, and those of the animals. All applications for testing cosmetics are submitted to it. The Committee should have two-thirds of its members drawn from medical, veterinary or biological backgrounds, one member shall be a lawyer, and in its final constitution not more than 50 per cent of the Committee shall have held a Home Office licence in the past six years. The power of the Committee to form sub-committees may lead to those with vested interests appointing others with the same interests. With the scientific community representing two-thirds of the Committee this could, in time, lead to biased advice being generated.

The Secretary of State publishes Codes of Practice for the care of protected animals and their use in experiments, similar to the Codes for farm animals, as well as guidelines on how the Act is administered. A criticism of the guidelines is that they have no legal standing, are not explicitly admissible as evidence in proceedings, and can be revoked or changed without the approval of Parliament.

The new Act was implemented on 1 January 1987 and took some five years to become fully operational. It permitted the licences that were issued under the Cruelty to Animals Act 1876 [page 104] to run until their expiry date. New licences have to be applied for every five years.

The Act has been seen by many to be the dawning of a new era of communication and co-operation between the scientific community and those at pains to safeguard the welfare of animals. However, it is viewed by anti-vivisectionists as a 'Vivisectors' Charter', empty of any prohibitions or guarantees that animals will be protected from pain, and even failing to prohibit any non-medical research.

Protection of Animals (Penalties) Act 1987

One of the major criticisms of the Protection of Animals Act 1911 [page 105] has always been that the penalties imposed for contravening it are too lenient, bear no relation to the offences committed and fail to represent an effective deterrent. In 1987 the Protection of Animals (Penalties) Act amended the 1911 Act so as to increase the penalties that magistrates could impose on those committing acts of cruelty and found guilty under the 1911 Act. The offender could be liable to imprisonment for a term not exceeding six months and/or to a fine not exceeding a maximum of £5,000. The Act does not extend to Scotland or Northern Ireland.

Protection of Animals (Amendment) Act 1988

This later piece of legislation also came about to strengthen the Protection of Animals Act 1911. It changed the law so that a court could disqualify a person from having custody of an animal on a first conviction of cruelty. Previously anyone convicted of cruelty to animals could continue to keep them until they were successfully prosecuted for a subsequent offence of cruelty.

The 1980s saw a tremendous upsurge of interest in illegal bloodsports such as dog fighting [page 10] and badger baiting [page 9] and the surge of public feeling against these practices brought pressure to bear on the government to tighten up the laws and to increase the penalties. Therefore the 1988 Act not only increased the penalties for offences relating to animal fights but also made it an offence to advertise or attend one. The great secrecy surrounding illegal fights has included coded advertisements in certain 'sporting' magazines. The Act covers Scotland but not Northern Ireland.

Protection Against Cruel Tethering Act 1988

Horses, ponies, donkeys and mules have been found tethered on common land and waste ground, sometimes for years, with little to eat, sometimes without a fresh water supply, with no shelter from the sun or bad weather. These animals have been victims of attacks from hooligans, and some have been found tethered with chains, barbed wire or tyres, while others have choked to death after becoming entangled in their own tethers. The nationwide plight of these animals led to such pressure being brought on the government that in 1988 the above Act was passed. This makes it an offence to tether any horse, ass or mule under such conditions or in such manner as to cause that animal unnecessary suffering. While the wording of this Act again brings into debate the term 'unnecessary suffering', thus displaying an acceptance of 'necessary suffering' [see page 105], the welfare societies may now at least have a tool with which to end this cruel practice. The Act does not apply to Scotland.

Dangerous Dogs Act 1991

The late 1980s and early 1990s saw a seemingly dramatic rise in the number of attacks on people by dogs; some of these attacks were fatal. When a succession of these attacks proved to be by a particular breed of dog, the American Pit Bull terrier, the ensuing public outcry led the government hastily to enact legislation covering this and three other breeds: the Japanese Tosa, the Fila Braziliera and the Dogo Argentino.

More than a decade earlier, when the first of the Pit Bull terriers were being imported into this country, dog welfare organizations had requested that the government ban them. The government refused, stating that it was not possible to legislate against one type of dog. The number of Pit Bulls in the UK rose to around 10,000, and whilst many of them were family pets, many were being used illegally in dog fights [page 10], as body-guards for villains, and to guard drugs and stolen goods due to their in-bred aggressive nature.

The 1991 Act made it an offence to keep a dog of the aforementioned breeds unless the owner has notified the police and been issued with a Certificate of Exemption for which the dog must have been neutered and identified with a permanent unique mark (a numbered tattoo and a transponder implant), and covered by a third party liability insurance. Failure to obtain a certificate by the end of the six months' grace allowed by the government meant automatic destruction for the dog. The government also offered to pay owners an incentive of £50 for each dog to be destroyed within the six months. The licensed dogs must also be muzzled and kept on a lead in public places, and securely held by a person over the age of sixteen years. It is also an offence to breed, sell or exchange, give away or abandon these dogs.

These restrictions on the ownership of such fighting dogs will perhaps minimize further attacks taking place and limit the spread of dog fighting, but may also send the breeding of them underground, making monitoring difficult. In July 1992, for example, after a long undercover operation, the police and the RSPCA [page 204] raided a breeding farm in a Welsh quarry where Pit Bulls were being illegally bred for fighting.

The Act makes it an offence to have any dog dangerously out of control in public, and if injury is caused, the person in charge of the dog may face up to two years in prison and/or an unlimited fine. The Act also provides for the Secretary of State to make Orders imposing restrictions on other dogs which may present a serious danger to the public. Courts have the power to order any dog to be muzzled in public and to order its exclusion from certain places.

The Badgers Act 1991

(NB. All badger legislation has now been consolidated under the Protection of Badgers Act 1992).

Badgers had been protected to a large extent by the Badgers Act 1973 [page 135] and by the Wildlife and Countryside (Amendment) Act 1985 [page 138], but there still remained a loophole in the law which was enabling people to abuse these animals. The 1991 Act closed this by making it an offence to damage a badger sett or any part of it; to destroy a sett; to obstruct access to any entrance of a sett; to enter a dog into a sett, or to disturb a badger in a sett. The badger has been the target of much abuse from farmers believing the animals were carrying tuberculosis [page 88], from badger baiters digging them out for sport [page 9], and from hunters stopping up the setts to prevent foxes going to ground [page 16].

The MAFF [page 216] or the Nature Conservancy Council (as was; see page 216) are responsible for issuing exempting licences to those specified in the Act. This includes fox hunts recognized by the Masters of Fox Hounds Association, the Association of Masters of Harriers and Beagles and the Central Committee of Fell Packs, which require a licence to enable them to lightly stop up badger setts on the day of a fox hunt. The master of foxhounds and four named officials in each hunt are to be responsible for the policing of the badger setts within the hunt's area, and those stopping up the setts must also be authorized by the landowner or occupier. The hunt can only stop up a sett with either: (a) untainted straw, hay, leaf litter or loose soil (to be placed in the entrance on the day of the hunt or after midday the day before); or (b) a bundle of sticks or paper sacks filled with the above (placed in the entrance on the day of the hunt and removed the same day). Previously hunts would stop up setts with oil drums, rocks, logs, or stamp the entrances closed.

Licences may also be granted to those tracking down infected badgers likely to spread disease; to those seeking to protect river banks or drainage works from undermining by badgers; and to those trying to control foxes which are thought to be menacing livestock and taking refuge in badger setts. It is thought that these provisions could have the ultimate effect of unravelling so much good work done in achieving the legal protection of badgers.

The Badgers (Further Protection) Act 1991

(NB. All badger legislation has now been consolidated under the Protection of Badgers Act 1992).

Further protection was given to badgers by this Act which states that where a dog has been used in or was present at an offence committed under the Badgers Act 1973 [page 135] (taking, injuring, killing or cruelly treating badgers), the court, on convicting the offender, may also order the destruction or other disposal of the dog, and/or disqualify the offender from owning a dog for such a time as it thinks fit. This Act does not apply to Northern Ireland.

The Breeding of Dogs Act 1991

The Breeding of Dogs Act 1973 [page 135] basically prohibited the keeping of a breeding establishment (any premises where more than two bitches are kept for the purpose of breeding dogs to sell) without a licence issued by the Local Authority (LA). The flaw in this piece of legislation was that the LA had no powers of entry to an establishment suspected of being run as a breeding kennels. With the increase in the number of puppy farms in the UK (especially in Wales) there was great concern for the welfare of the dogs, many of which had been found to be kept in dreadful conditions [page 78]. Such puppy farms were being run illegally without a licence, and inspections of them could not be easily made.

The Breeding of Dogs Act 1991 strengthened the original Act by giving a Justice of the Peace the power to issue a warrant if s/he is satisfied by information given by any officer of the LA, or by a veterinary surgeon/practitioner, that there are reasonable grounds to suspect that an offence has been committed against the 1973 Act in any premises in the LA's area. The warrant permits the officer or vet to enter those premises, using reasonable force if need be, to inspect them and any animals or anything there.

A warrant cannot be issued for inspection of a private dwelling, but this does not include any garage, out-house or other structure which is part of the premises. Anyone obstructing or delaying inspection will be committing an offence, and anyone convicted of an offence under this Act may be disqualified from keeping a breeding establishment for dogs for such period as the court thinks fit.

The Deer Act 1991

Many pieces of legislation deal with the protection, slaughter and sale of deer, such as the Deer Act 1963, the Nature Conservancy Act 1973, the Deer Act 1980. These were repealed in 1991 and the law consolidated to cover many areas including: the poaching of deer; the definition of close seasons for the various species of deer (with exemptions for farmed deer [page 60], whether kept in enclosures, or kept wild but marked conspicuously); the taking or killing of deer at night; the use of prohibited weapons, etc. and exemptions for occupiers of land where deer roam, and for persons licensed by the Nature Conservancy Council [page 216] or the Countryside Council for Wales [page 213]. The Act also covers the offences relating to venison, and the powers of enforcement of the Act such as powers of search, arrest and seizure, plus penalties and disqualifications for convicted persons.

Summary

The Act prohibits:

(a) intentionally taking, killing, injuring or attempting to do so, or searching or pursuing with the intention of doing so, any deer, or removing the carcase of any deer without the consent of the owner or the occupier of the land or other lawful authority;

(b) taking or killing deer at night;

(c) the use of traps, snares, poisoned or stupefying bait, any net to take or kill deer;

(d) the use of any smooth-bore gun, any rifle having a calibre of less than .240 inches or a muzzle energy of less than 2,305 joules, any air-gun, air-rifle or air-pistol;

(e) the use of any cartridge for use in a smooth-bore gun, any bullet for use in a rifle other than a soft-nosed or hollow-nosed bullet;

(f) the use of any arrow, spear or similar missile, or any missile whether discharged from a firearm or otherwise, carrying or containing any poison, stupefying drug or muscle-relaxing agent;

(g) the discharging of any firearm or projecting any missile at any deer from any mechanically propelled vehicle;

(h) the use of any mechanically propelled vehicle for the purpose of driving deer.

Owners and occupiers of any enclosed land where deer are usually kept have certain exemptions depending on a number of factors such as the risk of deer damaging crops; anything done in pursuance of a requirement by the MAFF [page 216] under the Agriculture Act 1947; anything done to prevent the suffering of an injured or diseased deer, including using a trap, net or smooth-bore gun; the use, as a slaughtering instrument, of a smooth-bore gun which is of not less gauge than 12 bore, has a barrel less than twenty-four inches in length and is loaded with a cartridge purporting to contain shot none of which is less than .203 inches in diameter.

The Wildlife and Countryside (Amendment) Act 1991

Makes it an offence knowingly to cause or permit to be done certain acts mentioned in sections 5 and 11 of the Wildlife and Countryside Act 1981 [page 120].

Other Statutes

Dogs Act 1906 (and Dogs [Amendment] Act 1928)

Gives the police powers to seize stray dogs, keep them for seven days and then, if the dog is not claimed and all expenses paid, it can be sold or destroyed though it may not be sent for vivisection. The police and all strays' homes must keep a register of such stray dogs. Anyone who finds a stray dog must return it to its owner or take it to a police station after which, if s/he wishes to keep the dog, s/he must obtain a certificate from the police and keep the dog not less than one month. (See also the Environment Protection Act 1991 [page 78]). The Act prohibits the leaving of cattle carcases where dogs can have access to them. (*Cattle* here includes horses, mules, asses, sheep, goats, pigs).

Protection of Animals (Cruelty to Dogs) Act 1933

Deals with the disqualification of any person from keeping a dog if convicted of cruelty to a dog under the Protection of Animals Act 1911 [page 105]. Such disqualification also prohibits a person from holding a licence to run a dog-breeding kennels, a boarding establishment for dogs or cats, or a riding school. (This Act was repealed by the Protection of Animals (Amendment) Act 1988 [page 126]).

Cockfighting Act 1952

Prohibits possession of instruments that are used, or can be adapted for use, for cock fighting with domestic fowl.

Animal Boarding Establishments Act 1963

Prohibits the keeping of any animal boarding establishment without a licence issued by the Local Authority (LA) which must try to ensure that the conditions for the animals are adequate. Further conditions can also be specified on the licence. Gives the LA the power to authorize officers to inspect the premises at reasonable times, to ensure the conditions of the licence are being followed. Licences can be revoked and anyone disqualified from holding a licence if convicted under this Act, the Protection of Animals Act 1911 [page 105] or the Pet Animals Act 1951 [page 113].

Definitions
Animal – any dog or cat.
Boarding establishment – accommodation for other people's animals run as a business, but only covered by this Act if this business is the main activity.

Riding Establishments Act 1964 and 1970

The Act prohibits:

(a) running a riding establishment without a licence granted by the Local Authority (LA), or without liability insurance against injury to other persons;

(b) holding a licence for running a riding establishment if disqualified under this Act, the Protection of Animals (Cruelty to Dogs) Act 1933 [above], the Pet Animals Act 1951 [page 113], the Protection of Animals (Anaesthetics) Act 1954 [page 114] or the Animal Boarding Establishments Act 1963 [above];

(c) leaving a riding establishment in the charge of anyone under the age of sixteen years;

(d) hiring out horses for riding or unsupervised instruction unless by a responsible person of over sixteen years (unless the licence holder is satisfied that they are competent);

(e) the return to work of a horse deemed unfit by authorized inspection unless a veterinary certificate is lodged with the LA;

(f) allowing a horse to be ridden for hire, etc. when it is in a condition that riding it will cause it to suffer, or when it is three years old or under, or is a mare that is either heavily in foal or is within three months of having had a foal;

(g) allowing a horse to be ridden for hire, etc. when its tack will cause either suffering to the horse or an accident to the rider;

(h) failing to provide cover for sick or injured horses that are kept for hiring out;

(i) allowing a person who is disqualified from keeping a riding school to have charge of or manage a riding establishment;

(j) concealing horses used by the riding establishment from authorized inspections.

The LA cannot grant a licence to anyone unless: the applicant is over the age of eighteen years; a vet has inspected the premises; the LA has considered the suitability of the applicant and the conditions for the horses with regard to health and safety; there is a notice prominently displayed giving instructions for the safety of the horses in case of fire, with an appropriate person's name and address on it. The LA can authorize officers or a vet to enter at all reasonable times for inspection all premises that hold a licence under this Act or have applied for a licence, or are believed to be run as a riding establishment.

Exemptions: military premises; police establishments; premises run by the Zoological Society of London, or the Zoological Society of Scotland, or by veterinary colleges for the instruction of students.

Definitions
Riding establishments – premises (including land) from which are run a business hiring out horses for riding and/or instruction in riding.
Horse– any age or sex of horse or pony, including ass, mule or jennet.

Veterinary Surgeons Act 1966

Prohibits persons carrying out treatment and operations on animals, unless registered with the Royal College of Veterinary Surgeons (RCVS) [page 216] after obtaining a degree in veterinary medicine at one of the six veterinary colleges in the UK.

Exemptions include (and are drastically paraphrased here): any minor medical treatment given to an animal by its owner, a member of the owner's household or employees of the same; any free, but essentially minor, treatment given to an animal that is used in agriculture, given by the owner, or a stockman involved with such animal, with the exception of entry into the body cavity; castrations of animals under certain ages, tail-docking of lambs, docking of a dog's tail and amputation of its dew claws before its eyes are open, unless the person is less than eighteen years of age, although a seventeen-year-old may carry out these operations during a training course in husbandry, etc. if certain conditions are fulfilled; first aid to relieve suffering or save life. A 1991 Amendment allows a veterinary nurse to carry out medical treatment or minor surgery to a companion animal in specified circumstances.

Slaughter of Poultry Act 1967

The Act prohibits:
(a) the slaughter of domestic fowl and turkeys for commercial use on unregistered premises, the Local Authority (LA) being responsible for keeping a register;
(b) the slaughter of domestic fowl and turkeys other than instantaneously by decapitation or dislocation of the neck, or by a method approved by the Ministers; or stunned instantaneously and insensible to pain until killed by an instrument in good repair and approved by the Ministers.

Exemptions: any slaughter to prevent injury or suffering to either person or bird or both; any slaughter of birds by the Jewish method (conducted by a licensed Jew) for the food of Jews, or by the Muslim method (conducted by a Muslim) for the food of Muslims, so long as no unnecessary suffering is caused [see page 66].

Badgers Act 1973

(NB. All badger legislation has now been consolidated under the Protection of Badgers Act 1992).
The Act prohibits:
(a) the killing, injuring, taking and cruel treatment of badgers;
(b) possession of whole or part of a dead badger, or a live badger;
(c) use of badger tongs, or firearms other than those specified;
(d) digging for badgers;
(e) selling live badgers;
(f) marking or ringing badgers.

Exemptions: acts lawful under the Animals (Scientific Procedures) Act 1986 [page 123]; acts carried out under licence from the National Environment Research Council or Ministry of Agriculture, Fisheries and Food (MAFF) [page 216]; taking or killing an injured badger for the purpose of preventing it suffering; taking a dead badger that had already died; buying an illegally killed badger when ignorant of this fact; killing a badger to prevent serious damage to crops, land or poultry.

The police are given wide powers to search suspects, vehicles, etc. and to arrest suspects and seize articles which may be used as evidence. This Act has since been strengthened by further legislation [pages 128 and 129].

Breeding of Dogs Act 1973

The Act prohibits:
(a) the keeping of a breeding establishment for dogs without a licence issued by the Local Authority (LA);
(b) holding such a licence if disqualified under certain other Acts;
(c) obstructing an inspector or veterinarian authorized by the LA while carrying out an inspection (at any reasonable time) to ensure conditions of the licence are being adhered to.

This Act was later strengthened by further legislation [page 130].

Definition

Breeding establishment – any premises, including private dwellings, where more than two bitches are kept for the purpose of breeding dogs to sell, whether sold by the breeder or by someone else.

Slaughterhouses Act 1974

The Act deals with the licensing of slaughtermen, slaughterhouses and knackers' yards, which are all the responsibility of the Local

Authority. It also deals with permissible methods of slaughter. Animals must be rendered instantaneously insensible to pain until death by a mechanically operated instrument, by means of electricity or by some method stated in regulations made under this Act.

Exemptions: slaughter in an emergency to prevent injury or suffering to any person or animal; slaughter by the Jewish method by a licensed Jew for the food of Jews, and slaughter by the Muslim method by a Muslim for food for Muslims, so long as no unnecessary suffering is caused [see page 66]; pigs up to twelve weeks of age.

The Act prohibits the obstruction of an authorized person who may enter and inspect for infringements at any time when slaughter is in progress or during normal business hours.

Provisions are given for the making of regulations to cover: the humane treatment of animals prior to, and at, slaughter; the design and layout of slaughterhouses and knackers' yards; the slaughter of different animals.

Slaughter legislation has since been strengthened. The Slaughter of Animals (Humane Conditions) Regulations 1990 requires that a form of head restraint equipment be used to assist in the stunning of cattle; that electrical stunning equipment be fitted with a device to prevent an under-strength current from being delivered to animals being stunned; that (from July 1992) animals to be ritually slaughtered shall be standing upright in a restraining pen (i.e. not in a rotary casting pen). The Welfare of Animals at Slaughter Act 1991 gives the government new regulation-making powers (not yet exercised) to enable it to implement a number of recommendations made by the Farm Animal Welfare Council (FAWC) [page 214] in its 1984 report on *The Welfare of Livestock (Red Meat Animals) at the Time of Slaughter* [page 146]. The Act provides that at every slaughterhouse the Local Authority must designate a particular official as the person responsible for ensuring compliance with welfare rules. The Act also enables the Minister to require that a trainee slaughterman pass a test before being granted a licence.

The corresponding legislation in Scotland is the Slaughter of Animals (Scotland) Act 1980.

Definitions

Slaughterhouse – premises used for killing animals for human consumption.

Knackers' yard – premises used for killing animals not for human consumption.

Endangered Species (Import and Export) Act 1976

The Act prohibits the export or import of any animal listed in the Act, whether dead or alive, unless under a licence issued by the Secretary of State. Includes mammals, birds, reptiles, amphibians, fish, insects, molluscs and any products or parts of them.

Certain listed animals may not be sold, offered for sale, possessed or transported for the purpose of sale, or displayed to the public, whether dead or alive, whole or part, or egg or any other immature stage. The Secretary of State can change the lists at any time. S/he can also direct an imported animal to be taken to premises nominated by him/her, after it has been in quarantine, until such time as s/he requires it to be moved or until the direction is revoked.

The animals excluded by this Act include; Eastern and Western grey kangaroo, the domestic rabbit, cat, dog, pig, llama, alpaca, camel, reindeer, ferret, musquash, guinea pig, chinchilla, horse, hinny, mule, donkey, goat, sheep, ox, yak, water buffalo, European fallow deer, common rat, house mouse, hamster and the common red fox. However, the import of all animals, poultry and others are covered by regulations and restrictions designed to minimize the spread of disease, etc. under the Animal Health Act 1981 (see below).

There are various other matters relating to this Act, including regulations and Euro-regulations implementing the CITES Treaty [page 213].

Animal Health Act 1981

The Act gives the Ministers extensive powers to make Orders to control and minimize the introduction and spread of disease within Britain, and to maximize control and eradication of disease within Britain.

The list of Orders is wide-ranging and includes controls for: methods of transport; points of entry to Britain; quarantine for imports and exports; seizure and disposal of animals including dogs and wildlife; movement of people and animals within Britain and the use of transport of all kinds; disinfection of persons, places and vehicles; entry of authorized persons to places (excluding dwellings) in relation to diseases; dipping sheep (e.g. for the eradication of sheep scab); the humane transport of animals within Britain, including air travel. Particular Orders cover provision for rabies, such as the muzzling of dogs, and foot and mouth disease. Conditions are laid down for the export of live animals, horses in particular.

Video Recordings Act 1984

The Act creates offences which, among other things, concern video works which depict the mutilation or torture of, or other acts of gross violence towards, humans and animals. The Act came into force during 1985 except as it applied to existing video recordings.

Wildlife and Countryside (Amendment) Act 1985

Provides increased protection for badgers by blocking the loophole in the Badgers Act 1973 [page 135] which enabled the accused to escape conviction by claiming to be digging for foxes when caught at badger setts. (NB. All badger legislation has now been consolidated under the Protection of Badgers Act 1992).

Chapter Seven
RESOURCES

This selective listing of titles available in the UK covers books, audio-visual materials and magazines but does not include records, recipe books or fiction titles. A great many additional resources are available and details of these can be obtained from the relevant organizations listed in Chapter Eight: Directory of Organizations, pages of which are referred to below in squared brackets, e.g. [page 197]. The reader is also advised to consult Magel (1989) [page 157] for further information on the works shown here, on international titles, and on earlier works dating back to Ovid and Plutarch.

The inclusion of any title should not be taken as a recommendation. This Resources section is offered merely as an introductory guide to the materials available on the subject(s) of animal rights and welfare.

BOOKS

SPORTS AND ENTERTAINMENT

Circuses

JOHNSON, William. (1990). *The Rose-Tinted Menagerie*, Heretic Books, London. 336pp. Powerful condemnation of an international performing animal business still based on cruelty and deprivation. Strong historical perspective.

JORDAN, Bill and ORMROD, Stefan. (1978). See below: **Zoos**.

KILEY-WORTHINGTON, Marthe. (1990). *Animals in Circuses and Zoos – Chiron's World?*, Little Eco-Farms Publishing, Basildon. 240pp. The results of an eighteen-month investigation. Includes publication of a controversial report on circuses sponsored by the Royal Society for the Prevention of Cruelty to Animals (RSPCA) [page 204] which disagreed with the author's conclusions. The Society sees in the collected data clear evidence of widespread stress and suffering experienced by circus animals, whilst the Association of Circus Proprietors [page 212] uses selected extracts to promote circuses.

WESTACOTT, E. (1962). *Spotlights on Performing Animals*, Daniel, Saffron Walden. 222pp. Fascinating extracts from evidence given before the Select Committee of 1921 and 1922 which led to the Performing Animals (Regulations) Act of 1925. Plus disturbing accounts of circus animal conditions.

Hunting, Shooting, Fishing

COBHAM RESOURCE CONSULTANTS. (1983 and 1992). *Countryside Sports: Their Economic Significance*, CRS, Oxford. 102pp incl. summary of 9pp available separately. (Available from the Estate Management Dept., University of Reading, Whiteknights, Reading, Berks). Reports prepared for the Standing Committee on Countryside Sports mainly backed by the British Field Sports Society. Statistics, survey material, etc.

HEWSON, Ray. (1990).*Victim of Myth*, League Against Cruel Sports [page 196]. 16pp. Report of study of foxes in the Highlands. Shows how the killing of foxes in the interests of sheep farming cannot be justified.

HUSKISSON, Mike. (1983). *Outfoxed*, Huskisson, London. 192pp. Account of two of the author's years as a 'mole' in hunting circles.

LEAGUE AGAINST CRUEL SPORTS. (1992). *Wildlife Protection*, League Against Cruel Sports [page 196]. 42pp. Provides the definitive case for the abolition of hunting and snaring, with sections on all forms of hunting with hounds and other forms of cruelty in the countryside.

MEDWAY, Lord. (Chair). (1980). *Report of the Panel of Enquiry into Shooting and Angling*, Panel of Enquiry into Shooting and Angling, RSPCA [page 204]. 63pp. Panel sat between 1976 and 1979, chaired by Lord Medway. Concentrating its attention on pain, one of its breakthroughs was to lay to rest the assumption that fish do not feel pain. A landmark.

PARKES, Charlie and THORNLEY, John. (1987). *Fair Game*, Pelham Books, London. 268pp. A detailed outline of the legislation relating to country sports.

PINE, Leslie. (1966). *After Their Blood*, Kimber, London. 144pp. Descriptive statement of the case against bloodsports founded on the facts known through the special study and personal testimony of a former editor of *Shooting Times*.

ROBINSON, Peter. (1991). *Falconry in Britain*, League Against Cruel Sports [page 196]. 27pp. Shows that falconry is virtually uncontrolled and conflicts with the conservation principles and spirit of EC legislation for bird protection. Strengthens the case for abolition.

ROYAL SOCIETY FOR THE PROTECTION OF BIRDS. (1991). *Death by Design*, RSPB [page 204]. 28pp. Details research into numbers of wild birds (mainly raptors) deliberately killed by shooting estates to protect game.

SHEPPARD, Vera. (1979). *My Head Against the Wall*, Moonraker, Bradford-on-Avon. 138pp. Documents a decade in the late author's fight against bloodsports.

THOMAS, Richard H. (1983). *The Politics of Hunting*, Gower, Aldershot. 312pp. Describes attempts to abolish hunting and coursing, and why they failed.

WINDEATT, P. (1982). *The Hunt and the Anti-Hunt*, Pluto Press, London. 64pp. Traces hunting's history and opposition, describing fox, deer, hare and otter hunting, showing how they can be stopped. Explores the arguments for and against.

Zoos

JORDAN, Bill and ORMROD, Stefan. (1978). *The Last Great Wild Beast Show*, Constable, London. 272pp. Shocking exposé of the fate of animals captured in the wild and transported across the world to spend their lives in zoos, safari parks and circuses, written after Jordan had conducted a survey of zoos in the UK while working for the RSPCA. Credited with influencing government to implement the Zoo Licensing Act 1981.

KILEY-WORTHINGTON, Marthe. (1989). See above: **Circuses**.

McKENNA, Virginia, TRAVERS, William and WRAY, Jonathan (eds). (1987). *Beyond the Bars*, Thorsons, Wellingborough. 208pp. Distinguished contributors discuss conservation and the immorality of keeping animals in captivity.

ANIMAL EXPERIMENTATION

ANIMAL AID. (1991). *The Ethical Scientist*, Animal Aid [page 175]. 12pp. Aims to raise healthy debate on the use of animals in education and research within life science departments at universities.

BEDDARD, Steve. (1989). *Transplants – A Report on Transplant Surgery in Humans and Animals*, Arc Print, London. 62pp. An opposed view to that presented by advocates of transplants, outlining the human and animal suffering, species differences, failures, and the immense misdirection of resources.

BRITISH UNION FOR THE ABOLITION OF VIVISECTION. (1987).*What is Vivisection?*, British Union for the Abolition of Vivisection [page 180]. 24pp. Basic introduction in prose and picture.

COLEMAN, Vernon. (1991). *Why Animal Experiments Must Stop, and How You Can Help to Stop Them*, Green Print, London. 128pp. Basic handbook examining the justifications used by scientists, considering both ethical and scientific aspects of vivisection. Describes why animal experiments are useless, analyses the alternatives and shows readers how they can help fight vivisection.

CRAWFORD, James. (1988).*Kill or Cure?*, Arc Print, London. 80pp. Exposé of profit-oriented pharmaceutical companies and their products.

CROCE, Pietro. (1991). *Vivisection or Science: a Choice to Make*, CIVIS, Klosters, Switzerland. 230pp. (Available from Doctors in Britain Against Animal Experiments [page 184]). Ex-animal experimenter examines the scientific invalidity of animal-based research, showing how the demand for abolition is responsibly based on a concern for human health. Covers 'alternative' methods.

DEPARTMENT OF HEALTH AND SOCIAL SERVICES. *Statistics of Scientific Procedures on Living Animals, Northern Ireland*, HMSO, Belfast. Annually published statistics on live animals used in experiments.

GUNN, Brian. (1988). *Entering the Gates of Hell*, International Association Against Painful Experiments on Animals (IAAPEA) [page 192]. 58pp. Compilation of colour photographs taken during numerous visits to vivisection laboratories throughout the world.

HOME OFFICE. *Statistics of Scientific Procedures on Living Animals, Great Britain*, HMSO, London. Annually published statistics on live animals used for experimental procedures.

KITE, Sarah. (1991). *Secret Suffering*, British Union for the Abolition of Vivisection [page 180]. 80pp. First-hand information about what some members of the scientific community are doing to various species in laboratories.

LANGLEY, Gill. (1991). *Faith, Hope and Charity*, British Union for the Abolition of Vivisection [page 180]. 39pp. An overview of research into cancer, heart disease and arthritis, with a summary of the roles of the charities that commission or perform misleading and painful experiments on animals.

LANGLEY, Gill (ed.). (1990). *Animal Experimentation: The Consensus Changes*, Macmillan, London. 260pp. Collection of essays from abolitionists and reformers marking a reassessment in the attitudes of those who sense a sea-change in morality, alongside a reinforcement of an animal rights ethic.

McIVOR, Steve (ed.). (1990). *Health with Humanity*, British Union for the Abolition of Vivisection [page 180]. 80pp. Seven short chapters from five contributors on ethics, disease prevention, development, futility of and alternatives to animal experimentation.

REGAN, Tom (ed.). (1986). *Animal Sacrifices: Religious Perspectives on the Use of Animals in Science*, Temple University Press, Pa, USA. 270pp. (Available from International Association Against Painful Experiments on Animals (IAAPEA) [page 192]). Collection of nine solo papers from the 1984 IAAPEA conference, examining the teachings of major religious systems concerning animals.

RUESCH, Hans. (1978). *Slaughter of the Innocent*, Campaign to End Fraudulent Medical Research [page 181]. 445pp. A breakthrough book detailing the suffering deliberately inflicted on animals in laboratories, demonstrating how the spread of vivisection has been possible through a conspiracy of secrecy and deception.

RUESCH, Hans. (1979). *Vivisection is Scientific Fraud*, CIVIS, Klosters, Switzerland. 42pp. (Available from Animal Research Kills (ARK) [page 177]). Photographs from laboratories with explanatory captions and statements, demonstrating the cruelty and futility of vivisection.

RUESCH, Hans. (1982). *Naked Empress: The Great Medical Fraud*, CIVIS, Klosters, Switzerland. 202pp. (Available from Animal Research Kills (ARK) [page 177]). Sets out to show how modern vivisection-based medicine has become the principal cause of human disease. Proposes greater emphasis on disease prevention, abolition of animal experimentation and reduction of drugs.

RUESCH, Hans. (ed.). (1991). *1000 Doctors (and many more) Against Vivisection*, CIVIS, Klosters, Switzerland. 286pp. (Available from Animal Research Kills (ARK) [page 177]). Chronologically ordered collection of quotations from doctors criticizing or condemning vivisection.

RUSSELL, W. M. S. and BURCH, R. L. (1959). *Principles of Humane Experimental Technique*, Methuen, London. See page 42.

RYDER, Richard D. (1983). *Victims of Science: The Use of Animals in Research*, National Anti-Vivisection Society [page 198]. 200pp. (Distributed by Centaur Press, Fontwell). Originally published in 1975, this book was for long the standard-bearer for the anti-vivisection movement. Packed with facts and excerpts from scientific journals. A cogent, compelling presentation using the author's term 'speciesism' to describe human discrimination against other species.

SHARPE, Robert. (1989). *The Cruel Deception: The Use of Animals in Medical Research,* Thorsons, Wellingborough. 288pp. A detailed study demonstrating both the barbarity and scientific invalidity of vivisection.

SMITH, Colin (ed.). (1982). *Reason Against Vivisection,* International Association Against Painful Experiments on Animals [page 192]. 124pp. Key-note speeches delivered at the IAAPEA General Assembly 1981.

SPERLINGER, David (ed.). (1981). *Animals in Research: New Perspectives in Animal Experimentation,* Wiley & Sons, London. 373pp. Collection of sixteen essays by different authors with a wide range of views represented. Main section describes the use of animals in different forms of research in the UK and USA, with the remaining sections devoted to broader legal, social and ethical issues.

VYVYAN, John. (1987). *In Pity and In Anger. A Study of the Use of Animals in Science,* Micah Publications, 255 Humphrey St, Marblehead, Massachusetts 01945, USA. 250pp. Reprint of the 1969 (Michael Joseph) classic chronicling the rise of the UK anti-vivisection movement in the last quarter of the nineteenth century. Propounds that acquisition of knowledge must be by humane means.

VYVYAN, John. (1989). *The Dark Face of Science,* Micah Publications, 255 Humphrey St., Marblehead, Massachusetts 01945, USA. (Originally published in 1971 by Michael Joseph, London). 250pp. Powerfully, eloquently completes the story started in the author's *In Pity and Anger,* recounting the history of the UK anti-vivisection movement in the twentieth century.

WALLIS, Louise. (1991). *Vivisection in Britain – Animals in Medical Research: An Investigation,* National Anti-Vivisection Society (NAVS) [page 198]. 16pp. Disturbing report on laboratory procedures and conditions by anti-vivisection campaigner working incognito as a technician at SmithKline Beecham laboratories and St Bartholomew's Hospital Medical School.

WHITTAL, J. D. (1981). *People and Animals,* National Anti-Vivisection Society (NAVS) [page 198]. 169pp. Paints a picture of the true meaning and implications of animal experimentation, stressing its cruelty and futility.

ANIMAL PRODUCTION/FARMING

ANIMAL WELFARE INSTITUTE. (1988). *Factory Farming: The Experiment that Failed,* Animal Welfare Institute, PO Box 3650, Washington, DC 20007, USA. 86pp. Packed with information and illustrations about the failings of intensive livestock systems on both welfare and economic grounds, despite the use of specialized language to defend them.

APPLEBY, Michael. (1991). *Do Hens Suffer in Battery Cages?*, The Athene Trust [page 178]. 20pp. Review of current scientific evidence about cages, confirming the major disadvantages of hens' inability to move and perform natural behaviours; increased foot damage and bone weakness; feather damage, etc.

BODY, Richard. (1991). *Our Food, Our Land,* Rider, London. 330pp. Shows how agriculture has been placed on a high-imput/high-output treadmill to the detriment of taxpayers, consumers, the environment, farmers and animals. Proposes new plan to improve food production systems and end factory farming.

BRAMBELL, F. W. (Chair). (1965). *Report of the Technical Committee to Enquire into the Welfare of Animals Kept under Intensive Livestock Husbandry Systems*, HMSO, London. 85pp. Also known as the Brambell Report, this was the outcome of the government's response to the outcry following the publication of Harrison (1964) [see page 146]. Some of its recommendations, e.g. the setting up of a Farm Animal Welfare Advisory Committee, were implemented but most, e.g. to give an animal sufficient freedom of movement to be able, without difficulty, to turn round, groom itself, get up, lie down and stretch its limbs, were not, and twenty-five years elapsed before the veal crate was banned in the UK.

CARNELL, Paul. (1983). *Alternatives to Factory Farming*, Earth Resources Research, London. 96pp. An economic appraisal of the alternatives to factory farming, challenging the claim that intensive systems produce food more cheaply.

CHICKENS' LIB. (1990). *Intensive Egg, Chicken and Turkey Production*, Chickens' Lib [page 182]. 28pp. Listing of 136 facts about the intensive bird and egg industries.

DRUCE, Clare. (1989). *Chicken and Egg: Who Pays the Price?* Green Print, London. 102pp. A constructive attack on the egg and poultry industry, examining birds' poor health, living conditions, drug industry activity and human health hazards.

DURNING, Alan B. and BROUGH, Holly B. (1991). *Taking Stock: Animal Farming and the Environment* (Worldwatch Paper 103), Worldwatch Institute, 1776 Massachusetts Avenue, N. W., Washington, DC 20036-1904, USA. 62pp. Study of how animal farming worldwide is exerting great pressure on the environment. Covers land wastage and soil, waterway and air pollution, showing how environmental degradation partners animal exploitation.

FARM ANIMAL WELFARE COUNCIL. Reports of FAWC examinations of animal production practices, published by HMSO. *Antlers in Velvet* (1980). *The Control of Mutilations* (1981). *The Welfare of Poultry at Slaughter* (1982). *The Welfare of Livestock (Redmeat Animals) at the Time of Slaughter* (1984).*The Welfare of Farmed Deer* (1985). *The Welfare of Livestock when Slaughtered by Religious Methods* (1985). *Egg Production Systems; An Assessment* (1986). *The Welfare of Livestock at Markets* (1986). *The Welfare of Livestock in Transit* (1987). *Report on Priorities in Animal Welfare Research and Development* (1988). *Assessment of Pig Production Systems* (1988). *Statement on Mink and Fox Farming* (1989). *Handling and Transport of Poultry* (1990). *Animals Slaughtered by Jewish and Muslim Methods* (1990). *The Welfare of Laying Hens in Colony Systems* (Official and Minority reports) (1991).

FRASER, Andrew F. and BROOM, Donald. (1990). *Farm Animal Behaviour and Welfare*, Balliere Tindall, London. 437pp. Provides a text for veterinary courses and farmers, taking in fundamental process, social and reproductive, early and parental, and abnormal behaviours, with section on welfare.

GOLD, Mark. (1983). *Assault and Battery*, Pluto, London. 184pp. Documents the effects of factory farming on animals, people and the environment, attacking the five main myths used to defend intensive systems.

HARRISON, Ruth. (1964). *Animal Machines*, Vincent Stuart, London. 186pp. Probably the first detailed investigation, analysis and coining of 'factory farming'. A pioneering work widely acknowledged as the stimulus which forced the UK government to set up a committee of enquiry into the welfare of intensively farmed livestock [see Brambell (1965) page 145]. Although dated, it still makes interesting reading and many of the points and recommendations made are still valid today.

JOHNSON, Andrew. (1991). *Factory Farming*, Blackwell, Oxford. 272pp. Deals factually with factory farming as a function of the profit motive of transnational corporations, considering health and environmental effects and animal suffering, with historical overview.

LYMBERY, Philip. (1992). *The Welfare of Farmed Fish*, Compassion in World Farming (CIWF) [page 183]. 20pp. Concise report on the intensive production of fish, covering methods, welfare, diseases, biotechnology, environmental impact and inefficiency.

LYNX and COMPASSION IN WORLD FARMING (1988). *Mink Factories*, Lynx and Compassion in World Farming (CIWF) [pages 198 and 183]. 53pp. An investigation of mink breeding and the associated animal welfare problems. Covers natural history, physiology and behaviour, husbandry, welfare, production figures, legislation.

MASON, Jim and SINGER, Peter. (1980). *Animal Factories*, Crown Publishers, New York. 174pp. Short, well-illustrated book revealing what the authors see as the truth about bio-machines, i.e. livestock in factory farms. Information largely relayed in pictures and descriptions rather than precise factual information.

MINISTRY OF AGRICULTURE, FISHERIES AND FOOD. (1990). *Codes of Recommendations for the Welfare of Livestock.* MAFF Publications, London. Published in separate booklets (approx. 14pp each) for cattle, deer, ducks, fowls, goats, pigs, rabbits, sheep and turkeys. Give basic welfare advice to farmers on livestock housing, feeding, etc.

NILSSON, Greta, *et al.* (1980). *Facts About Furs*, Animal Welfare Institute, USA. 258pp. (Available from LYNX [page 198]). Outlines fur-trapping and fur farming methods; the cruelty and the costs.

SCOTTISH FARM BUILDINGS INVESTIGATION UNIT. (1986). *Does Close Confinement Cause Distress in Sows?*, Scottish Farm Buildings Investigation Unit. 7pp. Available from the Athene Trust [page 178]. Explains why the answer is yes.

SCOTTISH WILDLIFE AND COUNTRYSIDE LINK. (1988 and 1990). *Marine Fishfarming in Scotland* and *Marine Salmon Farming in Scotland*, SWCL, St Magdalene's Lane, Perth. 70pp and 35pp. A discussion paper and its review covering industry status, impacts on environment, controls, research and advice.

TOWNEND, Christine. (1985). *Pulling the Wool*, Hale & Iremonger, Sydney, Australia. 157pp. (Available from Compassion in World Farming (CIWF) [page 183]). Exposé of the Australian sheep/wool industry, revealing in particular inadequate husbandry, the horrors of the live export trade to the Middle East and the practice of mulesing [see page 58].

UNIVERSITIES FEDERATION FOR ANIMAL WELFARE. (1988). *Management and Welfare of Farm Animals*, Balliere Tindall, London. 260pp. Describes the contemporary designs for improvement of animal welfare with practical advice emphasizing the welfare implications of modern methods, attempting to promote a humane attitude in those charged with the responsibility of rearing animals for slaughter.

Diet Ethics

ADAMS, Carol J. (1990). *The Sexual Politics of Meat*, Polity Press, London. 256pp. An innovative approach to the violence perpetrated against animals and women. Illustrates the links between patriarchy and meat production in language, symbolism and action.

CLEMENTS, Kath. (1986). *Why Vegan?* GMP Books, London. 96pp. A mass of facts and figures ably presented in a simple and straightforward exposition of the case for veganism, with practical tips.

COX, Peter. (1993). *The New Why You Don't Need Meat,* Bloomsbury, London. 256pp. Total rewrite of the 1986 bestseller which promoted non-meat eating from a health aspect. Now wider in scope, dealing with all meat issues.

DOMBROWSKI, Daniel A. (1985). *Vegetarianism: The Philosophy Behind the Ethical Diet,* Thorsons, Wellingborough. 186pp. An examination of vegetarianism and its intellectual origins in ancient philosophy, with annotated bibliography of current debates.

KAPLEAU, Philip. (1983). See below: **Animal Rights and Welfare: Theological Perspective.**

MORAN, Victoria. (1991). *Compassion: The Ultimate Ethic,* American Vegan Society, NJ, USA. 108pp. (Available from the Vegan Society [page 208]). An exploration of veganism, first published (in the UK) in 1985. Explains why people feel drawn to a more compassionate way of life, highlighting some roots in Eastern and Western religion and philosophy, outlining the application of its principles with practical advice on diet and nutrition.

WYNNE-TYSON, Jon. (1988). *Food For a Future: How World Hunger Could be Ended by the Twenty-First Century,* Thorsons, Wellingborough. 192pp. First published in 1975. A classic work, powerfully arguing the moral, economic, ecological, physiological and nutritional case for vegetarianism and veganism. Packed with information, statistics, literary quotations, nutritional and dietary data.

YATES, Geoffrey. (1986). *Food: Need, Greed and Myopia,* Earthright, Ryton. 104pp. The world food problem looked at from a vegetarian/vegan point of view.

COMPANION ANIMALS

BALLARD, Peter. (1990). *A Dog is for Life.* National Canine Defence League [page 199]. 120pp. History of the NDCL from 1891 to present day. Archive photographs of the way the lives of dogs have changed.

JORDAN, W. J. (1986). *A–Z Guide to Pet Health,* Care for the Wild [page 181]. 151pp. Assists pet owners to distinguish between the serious and trivial problems, helping to dispel anxiety caused by lack of knowledge. Not a book on home treatment.

SERPELL, James. (1986). *In the Company of Animals*, Blackwell, Oxford. 215pp. Survey of the pet–human relationship and of the theories which attempt to describe the phenomenon in its various manifestations. Examines the contradictions inherent in our treatment of different domesticated species.

WOOD GREEN ANIMAL SHELTERS (1991). See page 160: **Teachers'**.

WOOD, Philip (ed.). (1987). *A Passion for Cats*, Cats' Protection League [page 182]. 208pp. Anecdotal, historic, health and general cat care.

WILDLIFE

ANIMAL WELFARE INSTITUTE/ENVIRONMENTAL INVESTIGATION AGENCY. (1992). *Flight to Extinction: The Wild-Caught Bird Trade*, Animal Welfare Institute/Environmental Investigation Agency [page 186]. 27pp. Shows how the multi-million dollar international trade in wild-caught birds is devastating wild bird populations and causing terrible suffering.

BARSTOW, R., HOLT, S., SCHEFFER, V. and PAYNE, R. (1991). *Why Whales?*, Whale and Dolphin Conservation Society [page 210]. 24pp. Four scientists argue the ethical and scientific reasons against whaling.

DAVIES, Brian. (1989). *Red Ice*, Methuen, London. 228pp. Graphic history of the twenty-year Davies/International Fund for Animal Welfare (IFAW) [page 193] fight to save seals from the Canadian seal hunt.

ENVIRONMENTAL INVESTIGATION AGENCY. (1990). *The Global War Against Small Cetaceans: The IWC and the Politics of Extinct*, Environmental Investigation Agency [page 186]. 57pp.

ENVIRONMENTAL INVESTIGATION AGENCY. (1991). *The Global War Against Small Cetaceans II*, Environmental Investigation Agency [page 186]. 63pp. The first report documents dolphin kills around the world on a country-to-country basis. The second report provides an up-date on the global killing with specific focus on the greatest threats to cetacean populations.

ENVIRONMENTAL INVESTIGATION AGENCY. (1992). *Under Fire: Elephants in the Front Line*, Environmental Investigation Agency [page 186]. 57pp. Country-to-country report documenting major threats to survival of the African elephant due to poaching and the trade in ivory.

HOLT, Sidney and CARLSON, Carole. (1991). *Implementation of a Revised Management Procedure for Commercial Whaling.* International Fund for Animal Welfare (IFAW) [page 193]. 52pp.

JORDAN, William J. and ORMROD, Stefan. (1978). See above: **Zoos**.

JORDAN, William J. and HUGHES, J. (1988). *Care for the Wild.* Care for the Wild [page 181]. 199pp. Comprehensive guide to first aid care for sick, injured and orphaned wildlife.

LEAGUE AGAINST CRUEL SPORTS (1992). See above: **Hunting, Shooting, Fishing**.

MCKENNA, TRAVERS, WRAY (1987). See above: **Zoos**.

REGENSTEIN, Lewis. (1975). *The Politics of Extinction,* Collier Macmillan, London. 304pp. Shocking story of the world's endangered wildlife. Probably the first book to expose those responsible for wildlife carnage.

SHELDRICK, Daphne and JORDAN, William J. (1992). *The Elephant Harvest? An Ethical Approach,* Care for the Wild [page 181]. 36pp. Argues against the downlisting of elephants on CITES Appendices. Highlights the problems to be faced by elephants if trade in ivory were to resume.

STOCKER, Les. (1992). *St Tiggywinkles Wildcare Handbook – First Aid & Care for Wildlife,* Chatto & Windus, London. 224pp. Sections on first aid for beginners; how to handle the casualty and where to keep it; diagnosis and treatment; feeding; long-term care; return to the wild.

THORNTON, Allan and CURREY, Dave. (1991). *To Save an Elephant,* Bantam, London. 273pp. Stirring, behind-the-scenes story of Environmental Investigation Agency's exposé of the illegal ivory trade responsible for the deaths of tens of thousands of elephants.

VEAL, Lowana. (1983). *Wildlife and the Atom,* London Greenpeace [page 197]. 12pp. How the nuclear industry exploits and affects the animal kingdom.

WARWICK, Clifford. (1990). *Reptiles – Misunderstood, Mistreated and Mass-Marketed,* Reptile Protection Trust [page 204]. 46pp. Dispels the myths surrounding reptiles, describing abuse and promoting a sympathetic understanding of an all too long-suffering class of other species.

WILSON, Susan S. and JORDAN, William. J. (1991). *Whaling? An Ethical Approach,* Care for the Wild [page 181]. 24pp. An argument against whaling, taken to the International Whaling Commission meeting 1991.

ANIMALS AND LEGISLATION

COOPER, M. E. (1987). *An Introduction to Animal Law*, Academic Press, London. 213pp. A detailed outline of basic UK legislation relating to animal welfare.

CROFTS, W. (1984). *A Summary of Statute Law Relating to Animal Welfare in England and Wales*, Universities Federation for Animal Welfare (UFAW) [page 208].

EUROGROUP FOR ANIMAL WELFARE. (1992). *Summary of Legislation Relative to Animal Welfare at the Levels of the European Economic Community and Council of Europe*, Eurogroup for Animal Welfare [page 186]. 174pp. Reference source of all EC and Council of Europe documents on animal welfare and current legislative position.

GARNER, J. F. and JONES, B. L. (1992). *Countryside Law*, Shaw & Sons, Dartford. 272pp. Outlines for the general reader how the laws of England and Wales tackle the twin problems of countryside and animal protection, and public demand for countryside use.

HALSBURY, Earl of. *Halsbury's Laws of England, Halsbury's Statutes* and *Halsbury's Statutory Instruments*, Butterworth, London. Standard reference works on all our legislation, including animal welfare.

JENKINS, Sid. (1992). See below: **Miscellaneous**.

PARKES, Charlie and THORNLEY, John. (1987). See above: **Hunting, Shooting, Fishing**.

ROBERTS, J. J. (1987). *Up Against the Law*, Arc Print, London. 38pp. A guide to the 1986 Public Order Act and how it relates to animal rights issues and protest.

SANDYS-WINSCH, G. (1984). *Animal Law*, Shaw & Sons, London. 260pp. Documents, comprehensively and for the layman, the many facets of the law which affect those who have any dealings with animals, whether their own or other people's.

SWEENEY, Noël. (1990). See below: **General Ethics**.

ANIMAL RIGHTS AND WELFARE – General Ethics

BRYANT, John. (1990). *Fettered Kingdoms*, Fox Press, Winchester. 92pp. First published in 1982. Second edition of one individual's animal rights philosophy with infamous critique of pet-keeping and a controversial re-written Epilogue regarding animal liberation tactics.

CLARK, Stephen R. L. (1977). *The Moral Status of Animals*, Oxford University Press, Oxford. 233pp. Lively, literary–philosophical analysis of the arguments and rationalizations offered in defence of our behaviour in farms, laboratories and at home, revealing their roots in the human preference for sentimental fantasy.

CLARK, Stephen R. L. (1982). *The Nature of the Beast: Are Animals Moral?*, Oxford University Press, Oxford. 127pp. Explores our contradictory tendencies that underlie human moralizing about animals, and discusses the evidence for animal intelligence.

CLARKE, Paul A. B. and LINZEY, Andrew. (1990). *Political Theory and Animal Rights*, Pluto Press, London. 193pp. Collection of extracts – from Plato and Aristotle through Kant and Locke to Regan and Singer – on the connections between politics and animal rights, social issues and morality.

DUFFY, Maureen. (1984). *Men and Beasts: An Animal Rights Handbook*, Paladin, London. 172pp. A statement of the case for an enlightened attitude towards animals, based on equality and respect for their rights. An action handbook with useful advice on how to make political pressure effective, etc.

GODLOVITCH, Stanley and Rosalind and HARRIS, John (eds.). (1971). *Animals, Men and Morals: An Enquiry into the Maltreatment of Non-Humans*, Victor Gollancz, London. 240pp. Collection of twelve essays by different authors on various aspects of animal abuse. Rather dated now re factual information, this was one of the earliest books on a wide range of welfare and rights issues. Edited by members of the Oxford Group. (See **Introduction** [page xiii]).

GRUEN, Lori, SINGER, Peter and HINE, David. (1987). *Animal Liberation: A Graphic Guide*, Camden Press, London. 159pp. Powerfully illustrated introduction to the subject.

HALL, Rebecca. (1984). *Voiceless Victims*, Wildwood House, Hounslow. 288pp. Wide-ranging examination of various forms of human abuse of animals and what to do about it. A campaigner's handbook, and one of the first to expose the milk industry's inherent cruelty.

HENDRICK, George and HENDRICK, Willene (eds.). (1989). *The Savour of Salt – A Henry Salt Anthology*, Centaur Press, Fontwell. 204pp. Wide range of extracts from the seminal, humanitarian writings of the author of the early classic, *Animals' Rights Considered in Relation to Social Progress* [page 154].

HUME, C. W. (1982). *Man and Beast*, Universities' Federation for Animal Welfare (UFAW) [page 208]. 222pp. Collection of essays by the founder of UFAW, written between 1943 and 1962. Technically dated, they bear testimony to a common-sense approach to animal welfare, though some points are eccentric. Argues in praise of anthropomorphism, suggesting that human empathy for animal feelings has a valuable role in animal welfare despite scientific disquiet. Emphasis on pain and suffering.

MIDGLEY, Mary. (1983). *Animals and Why They Matter: A Journey Around the Species Barrier,* Penguin, London. 158pp. An examination of the relationship between humans and other species, exploring the historical and philosophical background to our current treatment of animals.

MIDGLEY, Mary. (1979). *Beast and Man,* Harvester Press, Brighton. 400pp. Explores how humans have tried to deflect attention from their own ferocity by mythically attributing 'beastliness' to animals. How traditional views have distorted argument in ethics. Interdisciplinary approach.

MILLER, Harlan B. and WILLIAMS, William H. (eds.). (1987). *Ethics and Animals,* Humana/John Wiley, London. 400pp. (Originally published in USA in 1983). Collection of twenty-six papers, from conference held at Virginia Polytechnic Institute and State University, May 1979, discussing the ways in which morality has or has not viewed animals as beings deserving our consideration.

MORAN, Victoria. (1985). See above: **Diet Ethics.**

NOSKE, Barbara. (1989). *Humans and Other Animals,* Pluto Press, London. 256pp. Examination of (speciesist) scientific, political, feminist and conservationist thinking as failing to embrace a wider compassion.

PATERSON, David and PALMER, Mary (eds.). (1989). *The Status of Animals: Ethics, Education and Welfare,* CAB International, Wallingford. 257pp. Collection of papers – on ethics, education, farming, experimentation, human–animal interaction, role of veterinarians, animals and the media – presented at an international conference emphasizing the need for animal welfare reforms.

PATERSON, David and RYDER, Richard D. (eds.). (1979). *Animals' Rights – A Symposium,* Centaur Press, Fontwell. 255pp. Collection of papers on speciesism; religious and theological perspectives; philosophical imperatives; modern farming methods; dietethics; experimentation; sport and wildlife; political issues, from an RSPCA-hosted symposium at Cambridge University.

REGAN, Tom. (1982). *All That Dwell Therein: Essays on Animal Rights and Environmental Ethics,* University of California Press, USA. 249pp. Collection of ten essays, previously presented as papers, on vegetarianism and environmental issues. Interesting reading, though the author's animal rights philosophy is better displayed in his later books (below).

REGAN, Tom. (1987). *The Struggle for Animal Rights*, International Society for Animal Rights, Clarks Summit, USA. 212pp. (Available from the Vegan Society [page 208]). Lucidly puts the abbreviated case for animal rights. Chapters on farm and laboratory animals, hunting, dissection, plus autobiographical sketch.

REGAN, Tom. (1988). *The Case for Animal Rights*, Routledge, London. 425pp. (Originally published in 1983 in the USA). Classic, philosophically high-powered animal rights manifesto from an inherent-value-of-the-individual/subject-of-a-life angle, based upon justice and equality.

REGAN, Tom. (1990). *The Philosophy of Animal Rights*, Culture and Animals Foundation, NC, USA. 26pp. (Available from the Vegan Society [page 208]). Ten reasons for animal rights and their explanations, plus ten reasons against animal rights and their replies.

REGAN, Tom and SINGER, Peter (eds.). (1989). *Animal Rights and Human Obligations*, Prentice-Hall, NJ, USA. 256pp. Originally published in 1976. Fifty contrasting essays; Aquinas and Descartes to Linzey and Schweitzer, on animals and humans; use, abuse and non-use.

SALT, Henry S. (1980). *Animals' Rights Considered in Relation to Social Progress*, Centaur, Fontwell. 240pp. First published in 1892, this practical book sets forth the principle of animal rights, describing the ways and means of the sufferings imposed on animals as an inevitable consequence of the denial of their rights. Explores a basic universal sense of injustice.

SAPONTZIS, Steve F. (1987). *Morals, Reason and Animals*, Temple University Press, Pa, USA. 302pp. Discusses most of the important theoretical controversies emerging since the publication of Singer's *Animal Liberation* in 1975, proposing an everyday, common-sense morality rather than a revolutionary ethic of animal rights.

SINGER, Peter. (1990). *Animal Liberation: A New Ethic for our Treatment of Animals*, Thorsons, Wellingborough. 336pp. Classic utilitarianist text grounded on the concept of an animal's ability to suffer, originally published in 1975, which made modern-day animal liberationist philosophy easy-access. Once hailed as the 'bible' of animal rights.

SINGER, Peter (ed.). (1985). *In Defence of Animals*, Blackwell, Oxford. 224pp. Sixteen introductory, personal essays and reports on different aspects of the fight for animal rights from leading activists and philosophers.

SPIEGEL, Marjorie. (1988). *The Dreaded Comparison: Human and Animal Slavery*, Heretic Books, London. 105pp. A penetrating study in picture and prose, loaded with shocking comparisons of human and animal slavery, of racism and speciesism.

SWEENEY, Noël. (1990). *Animals and Cruelty and Law*, Alibi, Bristol. 119pp. A practising barrister argues that in sanctioning animal cruelty, English law fails to recognize the quintessence of natural rights: justice and morality.

ANIMAL RIGHTS AND WELFARE – Historical Perspective

HENSHAW, David. (1989). *Animal Warfare*, Fontana, London. 214pp. Traces, somewhat sensationally, the growth of direct action within the animal rights movement.

HOLLANDS, Clive. (1980). *Compassion is the Bugler: The Struggle for Animal Rights*, Macdonald, Edinburgh. 201pp. Unique account of UK animal welfare movement in the late 1970s when strenuous attempts were being made to establish a high political profile for animal welfare.

MOSS, A. W. (1961). *Valiant Crusade: the History of the RSPCA*, Cassell, London. 221pp. Begins the history of animal welfare with Roman times but focuses attention on the Victorian era onwards. A descriptive account of the people and events shaping the animal welfare movement.

NIVEN, Charles D. (1967). *History of the Humane Movement*, Johnson, London. 174pp. An account of the development in humane thinking from the pre-Christian era to the animal defence legislation of the day.

ROBERTS, J. J. (1986). *Against All Odds*, Arc Print, London. 116pp. Traces the growth of the animal rights movement from 1972, with a seven-point plan for future action.

RYDER, Richard D. (1989). *Animal Revolution*, Blackwell, Oxford. 385pp. A detailed overview of the history of the animal welfare and rights movements with especial emphasis on the RSPCA and with reference to the author's own considerable role in the development of an increasingly discussed ethic of concern.

SINGER, Peter. (1986). *The Animal Liberation Movement: Its Philosophy, Its Achievements and Its Future*, Old Hammond Press, Nottingham. 19pp. Brief overview by the author of *Animal Liberation* (see above).

THOMAS, Keith. (1991). *Man and the Natural World*, Penguin, London. 432pp. Originally published in 1983. History of changing attitudes towards animals and the natural environment, 1500–1800. Excellent source book.

TURNER, E. S. (1992). *All Heaven in a Rage,* Centaur Press/Kinship Library, Fontwell. 336pp. Originally published in 1964. Illustrated, historical account of human maltreatment of animals and the development of the animal welfare movement in Britain.

TURNER, James. (1980). *Reckoning with the Beast: Animals, Pain and Humanity in the Victorian Mind,* Johns Hopkins Press, London. 190pp. Deals with how the new acceptance of human animality, appreciation of science and the horror of pain all impinged on the question of how people ought to treat the animals around them.

VYVYAN (1971 and 1987). See above: **Animal Experimentation**.

ANIMAL RIGHTS AND WELFARE – Theological Perspective

CARPENTER, Edward. (ed.). (1980). *Animals and Ethics: A Report of the Working Party,* Watkins, London. 44pp. Report of working party of theologians, scientists and veterinarians, chaired by the Very Revd Dr. Edward Carpenter. Presents guidelines for human attitudes towards, and the needs and treatment of, other species.

KAPLEAU, Philip. (1983). *A Buddhist Case for Vegetarianism,* Rider, London. 104pp. Marshals the basic religious, humanitarian and scientific reasons for becoming vegetarian, expanding on the Buddhist principle of cherishing all life. Argues the causal relationship between ill-considered treatment of animals and violence towards humans.

LINZEY, Andrew. (1976). *Animal Rights: A Christian Assessment of Man's Treatment of Animals,* SCM Press, London. 120pp. Promotes an animal rights ethic based on sentiency as essential to a true reading of Christianity and God's will. Argues for vegetarianism and abolition of animal experiments.

LINZEY, Andrew. (1986). *The Status of Animals in the Christian Tradition,* Woodbroke EMS, Birmingham. 32pp. Emphasizing biblical, scholastic and saintly traditions, explores twelve ideas within Christianity that influence our understanding and treatment of animals, suggesting a rights approach.

LINZEY, Andrew. (1987). *Christianity and the Rights of Animals,* SPCK, London. 191pp. Demonstrates that hidden behind organized Christian religion's total dismissal of the claims of the animal world is a solid biblical basis for awarding rights to animals.

LINZEY, Andrew and REGAN, Tom (eds.). (1988). *Compassion for Animals,* SPCK, London. 140pp. With a rich variety of quotations from some of the greatest thinkers in the Christian tradition, explains how the Christian faith should care about and have compassion for animals.

LINZEY, Andrew and REGAN, Tom. (eds.). (1988). *Animals and Christianity: A Book of Readings*, SPCK, London. 210pp. Anthology of readings from revered Christian thinkers on the relationship between humans and animals, showing how the question of the place of animals in creation is one which has been a subject of debate right from the beginning.

MASRI, Al-Hafiz B. A. (1987). *Animals in Islam*, Athene Trust [page 178]. 37pp. Authoritative account of the status of animals within the Islamic tradition, using scripture to present a strong case for animal welfare.

REGAN (1986). See above: **Animal Experimentation**.

REGENSTEIN, Lewis G. (1991). *Replenish the Earth – A History of Organized Religion's Treatment of Animals and Nature*, SCM Press, London. 304pp. Contrasts some of the major religious texts' fine statements about animals with the reality of organized religions' treatment of them and their support for animal abuse.

REFERENCE

BOWLER, Jane. (1990). *The Vegetarian Handbook*, Vegetarian Society [page 209]. 190pp. Guidelines on nutrition, healthy eating, food additives, products, organizations, and presents arguments for vegetarianism.

EYTON, Audrey. (1991). *The Kind Food Guide*, Penguin, London. 246pp. A guide to how animal produce reaches the table, with practical advice on where to buy to avoid support of obvious cruelties.

FARHALL, Richard, LUCAS, Richard and ROFE, Amanda (eds.). (1991). *The Animal-Free Shopper*, Vegan Society [page 208]. 185pp. A shopping guide for those wishing to buy goods – food, drink, toiletries, cosmetics, remedies, footwear, clothing, etc. – which are entirely free of animal ingredients and involve no animal testing.

KEW, Barry. (1991). *The Pocketbook of Animal Facts and Figures*, Green Print, London. 192pp. Single-volume collection of extraordinary facts and figures about the millions of animals used every day by humans as pets, for food and clothing, as sport or entertainment, as transport or as subjects in scientific experiments.

MAGEL, Charles. (1989). *Keyguide to Information Sources in Animal Rights*, Mansell Publishing, London. 267pp. A detailed overview of animal rights and welfare literature, history and organizations worldwide. Essential reference work also for researchers in natural and social sciences, philosophy, religion, human and veterinary medicine, agriculture, nutrition.

NEWKIRK, Ingrid. (1991). *Save the Animals! 101 easy things you can do*, Angus and Robertson, London. 213pp. Written for the US market, adapted for British readers. Packed with practical advice on letter-writing, dealing with MPs, shopping, animal first-aid, etc.

VEGGIES. *The Animals' Contact List*, Veggies [page 209]. Subscription-based, regularly updated listing of over 2,000 international, national and local welfare/rights groups; sanctuaries; rescue centres; complementary health centres; trading organizations, etc.

WYNNE-TYSON, Jon. (ed.). (1990). *The Extended Circle: An Anthology of Humane Thought*, Cardinal, London. 648pp. A telling collection of quotations from Aristotle to Zola concerning our treatment of non-human species. The definitive dictionary of quotations for animal rights and welfare.

MISCELLANEOUS

ALTMAN, Nathaniel. (1988). *The Non-Violent Revolution – A Comprehensive Guide to Ahimsa*, Element Books, Shaftesbury. 180pp. Provides a grounding in a philosophy that has been practised by Merton, Gandhi, Russell and Martin Luther King, showing how dynamic harmlessness can be applied in our own daily lives.

DAWKINS, Marian S. (1980). *Animal Suffering: The Science of Animal Welfare*, Chapman and Hall, London. 149pp. Investigation into how to determine animal suffering, suggesting simultaneous use of several criteria (productivity not *bona fide*) as the basis for scientific study.

DAWKINS, Marian S. (1986). *Unravelling Animal Behaviour*, Longman, London. 176pp. Written for the researcher/student rather than the lay person, tackles several problematic or controversial topics, including innate behaviour and evolutionary stable strategies.

GOLD, Mark. (1988). *Living Without Cruelty*, Green Print, London. 192pp. Practical promotion of a cruelty-free lifestyle, stressing the power of the individual to force change for the better. As with the author's *Assault and Battery* [page 146] the connections are drawn between human, animal and environmental abuse.

JANNAWAY, Kathleen. (1991). *Abundant Living in the Coming Age of the Tree*, Movement for Compassionate Living [page 198]. 40pp. Foresees the abundance of a tree-based culture as a means of encouraging the end of the second population explosion (of exploited farm animals).

JENKINS, Sid. (1992). *Animal Rights and Human Wrongs*, Lennard Publishing, Harpenden. 208pp. Based on the experiences of an RSPCA officer, outlines the ways people abuse animals and exposes the lack of adequate animal protection legislation.

NORTH, Richard. (1983). *The Animals Report*, Penguin, London. 176pp. An introduction to animal welfare issues.

NORTH, Richard. (1986). *The Real Cost*, Chatto and Windus, London. 192pp. Outlines the real, wider costs of many foods and Western 'necessities'. Strong emphasis on animal products and welfare.

WALKER, S. (1983). *Animal Thought*, Routledge, London. 442pp. Review of the mental capacities of animals, with information drawn from many disciplines such as philosophy, biology, psychology, ethology and neurophysiology. An in-depth insight into animal minds. Aimed at the student and researcher.

WHEALE, Peter and McNALLY, Ruth. (1990). *The Bio-Revolution: Cornucopia or Pandora's Box?*, Pluto, London. 318pp. Based on the Athene Trust's [page 176] 1988 conference, an introduction to the issues surrounding genetic engineering and its bearing upon animals.

WILKINS, David B. (1991). *Analysis of Major Areas of Concern for Animal Welfare in Europe*, Eurogroup for Animal Welfare [page 186]. 83pp. Analyses reasons for concern, economic and consumer factors, existing legislation and suggested initiatives, for all areas of animal welfare in Europe.

CHILDREN'S AND EDUCATIONAL

Other materials prepared specifically for children will be found listed under **Videos**, **Slides** and **Slide/Tapes**, starting on page 161.

BARTON, Miles. (1988). *Zoos and Game Reserves*, Franklin Watts, London. 32pp. Presents arguments for and against the various ways in which different species are held in captivity.

BRIGHT, Michael. (1987). *Animal Rights*, Franklin Watts, London. 32pp. Introductory outline of animal abuse in farming, science, hunting, zoos, circuses, films, etc.

BRIGHT, Michael. (1987). *Saving the Whale*, Franklin Watts, London. 32pp. Asks if the slaughter of whales can ever be justified or whether the present ban should be made permanent. Also deals with cetaceans in captivity.

BRIGHT, Michael. (1988). *Killing for Luxury*, Franklin Watts, London. 32pp. Outline of the fur trade, horns, ivory, trophies and curios, luxury foods, etc., all taken from animals.

BRIGHT, Michael. (1992). *The Dying Sea*, Franklin Watts, London. 32pp. Catalogues the deadly effects of our pollution on the seas and their creatures.

BURTON, John. (1988). *Close to Extinction*, Franklin Watts, London. 32pp. Looks at the many species which humans have driven off the face of the earth and the many others that face a similar fate unless our current practices are modified or halted.

CRABTREE, Vickie. (1982). *Farming Today*, Frederick Muller Ltd, London. 128pp. Simple introduction to modern farming written for young people, covering all animal and crop production systems, including the biological bases of production and the practicalities of farming methods. Little mention of animal welfare, but no attempt is made to glamorize or conceal the realities of animal production.

CRUDDAS, Helen. (1989). *Why Animal Rights?*, Animal Aid [page 175]. 16pp. Introduction to the issues; vivisection, factory farming, slaughter, vegetarianism and living without cruelty.

EARLY TIMES. (1991). *Animal Kind*, Puffin, London. 149pp. Outlines what humans are doing to animals and what they could be doing for animals.

INGLIS, Jane. (1987). *Some People Don't Eat Meat*, Oakroyd Press, London. 32pp. For children under twelve. Looks at the reasons why so many people are vegetarians.

JAMES, Barbara. (1992). *The Young Person's Action Guide to Animal Rights*, Virago Press. 158pp. Asks a series of Where do you stand? questions, offering What-you-can-do suggestions. Explanatory, informative A–Z format.

WATSON, Zoë R. (1989). *The Use and Abuse of Animals*, Simon and Schuster, London. 64pp. Facts and photos on factory farming, vivisection and hunting.

WILSON, Ron. (1986). *Nature in Your Town*, Earthkind [page 185]. 32pp. Originally published in 1970. Where to find wildlife in towns.

TEACHERS'

Other materials suitable for use in schools will be found listed, marked [C], under **Videos**, **Slides** and **Slides/Tapes**, starting on page 161.

ATHENE TRUST. (1989). *Choices: The Farm and You*, Athene Trust [page 178]. 33pp. Teacher's book full of class work ideas for primary and middle schools. Includes poster.

CLOSE, B. S., DOLINS, F. and MASON, G. (1990). *Animal Use in Education*, Network of Individuals and Campaigns for Humane Education [page 200]. 243pp. Euroniche conference proceedings 1989: ethics; overview of animal use in Europe; alternatives; attitudes to animals in education; cross-cultural differences.

HUMANE RESEARCH TRUST. (1988). *Humane Research Education Pack*, Humane Research Trust [page 190]. Set of study cards for schools dealing with the use of animals in research.

SMITH, Alison. (1990). *Conserving Our Marine Environment (The World of Whales and Dolphins)*, Whale and Dolphin Conservation Society [page 210]. Educational resource pack which explores a range of topical issues including whaling, overfishing, marine pollution.

WOOD GREEN ANIMAL SHELTERS. (1991). *Pet Ownership*. Wood Green Animal Shelters [page 210]. 32pp. A handbook of advice covering choosing, buying and caring for a pet, preventing and curing illness plus the social responsibilities. Aimed at establishing responsible pet ownership as a GCSE subject.

VIDEOS

Videos made specifically for children are marked [C]. Most of the others are suitable for older schoolchildren and adults. Many are disturbing, some extremely so. Consult the relevant organization(s) for further details of suitability. Where a video, especially one made outside the UK, is listed as being 'available from' an organization it is most likely the case that it is also available from other organizations. Probably the most extensive library of relevant videos for local group hire is held by Co-ordinating Animal Welfare [page 183]. All videos are VHS format unless stated.

SPORTS AND ENTERTAINMENT

Angling: The Neglected Bloodsport. 20 minutes. (1992). Campaign for the Abolition of Angling [page 181]. All aspects of angling: fish and pain; tackle victims; environmental damage, and how to help CAA.

Fiesta: Sacrifice and Torture of Animals. 20 minutes. (1981). Asociacion Para la Defensa de los Derechos del Animal, Madrid, Spain. (Available from Advocates for Animals [page 174]). Catalogue of Spanish fiesta cruelties inflicted on bulls, geese, calf, cockerel, in pursuit of fun.

Hare Coursing – Conservation or Cruelty?. 8 minutes. (1992). League Against Cruel Sports [page 196]. Scenes of hare coursing, providing new evidence on hare relocation; transporting them hundreds of miles in order to be coursed.

Rural Vandals. 50 minutes. (1986). League Against Cruel Sports [page 196]. Hare coursing and mink, stag and fox hunting sections covering hunts from start to finish, contrasted with scenes of the animals in natural habitat.

The Spade and Terrier Brigade. 11 minutes. (1986). League Against Cruel Sports [page 196]. Exposes legal and illegal activities of fox hunts and traces links between hunting, badger baiting, dog fighting and cock fighting.

ANIMAL EXPERIMENTATION

An Important Role Working with Animals. 28 minutes (1991). National Anti-Vivisection Society (NAVS) [page 198]. Film from undercover work in an animal laboratory.

Breaking Barriers. 20 minutes. (1986). Jane Goodall Foundation through the BVA Animal Welfare Foundation [page 212]. (Available from Advocates for Animals [page 172]). Inside an American primate laboratory (Sema Labs). Shows chimps and other primates manically rocking and circling in cages, driven mad by the deprivation and isolation of laboratory life.

Britches. 15 minutes. (1986). People for the Ethical Treatment of Animals, USA. (Available from British Union for the Abolition of Vivisection (BUAV) [page 180]). Story of an infant stump-tailed macaque who was involved in blinding experiments at the University of California's Research Centre in Los Angeles and was rescued by animal liberationists in 1985. Film made from footage taken by the Animal Liberation Front during and after the raid when the macaque had eyesight restored by a vet and was adopted by an adult female macaque in a primate sanctuary.

Getting Away with Murder. 14 minutes. (1988). People for the Ethical Treatment of Animals, USA. (Available from British Union for the Abolition of Vivisection [page 180]). Footage shot by researchers at the Life Science Centre of the State University of New York, showing mice, rats and rabbits thrown into plastic tub to be killed by domestic ferrets.

Health with Humanity. 27 minutes. (1988). British Union for the Abolition of Vivisection [page 180]. Presents the scientific arguments against vivisection, proposing an alternative approach of disease prevention, non-animal research techniques, complementary medicine, etc.

Hidden Crimes. 78 minutes. (1986). Students United Protesting Research on Sentient Subjects. (Available from British Union for the Abolition of Vivisection [page 180]). A powerful attack on vivisection on ethical and scientific grounds, with especial emphasis on drugs causing human ill-health and damage after being passed as safe following animal tests.

Inside Biosearch. 14 minutes. (1988). People for the Ethical Treatment of Animals, USA. (Available from British Union for the Abolition of Vivisection [page 180]). Commercial testing laboratory footage obtained by undercover investigator, exposing violations of federal and state law.

The Parliament of the Doomed. 17 minutes. (1992). International Association Against Painful Experiments on Animals [page 192]. Presents the case against animal experiments, spotlighting the failure of animal tests and the need for the adoption of more reliable forms of research.

Products of Pain. 15 minutes. (1986). People for the Ethical Treatment of Animals, USA. (Available from British Union for the Abolition of Vivisection [page 180]). The horror story behind household-name cosmetics.

Progress Without Pain. 55 minutes. (1985). Lord Dowding Fund/NAVS [page 198]. Concentrates on scientific research and the alternatives to animal experimentation.

Rabbits Don't Cry. 40 minutes. (1983). BBC. (Available from British Union for the Abolition of Vivisection [page 180]). Documentary dealing with animal experimentation (and factory farming) and animal rights movement campaigns.

Rags. 16 minutes. (1987). People for the Ethical Treatment of Animals, Washington, DC, USA. (Available from Advocates for Animals [page 174]). Footage from Eastern Carolina University dog laboratory, showing dogs used as teaching tools to demonstrate already-known facts.

Silver Spring Monkeys. 20 minutes. (1981). People for the Ethical Treatment of Animals, Washington, DC, USA. (Available from Co-ordinating Animal Welfare [page 183]). Story of monkeys used in experiments at the Institute for Behavioural Research, whose limbs were surgically mutilated and who were forced to live in appalling conditions, as told by Alex Pacheco who worked under cover at the Institute collecting evidence, taking it to the police who carried out the first raid of a research facility in the USA. A long legal wrangle ensued over fate/ownership of the monkeys. The lab was closed, the chief researcher resigned and the funding for the work was rescinded. However, the monkeys were eventually taken to another research station.

Suffer the Animals. 23 minutes. (1982). National Anti-Vivisection Society [page 198]. Introduction to animal experimentation and the humane alternatives.

Through the Looking Glass. 13 minutes. (1987). British Union for the Abolition of Vivisection [page 180]. A journey through the world of animal suffering and death that lies concealed behind the glossy image of the mainstream cosmetics and toiletries industry.

Unnecessary Fuss. 20 minutes. (1985). People for the Ethical Treatment of Animals, USA. (Available from British Union for the Abolition of Vivisection [page 180]). Story of experiments and treatment of baboons used in work at the head injury clinic laboratory at the University of Pennsylvania, USA. Consists of film footage shot by researchers and stolen by the Animal Liberation Front in a raid on the laboratory. Shows researchers ridiculing the animals; unhygienic conditions; and the experiments, involving hammer blows to the head.

ANIMAL PRODUCTION/FARMING

Calves in the Dock. 7 minutes. (1991). Compassion in World Farming [page 183]. Traces the journey of week-old calves from Sturminster Newton market in Devon to Dutch veal farms, to be imported back as veal.

Chicken for Dinner. 15 minutes. (1987). Chickens' Lib [page 182]. Exposes the way in which broiler chickens are reared for the table.

[C].***The Choice is Yours: Animal Suffering or Cruelty-Free Food?*** 15 minutes. (1988). Athene Trust [page 178]. For eleven-to-eighteen-year-olds (and above) presenting the arguments against factory farming, making youngsters aware of the personal choices they have which affect the lives of farm animals. Teachers' notes.

Choose Your Diet. 60 minutes. (1991). International Vegetarian Union [page 194]. Presents the arguments for vegetarianism. Material based on experience in India but relevant to the whole world.

Down With Cruelty. 8 minutes. (1992). Beauty Without Cruelty [page 179]. Shows the cruelty involved in the live-plucking of geese for feathers and down for bedding, on Hungarian factory farm.

The Egg Machine. 15 minutes. (1989). Royal Society for the Prevention of Cruelty to Animals [page 204]. Questions the morality of confining hens in battery cages and discusses the effects of keeping poultry in such restricted conditions.

Enriched Family Pig Unit. 16 minutes. (1984). Edinburgh School of Agriculture. (Available from Advocates for Animals [page 174]).

Faces of Fur. 13 minutes. (1991). Friends of Animals USA. (Available from Beauty Without Cruelty [page 179]). Shows conditions on US fur farms.

[C]. *Food for Protest*. 19 minutes. (1986). Royal Society for the Prevention of Cruelty to Animals [page 204]. Film on factory farming aimed at senior secondary school pupils. Footage of battery hens, markets and farrowing crates.

[C]. *Food Without Fear*. 20 minutes. (1989). Vegetarian Society [page 209]. Deals with many of the questions raised by young people, dispelling myths of happy farm animals with the reality of conditions, pharmaceutical input, effects on human health and the environment.

Fur Factories. 16 minutes. (1991). LYNX [page 198]. Presents the body of scientific evidence on the cruelty of fur production, with much of the material obtained by undercover investigators.

Hens Might Fly. 8 minutes. (1992). Compassion in World Farming [page 183]. Stark picture of the living conditions of the battery hen, dispelling the myths surrounding this farming system.

Humane Slaughter. 20 minutes. (1986). Humane Slaughter Association [page 191]. Shows how cattle, sheep and pigs should be slaughtered according to the Slaughterhouses Act 1974. An instructional film.

[C]. *Kept in the Dark*. 20 minutes. (1986). Athene Trust. [page 178]. Concentrates on factory farming systems of food production. Follows a group of 9 year-olds on school project investigating farms.

Meathead. 15 minutes. (1991). Oxford Film and Video Makers, The Stables, North Place, Headington, Oxford OX3 9HY. Parody of Western meat-based culture, revealing how the demand for animal produce is satisfied; with farm and slaughterhouse footage.

Mink Kill. 13 minutes. (1991). Friends of Animals USA. (Available from Beauty Without Cruelty [page 179]). Conditions on US fur farms.

Paying the Price. 10 minutes. (1989). Compassion in World Farming [page 183]. The case against battery cages. Consumers have the power to stop the cruelty of the battery cage – all they need do is look at the label and refuse to buy battery eggs.

Putting Fur out of Fashion. 10 minutes. (1991). LYNX [page 198]. An insight into an important aspect of the campaign against the fur trade – the no-fur fashion show. Clips from several, featuring celebrities.

The Road to Misery. 16 minutes. (1992). Compassion in World Farming [page 183]. Shows the horrifying conditions in which millions of live animals are transported across Europe, and the brutal handling they often undergo both en route and at their destinations.

The Roar of Disapproval. 18 minutes. (1989). LYNX [page 198]. Exposé of trapping and fur factories. Includes two Lynx cinema commercials, 'Dumb Animals' and 'Scavengers'.

Screaming for Change. 9 minutes. (1987). Compassion in World Farming [page 183]. Depicts how almost 70 per cent of all bacon and pork comes from pigs tied in restrictive stalls and crates.

Sentenced for Life. 34 minutes. (1987). Chickens' Lib [page 182]. Explains the illegalities of battery cage systems under British animal law.

Spanish Slaughterhouses. 7 minutes. (1991). Compassion in World Farming [page 183]. Shows appalling conditions, non-stunning methods of sheep/lamb slaughter, and the maiming of cattle by incorrect use of captive bolt, in three slaughterhouses.

COMPANION ANIMALS

Cats' Protection League. 20 minutes. (1990). Cats' Protection League [page 182]. An insight into the work of the CPL.

Deadline. 30 minutes. (1989). Royal Society for the Prevention of Cruelty to Animals [page 204]. Drama documentary aiming to jolt an apathetic public into supporting a campaign to tackle irresponsible pet ownership.

[C]. *Lucky for Some.* 20 minutes. (1982). Horses and Ponies Protection Association [page 190]. An insight into the work of HAPPA.

[C]. *Pony Talk.* 20 minutes. (1989). Horses and Ponies Protection Association [page 190]. Explains the pitfalls to avoid when buying a pony.

Too Late for Tessie. 23 minutes. (1987). Royal Society for the Prevention of Cruelty to Animals [page 204]. Drama documentary highlighting the need for responsible pet ownership. Follows the life story of a dog who becomes the tragic casualty of thoughtless owners.

WILDLIFE

Back Where She Belongs. 13 minutes. (1988). Royal Society for the Prevention of Cruelty to Animals [page 204]. Shows the work of the RSPCA seal unit in Norfolk, telling the story of the first survivor to be nursed through the 1988 North Sea virus.

Cry From the Wild. 15 minutes. (1980). World Society for the Protection of Animals [page 210]. The fur trade.

Fur Factories. (1991). LYNX [page 198]. See above: **Animal Production/ Farming**.

Hare Coursing – Conservation or Cruelty? League Against Cruel Sports [page 196]. See above : **Sports and Entertainment**.

Hopping Madness. 9 minutes. (1987). Compassion in World Farming [page 183]. Shows the story of how frogs' legs appear on the menu courtesy of appalling cruelty and the death of 300 million frogs a year, disrupting the delicate balance of nature.

Let Them Live. 30 minutes. (1987). Environmental Investigation Agency [page 186]. Pilot whale slaughter in the Faroes.

Oh Elephant!. 5 minutes. (1991). Elefriends [page 186]. Report on Daphne Sheldrick's elephant orphanage in Nairobi.

Peace on Ice. 25 minutes. (1987). International Fund for Animal Welfare [page 193]. A journey to the winter wonderland of baby seals.

Putting Fur out of Fashion. (1991). LYNX [page 198]. See above: **Animal Production/Farming**.

The Roar of Disapproval. (1989). LYNX [page 198]. See above : **Animal Production/Farming**.

GENERAL

Action for Animals. 18 minutes. (1990). Royal Society for the Prevention of Cruelty to Animals [page 204]. Explains the history of the RSPCA, identifying some of the newer issues concerning it today.

Animal Liberation: The Movie. 20 minutes. (1991). Animaliberation [page 177]. Compilation of footage of unofficial raids by animal rights activists on, and inspections of, factory farms, vivisection laboratories and breeding centres. Counters media distortion.

The Animals' Film. 136 minutes. (1981). Victor Schonfeld and Myriam Alaux. Slick Pics International, London. (Available from British Union for the Abolition of Vivisection [page 180]). First powerful and comprehensive film documentary on various kinds of animal abuse and the people campaigning against them.

Animals, Nature and Religion. 35 minutes. (1988). Michael W. Fox. Humane Society of the USA. (Available from Zoo Check [page 211]). Concise, moving and lucid distillation of the great religions' teachings, calling for a one world/universal view of compassion towards animals.

Beauty Without Cruelty. 20 minutes. (1987). Beauty Without Cruelty [page 179]. Covers exploitation of whales, crocodiles, seal pups, karakul lambs, musk deer, civet, UK fur farming and cosmetics testing. Explicit slaughter scenes.

Beauty Without Cruelty (India). 20 minutes. (1987). Beauty Without Cruelty [page 179]. Animal cruelty in India, covering elephants, silk worms, snakes, musk deer, cattle, pigs, dogs, rabbits and karakul lambs. Explicit slaughter scenes.

Behind Closed Doors. (1988). Central Animal Liberation League. (Available from Co-ordinating Animal Welfare [page 183]. Footage of CALL's unofficial visits to places of animal abuse.

A Caring Society. 35 minutes. (1986). Scottish Society for the Prevention of Cruelty to Animals [page 205]. The work of the SSPCA.

Creatures of God. 30 minutes. (1988). International Association Against Painful Experiments on Animals [page 192]. An outline of Muslim theological teaching on a wide range of animal welfare topics.

Devoted to Donkeys. 30 minutes. (1991). Donkey Sanctuary [page 185]. Shows the work of the Donkey Sanctuary.

[C]. *No Treats for Animals*. 16 minutes. (1984). Animal Aid [page 175]. Made for eight-to-thirteen-year-olds and raises questions about the use of animals in everyday life.

Silent World: Genetic Engineering. 45 minutes. (1987). Michael Fox. Humane Society of the United States. (Available from Athene Trust [page 178]). Explores the ethical, environmental and animal welfare issues raised by technology's 'advance'.

[C]. *Their Future in Your Hands*. 13 minutes. (1992). Animal Aid [page 175]. Animal rights issues. Primarily for use in secondary education. Contrasts the vitality and intelligence of animals in their natural environment with the misery they endure in factory farms, slaughterhouses and vivisection laboratories.

Voices I Have Heard. 56 minutes. (1987). Tom Regan. Culture and Animals Foundation, USA. (Available from McCrimmon Publishing, Great Wakering). Presenting the case for compassion towards animals to the senior citizen community, includes interviews with long-time campaigners for animal rights and welfare.

We Are All Noah. 45 minutes. (1985). Tom Regan. Culture and Animals Foundation, USA. (Available from Compassion in World Farming [page 183]). Presents the case for compassion towards animals to the religious community, especially Christian and Jewish, with representative thinkers proposing a humane approach towards other species.

SLIDES (35mm)

[C]. *Animal Abuse*. (1983). Animal Aid [page 175]. Thirty-six slides covering factory farming, fur, zoos, circuses and animal experiments, with accompanying notes.

[C] *Companion Animals*. (1990). Royal Society for the Prevention of Cruelty to Animals [page 204]. Forty slides plus illustrated notes. Looks at a range of issues concerning companion animals: responsibilities of pet ownership; the cruelty sometimes involved; how to prevent suffering.

[C] *Food for Thought*. (1991). Royal Society for the Prevention of Cruelty to Animals [page 204]. Forty slides plus illustrated notes. Looks at farm animals and some of the animal welfare issues associated with food production.

[C]. *Modern Farming: Factory or Free Range?* (1989). Athene Trust [page 178]. Twenty-five slides with accompanying notes on main factory farming systems and the more humane alternatives.

[C]. *Wildlife Concerns*. (1990). Royal Society for the Prevention of Cruelty to Animals [page 204]. Forty slides plus illustrated notes. Looks at a range of issues concerning our treatment of wildlife, both in captivity and in the wild; animals in entertainment, sport, hunting, and environmental changes.

SLIDES (35mm)/TAPES (audio-cassette)

Vegetarianism. (1986). Mark Gold. Drake Educational Publications. (Available from Animal Aid [page 175]). Pack of four 15-minute audio-visual programmes on how vegetarianism relates to Animal Suffering; Human Hunger; Health; Living Without Cruelty.

The Work of the RSPCA. (1988). Royal Society for the Prevention of Cruelty to Animals [page 204]. Fifty slides plus 13-minute cassette introducing the work of the RSPCA. Includes notes.

[C]. *Youth for Animal Rights*. (1986). Youth for Animal Rights. (Available from Animal Aid [page 175]). 24-minute programme on a range of animal abuse issues.

TAPES (audio-cassette)

Getting it Taped: The Rights of Animals. (1987). Tom Regan and Andrew
Linzey. McCrimmon Publishing. Great Wakering. Three 30-minute cas-
settes. Discussion of animal rights and human wrongs, with philosopher
and theologian.

MAGAZINES

Most of the magazines and journals relating to animal welfare and animal
rights are published by the organizations listed in the **Directory** [page 173].
(See page references after each entry below). The selection listed consists primarily of British magazines and journals which deal constantly with controversial news and subjects and/or consider animal rights and welfare from the
perspective of that society's work. Members of the organizations generally
receive the publications as part of their membership. Where a magazine is
published independently contact details are given after its title.

Agscene. Quarterly. Compassion in World Farming [page 183].

Alternative News. Quarterly. Dr Hadwen Trust for Humane Research [page
184].

Animal International. Quarterly. World Society for the Protection of Animals [page 210].

Animal Life. Quarterly. Royal Society for the Prevention of Cruelty to
Animals [page 204].

Animals Matter. Quarterly. Wood Green Animal Shelters [page 210].

The Ark. Quarterly. Catholic Study Circle for Animal Welfare [page 182].

Arkangel. Quarterly. Independent. BCM 9240, London WC1N 3XX.

The Campaigner. Bi-monthly. National Anti-Vivisection Society [page 198].

The Cat. Quarterly. Cats' Protection League [page 182].

CAW Bulletin. Irregularly. Co-ordinating Animal Welfare [page 183].

Compassion. Two issues per year. Beauty Without Cruelty [page 179].

Dolphin. Quarterly. International Dolphin Watch [page 192].

Education News. Three issues per year. Royal Society for the Prevention of
Cruelty to Animals [page 204].

Eurobulletin of EC Developments in Animal Welfare. Monthly. Eurogroup for Animal Welfare [page 186].

Flesh and Blood. Quarterly. Independent. Caroline Publications, PO Box 84, Stevenage, Herts SG1 2SE.

FRAME News. Three issues per year. Fund for the Replacement of Animals in Medical Research [page 188].

Green Revolution. Quarterly. Independent. PO Box 845, Bristol BS99.

Howl. Quarterly. Hunt Saboteurs Association [page 191].

Humane Education Newsletter. Quarterly. Earthkind [page 185].

Jewish Vegetarian. Quarterly. Jewish Vegetarian and Ecological Society [page 196].

Living World. Quarterly. EarthKind [page 185].

Lynx. Quarterly. LYNX [page 198].

NEWS. Quarterly. Animal Concern [page 175].

NDCL News. Two issues per year. National Canine Defence League [page 199].

Oryx. Quarterly. Fauna and Flora Preservation Society [page 188].

Outrage. Bi-monthly. Animal Aid [page 175].

The Petwatcher. Three issues per year. National Petwatch [page 200].

Pisces. Quarterly. Campagn for the Abolition of Angling [page 181].

Puppy Watch News. Quarterly. Puppy Watch [page 202].

SONAR. Two issues per year. Whale and Dolphin Conservation Society [page 210].

SSPCA News. Quarterly. Scottish Society for the Prevention of Cruelty to Animals [page 205].

Today's Vegetarian. Quarterly. Independent. Future Publishing, Bath.

Trunkline. Quarterly. Elefriends [page 186].

Turning Point. Quarterly. Independent. PO Box 45, Northolt, Middx UB5 6SZ. Tel. 081 841 0503.

The Vegan. Quarterly. Vegan Society [page 208].

Vegan Views. Quarterly. Independent. 6 Hayes Avenue, Bournemouth BH7 7AD.

The Vegetarian. Ten issues per year. Vegetarian Society [page 209].

Vegetarian Living. Monthly. Independent. ESG Publishing, 59 High Street, Sutton, Surrey SM1 1EZ. Tel. 081 770 7337.

Whalewatch. Quarterly. International Wildlife Coalition [page 194].

Wildlife Guardian. Quarterly. League Against Cruel Sports [page 196].

Wildlife Times. Quarterly. Born Free Foundation [page 179].

Zoo Check News. Bi-monthly. Zoo Check [page 211].

Children's Magazines

Many of the above magazines and journals carry a young reader's page or section. Listed below are those magazines and journals which are published specifically for children or younger people.

All Living Things. Quarterly. Magazine for junior section of EarthKind [page 185].

Animal Express. Quarterly. Magazine for junior members of the Scottish Society for the Prevention of Cruelty to Animals [page 205].

Animal World. Quarterly. Magazine for junior members of the Royal Society for the Prevention of Cruelty to Animals [page 204].

Animals' Defender. Quarterly. Magazine for youth section of the National Anti-Vivisection Society [page 198].

Critters Club News. Three issues per year. Magazine for young friends of Wood Green Animal Shelters [page 210].

Farm Watch. Termly. Magazine of Compassion in World Farming's [page 183] youth group.

Greenscene. Quarterly. Magazine for young vegetarians. Vegetarian Society [page 209].

Trumpet. Two issues per year. Newsletter for junior members of Elefriends [page 186].

United Against Cruelty. Bi-monthly. Animals' Vigilantes [page 178].

Chapter Eight
DIRECTORY OF ORGANIZATIONS A–Z

It is very doubtful whether any animal welfare/rights Directory can be anything other than selective. To include every organization, society, university department or veterinary college dealing in some way with animal welfare would be to include also those establishments which additionally conduct work on animals and are thus at odds with the primary ethic of animal rights. Organizations which do not sit comfortably alongside those primarily concerned with animal rights and welfare, or which seek to promote the use of animals for various purposes, are listed in the Appendix [page 212].

This Directory deals mainly with national and (UK-based) international non-profit-making organizations and societies which set out to protect, and promote respect and justice for animals. However, it does not include local groups and animal sanctuaries (unless of a national appeal), mainly because space does not permit and because many of these tend to be short-lived.

Where applicable, each entry includes the title of the organization's regular magazine/newsletter, but the reader should note that a huge range of other printed materials is produced. Information packs, including details of merchandise, etc., are generally available from the listed organizations, which appreciate stamped addressed envelopes from enquirers.

Questionnaires to organizations were used in order to compile this Directory, and organizations which are still functioning but which failed to complete and return them are listed *without* an asterisk. Telephone numbers have been included in most cases and others have been omitted by request. The authors apologize in advance for any disappointment caused to organizations which have a legitimate claim to inclusion in the *Handbook* and invite contact from them for the next edition. Any information on organizations closing down or moving offices, or new ones being founded, would be gratefully received by the authors.

Great differences of philosophy and activity can be found to exist between these organizations, and the reader should not assume that the inclusion of an organization here links it in any way to the activities of any other. It must be recognized that while it is reasonable to assume that all of them respect the sanctity of human and other animal life, a minority of the organizations listed below take part in law-breaking activities, such as economic sabotage, which are disapproved of and publicly condemned by the majority.

The reader will notice that some organizations have been granted charitable status. This should not be read to mean that they are any better or worse than those without such benefit.

A

ABERDEEN ASSOCIATION FOR THE PREVENTION OF CRUELTY TO ANIMALS (AAPCA).
6 Bon Accord Square, Aberdeen AB9 1XU. Tel. 0224 581236. Registered Charity No. CR8770. Founded in 1870.
Aims and Methods. To repress all acts of cruelty, wanton and improper treatment of animals in the County and City of Aberdeen and neighbourhood (not covered by the Scottish SPCA [page 205]), and promote the habit of humanity and kindness towards all animals, by bringing into operation legislative enactments; by the circulation of suitable publications; by arranging for the delivery of lectures, and by other suitable means, including support of national and worldwide societies. Inspectorate visits animal-use establishments; investigates alleged cruelty; effects rescues, etc.

ADVOCATES FOR ANIMALS.*
10 Queensferry Street, Edinburgh EH2 4PG. Tel. 031 225 6039. Fax. 031 220 6377. Founded in 1912, by the Misses Ivory, as the Scottish Society for the Prevention of Vivisection. Changed name in 1989.
Aims and Methods. The protection of animals from cruelty, the prevention of the infliction of suffering, the abolition of vivisection. Campaigns for parliamentary legislation to protect animals. Exposés of institutionalized animal abuse. Has the St Andrew Animal Fund [page 205] as its sister organization, funding the search for alternatives to using animals in research. Youth membership. Publishes the *Annual Pictorial Review.*
Members/Supporters: 1,500.

ANGLICAN SOCIETY FOR THE WELFARE OF ANIMALS.
PO Box 54, Tunbridge Wells, Kent TN2 4TZ. Tel. 0892 525594.
Aims and Methods. To promote prayer, study and action on behalf of animals.

ANGLO-ITALIAN SOCIETY FOR THE PROTECTION OF ANIMALS.
136 Baker Street, London W1M 1FH. Tel. 071 435 2404.
Aims and Methods. To prevent cruelty to animals and encourage kindness.
Raises money to provide help to Italians who are fighting a tradition of animal cruelty. Campaigns against live animal export and helped to create the Italian Bird League conservation body.

ANGLO-VENETIAN GROUP FOR THE PROTECTION OF ANIMALS (DINGO).*
4 Hop Row, Haddenham, Ely, Cambridgeshire CB6 3SF. Tel. 0353 741201.
Registered Charity No. 259957. Founded in 1969 by Helena Sanders and Gina Scarpabolla.
Aims and Methods. The prevention and relief of cruelty, by veterinary treatment; neutering/spaying and humane destruction; and rescue of stray cats, in the commune of Venice and other parts of Italy. Has responsibility of removing cats from areas where they are not wanted and re-homing where possible. Dingo UK is the fundraising wing.

ANIMAL AID.*
7 Castle Street, Tonbridge, Kent TN9 1BH. Tel. 0732 364546. Fax. 0732 366533.
Founded in 1977 by Jean Pink.
Aims and Methods. Campaigns against all forms of animal abuse, principally vivisection and factory farming. Provides information and advice to the public to raise awareness of how animals are exploited and promotes a more compassionate attitude towards animals through its Living Without Cruelty message. Organizes the annual Living Without Cruelty exhibition, held in London. Co-organizer of Great British MeatOut. Launched the Humane Research Donor Card signifying that the carrier is willing to allow his/her human tissue to be used for medical research when he/she dies, with the aim of replacing animals in experimental work. Campaigning to convert 10 per cent of UK population to vegetarianism by year 2000. The Chickens' Lib campaign is now part of its work. Local groups. Youth group. Publishes *Outrage* magazine.
Members/Supporters: 15,000.

ANIMAL CHRISTIAN CONCERN (ACC).
46 St Margaret's Road, Horsforth, Leeds LS18 5BG. Tel. 0532 583517. Founded in 1985.
Aims and Methods. Expresses the view both inside and outside the Church, that cruelty of any kind is incompatible with Christ's teachings. Offers prayer and active support to peaceful animal welfare ventures.

ANIMAL CONCERN.*
62 Old Dumbarton Road, Glasgow G3 8RE. Tel. 041 334 6014. Founded in 1876 as the Scottish Anti-Vivisection Society, incorporated into the new Animal

Concern (Scotland) in 1988. Name changed to Animal Concern in 1992.
Aims and Methods. Total abolition of animal exploitation. Campaigns against
all forms of animal abuse in Scotland by exposing animal exploitation to the
public, lobbying and calling on the public to boycott exploitative goods,
companies and pastimes. Aiming at the abolition of vivisection by the year
2000. Monitoring the killing of seals in Scotland, opposing any new culling
proposals. Youth membership. Publishes *Animal Concern NEWS*.
Members/Supporters: 700.

ANIMAL CRUELTY INVESTIGATION GROUP.*
PO Box 8, Halesworth, Suffolk IP19 0JL and c/o LACS, 83–87 Union Street,
London SE1 1SG. Founded in 1989 by Mike Huskisson.
Aims and Methods. To acquire by any lawful means the hard evidence (photographs, videos, audio recordings, etc.) of the cruel abuse of our fellow
creatures, in order to expose and curtail it. Where possible the evidence is used
to prosecute offenders and, if no legislation exists, to force government to act.
Also promotes this style of investigative work throughout the animal wel-
fare/rights movement with programme of illustrated talks and production of
educational materials. Exposed the animal experimental work of Professor
Feldberg in 1989/90, and the practices of the Quorn Hunt in 1991. Publishes
ACIG News Bulletin.
Members/Supporters: 1,200.

ANIMAL LIBERATION FRONT (ALF).
Press Office: BM 4400, London WC1N 3XX. Tel. 0954 30542. Mobile Tel. 0836
310763.
Formed as the Band of Mercy in 1972 to embark on a campaign of direct action
against vehicles and property used by hunts. Campaign soon expanded to
include action against all forms of animal abuse. Became the ALF in 1976.
Aims and Methods. Animal rescue from laboratories and breeding farms, destruction of property of animal abusers; economic sabotage.

ANIMAL LIBERATION FRONT SUPPORTERS GROUP (ALF SG).
BM 1160, London WC1N 3XX. Tel. 0954 30542.
Aims and Methods. Raises money through sale of merchandise to support ALF
activists faced with fines and prison sentences.

ANIMAL LIBERATION INVESTIGATION UNIT (ALIU).*
PO Box 38, Manchester M60 1NX. Tel. 061 953 4039. Founded in 1990.
Specialist group of Animaliberation [page 175].
Aims and Methods. To shatter the secrecy surrounding animal abuse and
expose the plight of animals held behind closed doors. Gathers information
via daytime inspections of animal use establishments. Causes no damage to
property, etc. Launched with an uninvited visit to the Boots laboratory at
Thurgarton, Notts, taking videos and photos of the beagles held there for
experiments, prompting a nationwide campaign against Boots.

ANIMAL PROTECTION FOUNDATION.*
PO Box 168, Cardiff CF5 5YH. Tel. 0222 569914. Fax. 0222 238866. Founded in
1983 by Christopher Aston.
Aims and Methods. To promote the animal rights ethic; expose areas of violence
to animals; lobby the public to boycott cruelty; lobby local, regional, national
and international politicians to effect change that will benefit animals. Promotes literature, petitions, exhibitions, legal protest and media liaison to work
for change. Located, researched, exposed and closed in 1991 the last arctic fox
fur farm in England and Wales.

ANIMAL RESEARCH KILLS (ARK).*
PO Box 82, Kingswood, Bristol BS15 1YF. Founded 1992.
Aims and Methods. The abolition of vivisection. Distributes information exposing the scientific fraud of vivisection. Promotes the work of CIVIS [page 183]
and the books of Hans Ruesch [page 143]; warns of the dangers of a health care
system based on vivisection and the products of the petro-chemical industry.

ANIMAL RIGHTS BUREAU.
4 Garden Lane, Bradford, West Yorkshire BD9 5QJ. Tel. 0274 495847. (Or 19-
25 Sunbridge Road, Bradford BD1 2AY – Animals in Need).

ANIMAL RIGHTS COALITION.*
PO Box 155, Manchester M60 1FT. Tel. 061 953 4039. Founded in 1992 by Neil
Lea.
Aims and Methods. Formed to link up animal rights groups around the country
by setting up networks; to set up new animal rights groups in areas not already
covered; to organize fundraising events; to distribute funds to local independent groups.

ANIMAL WELFARE INVESTIGATION UNIT.
PO Box 589, Bristol, Avon BS99 1RW. Tel 0272 776261.

ANIMAL WELFARE TRUST.
Tyler's Way, Watford by-Pass, Watford, Herts WD2 8HQ. Tel. 081 950 8215/
0177. Registered Charity No. 262999. Founded in 1971.
Aims and Methods. Rescues unwanted animals, and runs an emergency pet
care scheme to ensure that pets are looked after if anything happens to their
owners. Cares for hundreds of unwanted pets every year until new homes can
be found. No healthy animal is ever destroyed.

ANIMALIBERATION.*
PO Box 38, Manchester M60 1NX. Tel. 061 953 4039. Founded in 1990.
Aims and Methods. To fight for animal liberation and to unite those involved
in the fight. Promotes direct action against all forms of animal abuse, e.g.
halting the Grand National; roof top demonstrations. Has no formal membership or groups. Operates as a banner under which various groups can take

action. Its specialist group, the Animal Liberation Investigation Unit [page 176], takes direct action to expose animal-abusing industries. Publishes *Animaliberation* newsletter.

ANIMALINE.
PO Box 10, Ryde, Isle of Wight PO33 1JX. Tel. 0983 616980.

ANIMALS' VIGILANTES.
James Mason House, 24 Salisbury Street, Fordingbridge, Hants SP6 1AF. Tel. 0425 53663.
Aims and Methods. To fight cruelty. Publishes *United Against Cruelty*.

ANIMUS.*
34 Marshall Street, London W1V 1LL. Founded in 1980.
Aims and Methods. Produces goods related to animal rights to promote awareness and to sell at low cost for groups' fundraising. Large range of badges; producers of the *Animals Diary* 1985–9; records; animals calendar. Mail order only.

ANTI-ANIMAL CARCASS CAMPAIGN.
PO Box 307, Ship Street, Brighton, East Sussex BN2 1HW. Founded 1992.
Aims and Methods. To seek legislation to prohibit the public display of animal carcasses. Petitions.

ARTISTS FOR ANIMALS.
12 Noble Street, Bradford BD7.
Aims and Methods. Promotes animal rights ethic and raises funds through exhibitions and record production.

ASSOCIATION OF BRITISH DOGS' HOMES.
c/o Dogs' Home Battersea [page 183].
Aims and Methods. To encourage those concerned with the running of animal shelters to exchange information and to speak with one voice on matters such as legislation concerning dogs.

ATHENE TRUST.*
5a Charles Street, Petersfield, Hants GU32 3EH. Tel. 0730 268070. Fax. 0730 260791. Registered Charity No. 295126. Founded in 1981 by Compassion in World Farming [page 181].
Aims and Methods. To promote the essential harmony which could and should exist between humankind and the natural world. Considers that human needs can be shown to be compatible with a regeneration of organic/veganic farming, conservation of and respect for wildlife of all kinds and with the welfare of animals. Staged first-ever public conference on genetic engineering, in UK in 1988.

B

BEAUTY WITHOUT CRUELTY (BWC).*
57 King Henry's Walk, London N1 4NH. Tel. 071 254 2929. Fax. 071 923 4702. Registered Charity No. 222884. Founded in 1959 by Lady Muriel Dowding and others. Launched, but now entirely separate from, the cosmetics company Beauty Without Cruelty Ltd.
Aims and Methods. To make people aware of the cruelty and suffering inflicted on animals for unnecessary items of fashion. Seeks to promote cruelty-free alternatives for furs, cosmetics, perfume, exotic skins and feathers, silk, bristles and down. Initiated EC fur import ban which will be implemented in 1994/5. Revealed live-plucking of geese for down-filled bedding. Publishes *Compassion*.

BLUE CROSS.*
Field Centre, Home Close Farm, Shilton Road, Burford, Oxfordshire OX18 4PF. Tel. 0993 822651. Fax. 0993 823083. Registered Charity No. 224392. Founded in 1897. Incorporates Our Dumb Friends League.
Aims and Methods. To encourage kindness to animals by providing free veterinary treatment for the pets of owners in genuine financial need; providing temporary accommodation for animals whose owners can no longer keep them, and finding good homes; providing a protection scheme for horses, ponies and donkeys; providing a welfare boarding service for the pets of owners who cannot afford commercial boarding fees. Operates animal hospitals (establishing possibly the world's first in 1906), clinics and re-homing centres. Publishes *Blue Cross Illustrated*, and *Pawprint* for young members. Members/Supporters: 50,000.

BORN FREE FOUNDATION. *
Cherry Tree Cottage, Coldharbour, Dorking, Surrey RH5 6HA. Tel. 0306 712091. Fax. 0306 713350. Registered Charity No. 296024. Founded in 1991 by Virginia McKenna, Bill Travers, Will Travers, Joanna Lumley and Terry Dickinson.
Aims and Methods. Co-ordinates the work of Zoo Check [page 211], Elefriends [page 186] and Into the Blue [page 195]. Committed to ending captive animal abuse and suffering; helping protect endangered wildlife; conserving natural habitats; inspiring and educating people to respect the natural world. In 1992, re-launched the Operation Wolf campaign, and launched the Great Ape Escape to raise funds for the rescue of chimps used by Spanish beach photographers and send them to the Primate Rescue Centre (formerly Monkey World) in Devon. Publishes *Wildlife Times*.
Members/Supporters: 1,000.

BRANSBY HOME OF REST FOR HORSES.
Bransby, Saxilby, Lincoln LN1 2PH. Tel. 0427 788464.
Aims and Methods. To rescue and care for horses, ponies and donkeys. Visits low-class sales, rescuing distressed animals. Campaigns against the indiscriminate breeding of foals, the tethering of underfed horses on waste/ common land, investigates cruelty complaints. Instrumental in passing of Dartmoor Commons Act 1986 [page 83].

BRITISH DIVERS MARINE LIFE RESCUE.
Unit 10, Maylan Road, Earlstrees Industrial Estate, Corby, Northamptonshire NN17 2DR. Tel. 0536 67374.

BRITISH HEDGEHOG PRESERVATION SOCIETY.
Knowbury House, Knowbury, Ludlow, Shropshire SY8 3LQ. Tel. 0584 890287. Founded in 1982 by Adrian Coles.
Aims and Methods. To prevent cruelty to hedgehogs, to protect them from unnecessary suffering and promote a more humane attitude towards them.

BRITISH TRUST FOR ORNITHOLOGY.*
The Nunnery, Nunnery Place, Thetford, Norfolk IP24 2PU. Tel. 0842 750050. Fax. 0842 750030. Registered Charity No. 216652. Founded in 1933. Britain's premier research organization in ornithology.
Aims and Methods. Through its network of volunteers it carries out fieldwork and the findings are analysed by its research staff. Licensed to carry out Britain's bird-ringing scheme. Many long-running schemes including the Common Bird Census, Nest Record Scheme, etc. Work is extensive and covers such topics as organic farming, bird distribution, pesticides. Publishes *BTO News*.
Members/Supporters: 9,000.

BRITISH UNION FOR THE ABOLITION OF VIVISECTION (BUAV).*
16a Crane Grove, Islington, London N7 8LB. Tel. 071 700 4888. Fax. 071 700 0252. Founded in 1898 by Frances Power Cobbe.
Aims and Methods. To end all experiments on living animals. Public and parliamentary campaigning in UK and Europe to end use of animals for testing cosmetic and hoseholad goods; challenge conventional views about animals in medical research, and promote alternatives to animal experiments. Success with undercover work providing insight into a British laboratory. Licenses use of its not-tested-on-animals logo (rabbit on triangle) for use on consumer product packaging.
Members: 13,000. Supporters: 50,000.

BROOKE HOSPITAL FOR ANIMALS.
British Columbia House, 1–3 Regent Street, London SW1Y 4PA. Tel. 071 930 0210. Founded in 1934 by D. Brooke.
Aims and Methods. To provide free veterinary treatment for those animals

whose owners cannot afford it, in Egypt. Operates hospitals, clinics, shelters and troughs and visits markets, etc. in that country.

C

CAMPAIGN AGAINST LEATHER AND FUR (CALF).*
CALF BM Box 8889, London WC1N 3XX. Founded in 1989 by Robin Lane and Ros Dadej.
Aims and Methods. To encourage the public to understand that leather must be opposed for the same reasons as fur. Promotes use of alternatives.

CAMPAIGN FOR THE ABOLITION OF ANGLING (CAA).*
PO Box 130, Sevenoaks, Kent TN14 5NR. Tel. 0836 279758. Founded in 1981 by Bill Maxwell-Brodie.
Aims and Methods. To promote public awareness of all forms of animal suffering engendered by angling; to campaign for the rights of such animals, particularly fish, *viz.* their right to life, liberty and to follow the dictates of nature; to draw together individuals and groups nationally and internationally to pursue the aforementioned aims. Pressurizes the angling community to justify its actions. Local groups. Publishes *PISCES*.
Members: 400.

CAMPAIGN FOR THE ADVANCEMENT OF RUESCH'S EXPOSÉS
23 Dunster Gardens, London NW6 7NG. Tel. 071 625 5935.
Aims and Methods. Promotion of the work of Hans Ruesch [page 143].

CAMPAIGN TO END FRAUDULENT MEDICAL RESEARCH.
PO Box 302, London N8 9HD.
Aims and Methods. Anti-vivisection from a scientific angle.

CAPTIVE ANIMALS PROTECTION SOCIETY (CAPS).
36 Braemore Court, Kingsway, Hove, East Sussex BN3 4FG. Tel. 0273 737756.
Inactive at time of writing.

CARE FOR THE WILD.*
1 Ashfolds, Horsham Road, Rusper, West Sussex RH12 4QX. Tel. 0293 871596. Fax. 0293 871022. Registered Charity No. 288802. Founded in 1984 by William J. Jordan.
Aims and Methods. To prevent suffering and cruelty inflicted by humans on wildlife. Sole funders of the elephant orphanage in Tsavo National Park. Exposed and halted the trade in elephant hide in Thailand. Campaigning to ensure the CITES [page 213] ban on ivory trading is not lifted. Represented at the International Whaling Commission. Local groups. Publishes *Care for the Wild News*.

CAT SURVIVAL TRUST.
The Centre, Codicote Road, Welwyn, Herts AL6 9TU. Tel. 043871 6873/6478.
Founded in 1976.
Aims and Methods. Concerned with the survival of wild endangered cats.
Takes in wild cats (some of which have been impounded by authorities from
unlicensed and unsuitable collections) as breeding stock to breed in captivity
to reintroduce to the wild. Habitat preservation and cat conservation.

CATHOLIC STUDY CIRCLE FOR ANIMAL WELFARE.
39 Onslow Gardens, South Woodford, London E18 1ND. Tel. 081 989 0478.
Founded in 1937.
Aims and Methods. To promote concern and respect for animals by prayer,
example and educational materials. To influence the Roman Catholic authorities to treat animal welfare as a matter of Christian morality.

CATS' PROTECTION LEAGUE.*
17 Kings Road, Horsham, West Sussex RH13 5PN. Tel. 0403 61947. Fax. 0403
218414. Registered Charity No. 203644. Founded in 1927 by a group chaired
by Miss J. Wade.
Aims and Methods. To rescue stray, unwanted and injured cats and rehabilitate
and rehome them where possible; to provide information on the care of cats
and kittens; to encourage the neutering of all cats not required for breeding.
Maintains shelters. Branches conduct rescue work at local level. Publishes *The
Cat* magazine.

CELIA HAMMOND ANIMAL TRUST.
Riverhall, Partridges Lane, Wadhurst, East Sussex TN5 6LB. Tel. 089 288 3367.
Founded in 1987 by Celia Hammond.
Aims and Methods. To set up a network of spaying clinics throughout the UK
to enable owners to have their animals neutered for less than private veteri-
nary fees.

CHICKENS' LIB.
See Animal Aid [page 175].
Aims and Methods. To abolish intensive chicken and egg production. Tempo-
rarily cannot deal with enquiries.

**CHRISTIAN CONSULTATIVE COUNCIL FOR THE WELFARE OF ANI-
MALS.**
11 Dagmar Road, London N4 4NY. Founded in 1978.
Aims and Methods. To promote active concern for animals within the Christian
Church; to encourage and facilitate the exchange of information.

CINNAMON TRUST.*
Poldarves, Trescowe Common, Penzance, Cornwall TR20 9RX. Tel. 0736
850291. Registered Charity No. 293399. Founded in 1985 by Mrs Avril R.
Jarvis.

Aims and Methods. To keep the elderly and their pets together for as long as possible. Volunteers provide help at home, e.g. walking dogs. Provides a short-term fostering service for pets whose owners face a spell in hospital, and also a variety of solutions for the long-term care of pets whose owners have died or moved to residential accommodation which will not accept pets. Members/Supporters: 3,000.

CIVIS.
PO Box 338, London E8 2AL.
Anti-vivisection organization.

COLLEGE OF ANIMAL WELFARE. *
Wood Green Animal Shelters, London Road, Godmanchester, Cambridge-shire PE18 8JL. Tel. 0480 831177. Fax. 0480 830556.
Offers a wide range of courses and seminars for staff (of the Shelters), members of the public and those wishing to pursue a career in animal welfare. The Shelters' nationally recognized Animal Welfare Training Course provides trained officers to work within local communities on contractual basis or full-time employment. Also veterinary nurse training, kennel and cattery management, YTS kennel craft and others.

COMMITTEE FOR THE REFORM OF ANIMAL EXPERIMENTATION (CRAE).
10 Queensferry Street, Edinburgh EH2 4PG. Founded in 1977.

COMPASSION IN WORLD FARMING (CIWF).*
Charles House, 5a Charles Street, Petersfield, Hants GU32 3EH. Tel. 0730 260791/268863. Fax. 0730 260791. Founded in 1967 by Peter Roberts.
Aims and Methods. Campaigns for an end to factory farming of animals and for better legal protection for animals on the farm, in transit and at slaughter. Prominent in efforts to ban live animal export and to gain improved status for animals in the Treaty of Rome. Instrumental in the phasing out of sow stalls and tethers. Co-organizer of the Great British MeatOut campaign. Publishes *Agscene* magazine and, for youth group members, *Farm Watch*.

CONSERVATIVE ANTI-HUNT COUNCIL.*
PO Box 193, Welwyn, Herts AL6 9HG. Tel. 0823 286398. Founded in 1981 by MPs and members of the Conservative Party.
Aims and Methods. To persuade the Conservative Party to adopt, as official Party policy, policies to legislate against the hunting of animals with two or more dogs; to ensure that, once the Party adopts such policies, legislation is brought before Parliament at the earliest opportunity to abolish the hunting of animals. Membership open only to members of the Conservative Party.

CO-ORDINATING ANIMAL WELFARE.*
PO Box 589, Bristol, Avon BS99 1RW. Tel. 0272 776261. Founded in the 1970s. Re-formed in 1985.

Aims and Methods. To bring together the active members of all animal rights societies and work for unity within the movement; to increase the flow of information in the movement and to encourage open discussions on successful tactics and campaigns; to promote and support strong local groups and to work for good relations between campaigners; to increase the general level of campaigning by drawing on the accumulated skills of experienced campaigners and encouraging enthusiasm. Operates an extensive video library plus desktop publishing and database systems for local groups. Local group networking now taken over by Animal Rights Coalition [page 175]. Publishes *CAW Bulletin*.
Members/Supporters: N/A.

D

DISABLED AGAINST ANIMAL RESEARCH AND EXPLOITATION (DAARE).*
PO Box 8, Daventry, Northamptonshire NN11 4QR. Tel. 0327 71568. Founded in 1986 by Sue Crowshaw.
Aims and Methods. To abolish the use of animals in experiments, and all animal abuse. Promotes the belief that it is in all disabled persons' interest to campaign for the total abolition of vivisection as artificially induced diseases in animals have no relevance to the human situation and results obtained therefrom cannot be reliably applied to people with disabilities and illnesses. Publishes Dare to Liberate Newsletter.

DR HADWEN TRUST FOR HUMANE RESEARCH.*
6c Brand Street, Hitchin, Herts SG5 1HX. Tel. 0462 436819. Fax. 0462 420863. Registered Charity No. 261096. Founded in 1970 by members of the British Union for the Abolition of Vivisection [page 178].
Aims and Methods. To promote the development of valid techniques to substitute for the use of animals in medical and associated fields of research. Believes that the use of live animals in experiments is ethically unjustifiable, and that human health can be more effectively improved by replacing the outdated 'animal model' with methods more relevant to the human situation. Sponsors humane research projects, making grants to scientists, and assists in organization and provision of facilities and equipment for such research. Local groups. Publishes *Alternative News*.
Members/Supporters: 5,500.

DOCTORS IN BRITAIN AGAINST ANIMAL EXPERIMENTS.
PO Box 302, London N8 9HD. Tel. 081 340 9813. Fax. 081 342 9878. Founded 1990.
Aims and Methods. Opposes animal experiments on scientific and medical

grounds. Campaigns for total, immediate and unconditional abolition. Proposes other, non-animal, research methods.

DOGS' HOME BATTERSEA.

Battersea Park Road, London SW8 4AA. Tel. 071 622 3626. Founded in 1869 by Mrs M. Tealby.

Aims and Methods. To restore lost dogs and cats to their owners; to give food and shelter to unwanted dogs and cats and find them good homes.

DONKEY SANCTUARY.*

Slade House Farm, Salcombe Regis, Sidmouth, Devon EX10 0NU. Tel. 0395 578222. Fax. 0395 579266. Registered Charity No. 264818. Founded in 1969 by Mrs E. D. Svendsen.

Aims and Methods. To actively help any donkey in trouble anywhere in the UK. Those that are admitted to the sanctuary(over 5,000 to date) are guaranteed care and protection for life. Arranges inspections and advises local authorities regarding the issue of licences appertaining to donkeys used for financial gain. Welfare officers throughout the UK. Conducts non-intrusive research into donkeys' physiology. Rescued donkey from Spanish fiesta in 1987 [page 11]. Publishes The Donkey Sanctuary Newsletter. Also at this address, the International Donkey Protection Trust which aims to help working donkeys (some 55 million exist) throughout the world.

E

EARTHKIND.*

Humane Education Centre, Bounds Green Road, London N22 4EU. Tel. 081 889 1595. Fax. 081 881 7662. Registered Charity No. 260708.

Founded in 1955 by Michael Fryer as the Crusade Against All Cruelty to Animals, campaigning to aid seals, whales and fur animals (1956), against factory farming (1960) and *foie gras* production (1963). Established the Humane Education Centre, with lecture theatre. Changed name in 1991.

Aims and Methods. Envisages a ten-year plan (the Animals Contract) to bring all areas of animal concern under one legislative umbrella. Works mainly through education to promote respect and compassion for animals, recognizing their inherent value and the interdependence of all life on earth. Working to produce educational resources aimed at the National Curriculum. Youth membership. Publishes *The Living World, All Living Things* (junior) and the Humane Education Newsletter.

Members/Supporters: 2,000.

ELEFRIENDS.*
Cherry Tree Cottage, Coldharbour, Nr Dorking, Surrey RH5 6HA. Tel. 0306 713320. Fax. 0306 713350. Registered Charity No. 296024. Founded in 1989 by Zoo Check Charitable Trust. Elefriends is now a project of the Born Free Foundation [page 177].
Aims and Methods. To support anti-poaching and conservation initiatives in the field and to tackle the consumer markets for ivory around the world through a public awareness campaign, the focal point of which has been the Elefriends Ivory Out Pledge. Raises money to provide equipment, sanctuary and undercover work. Campaigns to maintain the elephant on CITES Appendix 1 [page 213] – the 'most endangered' listing – effectively banning trade in elephant products like skins and ivory. Publishes *Trunkline* magazine and the youth group's *Trumpet*.
Members/Supporters: 20,000.

ELEVENTH HOUR GROUP.
86 Smithwood Close, London SW19 6JH. Tel. 081 788 7862.
Aims and Methods. Anti-vivisection from scientific angle.

ENOUGH.*
PO Box 10, Ryde, Isle of Wight PO33 1JX. Tel./Fax. 0983 811372. Founded in 1985 by Geoff Francis, Janet Hunt, Melody Lovelace and Mark Gold.
Aims and Methods. To promote the priorities of a vegetarian diet on both ethical and economic grounds, stressing the interconnections between livestock farming, Third World hunger and environmental destruction. Planning an annual festival based on these themes. Co-founder of the Great British MeatOut campaign.

ENVIRONMENTAL INVESTIGATION AGENCY (EIA).*
2 Pear Tree Court, London EC1R 0DS. Tel. 071 490 7040. Fax. 071 490 0436. Founded in 1984 by Allan Thornton, Dave Currey and Jennifer Lonsdale.
Aims and Methods. Works for the conservation and protection of wildlife and the environment. In-depth research is backed by on-site investigations. Information gathered is released to the international media. Played key role in winning international ban on trade in ivory in 1989 and in maintaining ban at CITES in 1992. Spearheading campaign to control indiscriminate killing of dolphins, porpoises and whales through International Whaling Commission. Leading the way in Europe and USA to ban import of wild birds for the pet trade. Publishes *EIA News*.
Members/Supporters: 8,000.

EUROGROUP FOR ANIMAL WELFARE.*
17 Square Marie-Louise, Bte 6, B-1040 Brussels. In UK, c/o Royal Society for the Prevention of Cruelty to Animals [page 204]. Founded in 1980 by major animal welfare organizations in each of the then nine member states of the EC.

Aims and Methods. To advise the European Community members [page 213] and their institutions and the Council of Europe [page 213] on all aspects of animal welfare; to seek the introduction and enforcement by the EC and member states of adequate and effective legislation to protect animals of all species; to establish a system of communication and the exchange of information between member societies on animal welfare matters. Instrumental in securing 1983 EC ban on seal product imports; 1986 EC Directive on animal experimentation; 1991 EC Regulation banning leghold trap and import of certain furs; introduction of EC budget for animal welfare projects. Publishes *Eurobulletin of EC Developments in Animal Welfare.*

Members/Supporters: twelve member organizations.

EUROPEAN COUNCIL FOR ANIMAL WELFARE.

c/o Royal Society for the Prevention of Cruelty to Animals, Causeway, Horsham, West Sussex RH12 1HG. Tel. 0403 64181. Founded in 1985.
Aims and Methods. Incorporates Eurogroup for Animal Welfare (see above) and was formed by them and the World Society for the Protection of Animals [page 210].

EUROPEAN PARLIAMENTARY INTERGROUP ON ANIMAL WELFARE.

See Intergroup on Animal Welfare [page 191].

EUROPEAN WILDLIFE TEACHING HOSPITAL.

The Wildlife Hospital Trust (St Tiggywinkles), Aston Road, Aylesbury, Bucks HP17 8AF.

F

FARM AND FOOD SOCIETY.*

4 Willifield Way, London NW11 7XT. Tel. 081 455 0634. Registered Charity No. 1000919. Founded in 1966.
Aims and Methods. To promote farming humane to animals, wholesome for consumers and fair to farmers. Aims at a non-violent system of farming in harmony with the environment, combining the best traditional methods with wise use of technology. Makes an annual award for a project designed to improve the conditions of farm animals at any stage from birth to slaughter. Special concerns include the patenting of new life-forms, genetic engineering, live export and factory farming. Publishes *Farm and Food News.*

FARM ANIMAL WELFARE CO-ORDINATING EXECUTIVE.*

Springhill House, 280 London Road, Cheltenham, Gloucestershire GL52 6HS. Tel. 0242 524725. Founded in 1977 during Animal Welfare Year.
Aims and Methods. To co-ordinate views on farm animal welfare within the

movement, acting as a joint consultative body to represent welfare opinion on matters relating to the improvement of conditions and/or protection of animals, birds and fish used for the production of food or farmed for other purposes. Played active role in outlawing the taking of antler velvet from live deer [page 60].

FAUNA AND FLORA PRESERVATION SOCIETY.

1 Kensington Gore, London SW7 2AT. Tel. 071 823 8899. Founded in 1903.
Aims and Methods. Focuses attention on the plight of endangered species by, e.g., involvement in the Mountain Gorilla Project.

FELLOWSHIP OF LIFE.*

43 Braichmelyn, Bethesda, Bangor, Gwynedd LL57 3RD. Founded in 1973 by Margaret Lawson.
Aims and Methods. To establish vegetarianism/veganism as a religious basis and way of life, and to unite believers of all faiths or none in a way of life which hurts neither life nor the environment, through the publication of literature. Members: 850.

FIGHT AGAINST ANIMAL CRUELTY IN EUROPE.

29 Shakespeare Street, Southport, Merseyside PR8 5AB. Tel. 0704 535922.
One of the organizations involved in monitoring Spanish fiestas [page 11].

FREE-RANGE EGG ASSOCIATION.

37 Tanza Road, London NW3 2UA. Tel. 071 435 2596. Founded in 1970s by A. Coghill.
Aims and Methods. Encourages the sale of genuine free-range eggs as opposed to those passed off as such. Highlights the conditions in battery systems, encouraging people to eat/produce free-range non-battery eggs. Issues a list of approved farms and shops, the shops displaying a yellow FREGG triangle containing the name and address of the supplying farmer. Involved in drawing up proposals put to the EC for the labelling of non-cage eggs, which have since been made into regulations.

FUND FOR THE REPLACEMENT OF ANIMALS IN MEDICAL EXPERIMENTS (FRAME).*

Eastgate House, 34 Stoney Street, Nottingham NG1 1NB. Tel. 0602 584740. Fax. 0602 503570. Registered Charity No. 259464. Founded in 1969 by Dorothy Hegarty and Charles Foister.
Aims and Methods. To seek a reduction in live animal experimentation, refinement of the procedures used, and the development, validation and acceptance of replacement alternative methods. Believes that the scale of live animal experimentation is unacceptable and must not be allowed to continue, although considers that the immediate and total abolition of animal experiments is not possible if medical research is to continue and overcome human and animal diseases, and if new consumer products and industrial chemicals

are to be adequately tested. Funds with commercial concerns alternative research at universities and other laboratories. A principal adviser to government during preparation and passage through Parliament of the Animals (Scientific Procedures) Act 1986 [page 123]. Consultant to EC [page 213]. Publishes *FRAME News* and *ATLA (Alternatives to Laboratory Animals)*. Members/Supporters: 1,000.

G

GREEK ANIMAL WELFARE FUND.*
11 Lower Barn Road, Purley, Surrey CR8 1HY. Tel./Fax. 081 668 0548. Registered Charity No. 233574. Founded in 1959 by Eleanor Close.
Aims and Methods. To raise funds to further humane behaviour towards animals on the mainland and islands of Greece; to assist the few animal welfare societies in Greece with financial aid; to supply veterinary drugs and equipment to clinics; to supply animal food; to supply vehicles for animal collection; and to maintain shelters. Following a programme of building new shelters and establishing mobile clinics for the Greek islands.

GREEN PARTY ANIMAL RIGHTS WORKING PARTY.*
23 Highfield South, Rock Ferry, Wirral L42 4NA. Tel. 051 648 0485. Fax. via TCSU 051 225 3389.
Aims and Methods. Long-term aim to eliminate wholesale exploitation of other species and protect natural habitats; to reduce consumption of animal products; to promote a ban on import/export of all furs, and on ivory and whale oil import; to outlaw fur farms; to phase out intensive farming, including fish; to phase out animal experimentation in five years with immediate ban on certain procedures; to ban dissection within three years; to ban hunting with hounds, shooting; to ban zoos. Such policy passed at party conference in 1990. To continuously update such policy; to inform public of such policies and influence other parties to adopt. Membership open only to Green Party members, who receive quarterly newsletter.

H

HOME OF REST FOR HORSES.
Westcroft Stables, Speen Farm, Slad Lane, Nr Lacey Green, Princes Risborough, Bucks HP27 0PP. Tel. 0494 488464. Founded in 1886.
Aims and Methods. To enable poorer owners to procure rest and skilled treatment for their animals when needed; to provide a place of refuge for

animals whose owners are proved guilty of cruelty or neglect in the Courts; to provide a suitable asylum for a limited number of 'old favourites'. Funds equine research, e.g. at University of Cambridge, University of Bristol (prevention and alleviation of respiratory diseases), Royal College of Veterinary Surgeons (RCVS) (research into laminitis) plus grants to the RCVS [page 216] to set up the Sefton Surgical Wing at the Equine Veterinary Hospital.

HORSES AND PONIES PROTECTION ASSOCIATION (HAPPA).*
Happa House, 64 Station Road, Padiham, Nr Burnley, Lancashire BB12 8EF. Tel./Fax. 0282 79138. Registered Charity No. 217161. Founded in 1937 by Miss Mona Huskie.
Aims and Methods. To improve equine welfare; to prevent unnecessary suffering to horses, ponies and donkeys caused by ignorance and idleness; to underline cost and responsibility of pony ownership. Investigates complaints; educates ignorant owners; removes ill-treated animals: nurses victims back to health; offers a permanent home; prosecutes for cruelty; operates lost and found horse register. Has Field Officers who are experts in horse welfare and the law, and who visit horse fairs, sales and markets. Presses Parliament to make better protective legislation for equines and was involved in bringing about the Riding Establishments Act 1964 [page 133] and the Ponies Act. Wishes to see animals auctioned from licensed premises only, more supervision of slaughterhouses and higher standards maintained; to prevent live export for overseas slaughter; to see fewer ponies turned out onto moors and common land; to secure an end to the indiscriminate breeding of foals, and to oversee new legislation to ban tethering [page 83]. HAPPA Club for Junior Members. Local groups. Publishes HAAPA Newsletter.
Members/Supporters: 13,000.

HUMANE RESEARCH TRUST (HRT).*
Brook House, 29 Bramhall Lane South, Bramhall, Stockport, Cheshire SK7 2DN. Tel. 061 439 8041. Fax. 061 439 3713. Registered Charity No. 267779. Founded in 1974 by the Lawson Tait Trust which has a restriction written into its deeds that no money may be given to any scientist holding a Home Office Licence to use animals.
Aims and Methods. To support research into the cause and cure of human illness and to replace the use of animals in laboratory experiments. Was formed to provide funds to licence-holders who wish to discover new methods, providing that they are drastically reducing the number of animals used in doing so, and that no live animals are used. Sponsors research with potential value to humanity and for sparing animals in the laboratory, and the capability of influencing medical research in the future. Local groups.
Members/Supporters: 7,500.

HUMANE SLAUGHTER ASSOCIATION (HSA).
34 Blanche Lane, Potters Bar, Herts EN6 3PA. Tel. 0707 59040. Founded in 1911 by Miss D. Sidley. Originally known as the Council of Justice and the Humane Slaughter Association.
Aims and Methods. To promote humane methods of slaughter, and to introduce reforms in livestock markets, including transport facilities. Promotes pre-slaughter stunning using proper equipment, giving demonstrations and advice. Campaigns against religious/ritual slaughter [page 66] and the export of live food animals. Supports symposia and meetings and is involved in giving advice to government bodies and to the Farm Animal Welfare Council [page 214]. Promotes use of mobile slaughterhouse for rural areas.
Members/Supporters: 400.

HUNT SABOTEURS ASSOCIATION (HSA).*
PO Box 1, Carlton, Nottingham NG4 2JY. Tel./Fax. 0602 590357. Founded in 1963 by John Prestidge in Brixham, Devon. First outing in Torquay on Boxing Day 1963 against the South Devon Foxhounds.
Aims and Methods. To abolish all bloodsports. Operates through local groups, taking non-violent direct action (though non-active members are welcomed), to sabotage hunts, hare coursing, angling and shooting, badger baiting, cock and dog fighting, poaching, seal culling, horse racing and dog racing. Hunt sabotage tactics include laying false trail masking that of hunted animal, and using horns to call off/redirect hounds from prey. Youth membership. Publishes *HOWL* magazine.
Members/Supporters: 3,000.

I

IDENTICAT (SCOTLAND).
Tel. 0383 610800. Traces lost cats.

INTERGROUP ON ANIMAL WELFARE.
Secretariat: Eurogroup for Animal Welfare [page 184]. Contact Address: c/o Royal Society for the Prevention of Cruelty to Animals [page 202].
Attended by the Euro-members of Parliament from all political parties, meets once a month in Strasbourg during the full session of the European Parliament. Secretariat is Eurogroup [page 186]. Attended by approximately 15–20 per cent of those Members attending the European Parliament.

INTERNATIONAL ANIMAL RESCUE.*
Animal Tracks, Ashmill, South Molton, Devon EX36 4QW. Tel./Fax. 0769 550277. Registered Charity No. 802132. Founded in 1990 by J. E. Hicks and Miss V. Tillyer.

Aims and Methods. To campaign on animal welfare issues worldwide; to establish rescue centres in Britain; to educate the public in all aspects of animal rights. Funded and campaigned to save whales in Turkey, meeting with Turkish ministers on animal welfare issues. Fighting deer hunting in the West Country.

INTERNATIONAL ASSOCIATION AGAINST PAINFUL EXPERIMENTS ON ANIMALS (IAAPEA).*

PO Box 215, St Albans, Herts AL3 4PU. Tel. 0727 835386. Founded in 1969.
Aims and Methods. The abolition of experiments on live animals. Promotes prevention of ill health and the use of alternatives to the use of animals in research. Organizes international conferences; funds work developing alternatives; maintains an international animal experimentation photo agency; established 24 April as World Day for Laboratory Animals; devised and promotes the International Charter for Health and Humane Research; supports new anti-vivisection societies. Has consultative status with the United Nations Economic and Social Council. Publishes *International Animal Action* and the IAAPEA Newsletter.
Members/Supporters: sixty member societies in thirty countries.

INTERNATIONAL COUNCIL FOR BIRD PRESERVATION.

32 Cambridge Road, Girton, Cambridge CB3 0PY. Tel. 0223 277318. Fax. 0223 277200. Founded in 1922.
Aims and Methods. To conserve birds and their habitats. Protects endangered birds all over the world and promotes public awareness of their ecological importance. Gathers and disseminates information, identifies and carries out priority projects, advocates and implements conservation measures where they are needed. Maintains a computerized databank from expert reports of threatened species and their habitats, and in conjunction with the International Union for the Conservation of Nature [page 214], compiles the *Bird Red Data Book.* Highlights the facts that birds are threatened in many ways such as from pesticide poisoning, habitat destruction, indiscriminate hunting and trapping, and pollution. Publishes *World Birdwatch.*
Members/Supporters: Over 300 member organizations in 100 countries.

INTERNATIONAL DOLPHIN WATCH.

3 Riverview Avenue, North Ferriby, Humberside HU14 3ET. Tel. 0482 632650/ 634899.
Aims and Methods. To study and conserve wild dolphins. Aims to help those with an interest in dolphins to gain a greater understanding and to encourage others to become aware. Members who have made a direct observation of a wild dolphin are asked to participate in the Dolphin Survey Project which is being used to build up a worldwide picture of the populations and movements of dolphins. Publishes Dolphin Newsletter.

INTERNATIONAL DONKEY PROTECTION TRUST.
Slade House Farm, Sidmouth, Devon EX10 0NU. Tel. 0395 578222. Registered Charity No. 271410.
Aims and Methods. To help improve conditions for donkeys and mules throughout the world. Many of the problems are associated with the ignorance and poverty of the owners, such as the cruel bits prevalent in the Middle East and North Africa. Highlights the short life-span of a donkey in these countries as due to the enormous burden of gut parasites each donkey carries, with the parasites eventually burrowing through the wall of the gut and causing death.

INTERNATIONAL FUND FOR ANIMAL WELFARE (IFAW).*
Tubwell House, New Road, Crowborough, East Sussex TN6 2QH. Tel. 0892 663374. Fax. 0892 665460. Founded in 1969 by Brian Davies.
Aims and Methods. To promote and ensure the just and kind treatment of animals as sentient beings; to improve the quality of the lives of animals and their environment; to preserve animals from extinction; to prevent and abolish animal cruelty and to ensure that offshore Canadian and Norwegian hunt for harp and hood seals in the NW Atlantic is brought to an end. Has run numerous campaigns, e.g Operation Bear-lift in the USA against bear shooting; saving otters in Thailand; halting cruelty to iguanas in Central America; protection for endangered vicuna in Peru; alleviating suffering of dogs and cats in food trade in Philippines and Korea. In UK, work includes campaigns to stop hunting and end testing of cosmetics on animals. Established Political Animal Lobby [page 202] in UK in 1991. Branches in eighty countries. Members/Supporters: 1 million.

INTERNATIONAL LEAGUE FOR THE PROTECTION OF HORSES (ILPH).
PO Box 166, 67a Camden High St, London NW1 7JL. Tel. 071 388 1449/8333. Overa House Farm, Larling, Norfolk NR16 2QX. Tel. 0953 717882/717309. Anne Colvin House, Snetterton, Norwich, Norfolk NR16 2LR. Tel. 0953 498682. Founded in 1937 by Miss A. Cole .
Aims and Methods. To promote the welfare of horses throughout the world. Campaigns for the better treatment of horses especially those transported for human consumption. Seeks to improve conditions and methods in horse slaughterhouses and transit worldwide. Rescues horses in UK and Ireland, placing them in its rest and rehabilitation centres, with animals being re-homed where possible. Inspectors investigate cruelty complaints and maintain watch on UK's native ponies.

INTERNATIONAL PRIMATE PROTECTION LEAGUE (IPPL) UK.*
116 Judd Street, London WC1H 9NS. Tel. 071 837 7227. Fax. 071 278 3317. Registered Charity No. 272723.
Founded in 1973 in the USA by Shirley McGreal. Established in UK in 1976.
Aims and Methods. The conservation and welfare of all non-human primates.

Has field representatives in twenty-six countries, with members in over forty. Many of its officers have lived for long periods with primates in their natural habitats. Highlights the plight of primates threatened on three fronts: loss of natural habitat; being hunted for food and trade; being captured for use in live animal experimentation and other purposes. Has achieved primate export bans in many tropical countries, and keeps close watch to ensure that these are not rescinded. Helps to create and preserve national parks and sanctuaries and campaigns for strict regulation of primate hunting, trapping and sale; has assisted establishment of anti-poaching patrols in Rwanda, and supports the Chimpanzee Rehabilitation project in the Gambia. Successful in exposing and ending the blackmarket in primates in Singapore. Exposed a smuggling ring trafficking gibbons from Thailand to the USA and other countries. Has drawn attention to the link between zoos breeding primates surplus to their requirements and selling them to laboratories for experimentation. Publishes IPPL Newsletter.
Members/Supporters: 12,000.

INTERNATIONAL VEGETARIAN UNION (IVU).*
10 King's Drive, Marple, Stockport, Cheshire SK6 6NQ. Tel./Fax. 061 427 5850. Founded in 1908 by various vegetarian societies worldwide, as successor to the Vegetarian Federal Union established in 1889.
Aims and Methods. To further vegetarianism worldwide by promoting knowledge of vegetarianism as a means of advancing the spiritual, moral, mental, physical and economic well-being of humankind. Promotes world and regional congresses and research into all aspects of vegetarianism; encourages formation of vegetarian organizations. Aims to publish and encourage publication of material on all aspects of vegetarianism and acts as contact for enquiries about all aspects of vegetarianism from any part of the world. Publishes the IVU Newsletter.
Members/Supporters: fifty national and regional societies.

INTERNATIONAL WILDLIFE COALITION.*
PO Box 73, Hartfield, East Sussex TN7 4EY. Tel. 0342 825482. Fax. 0342 824716. (USA HQ: North Falmouth, Massachusetts, USA). Founded in 1984 in USA firstly as the I KARE Wildlife Trust. In 1986 expanded into the IWC with other members, e.g. Care For The Wild [page 179]. IWC–UK founded in 1989.
Aims and Methods. To challenge wildlife exploitation worldwide. Specializes in campaigns that attack the large commercial slaughter of wildlife [page 88]. Major campaigns against kangeroo slaughter [page 92]; fur trapping [page 72]; whaling [page 93], especially the Faroe Isles Slaughter [page 94]; sealing [page 96]; bloodsports [page 14]; ivory trade [page 91], and animal experimentation [page 29]. Is active at government levels in Washington, DC, Ottawa, London and at the central offices of the EC [page 212] in Brussels. Developed an Emergency Campaign contingent for times when prompt action is necessary. Promotes conservation education through programmes such as the

Whale Adoption Project, for which a magazine, *Whalewatch*, is published, plus special reports on wild cats, walrus, kangaroos, etc. and monthly newsletter updates.
Members/Supporters: 10,000 (UK).

INTO THE BLUE.*
Dolphin rescue and rehabilitation programme currently held in abeyance.
See Born Free Foundation [page 179].

IRISH ANTI-VIVISECTION SOCIETY.
Crosshaven, Co. Cork, Eire. Tel. 021 831146. Founded in 1970 when the Irish Union for the Abolition of Vivisection merged with groups in Cork and Wicklow.

IRISH SOCIETY FOR THE PREVENTION OF CRUELTY TO ANIMALS.*
1 Grand Canal Quay, Dublin 2. Tel. 010 353 1 775922. Registered Charity No. 5619. Founded in 1949. Federation of the thirty county SPVAs in the Republic.
Aims and Methods. To prevent and alleviate both domestic and wild animal suffering; to educate people, particularly the young, in a sense of concern for all animals; to take a positive and objective view of problems concerning animals within the context of the social and economic conditions in Ireland. Investigates complaints of cruelty; visits ports, marts and slaughterhouses. Adviser to Department of Environment and agent for several authorities in implementation of Control of Dogs Act 1986. Maintains rest homes for horses, ponies and donkeys.
Members/Supporters: 250 associate members.

J

JAPAN ANIMAL WELFARE SOCIETY (JAWS).*
RMC House, Townmead Road, London SW6 2RZ. Tel. 071 736 9306. Registered Charity No. 244534. Founded in 1954 by Lady Gascoigne and Mrs E. M. Close.
Aims and Methods. To promote the welfare of animals and of humane attitudes towards animals in Japan. Raises funds by subscriptions, donations and other means for remittance to JAWS in Tokyo and to other animal welfare organizations in Japan in order that the suffering of animals there may be relieved. Maintains rescue centres in Japan, provides drugs and money to support voluntary field workers and to pay caretakers to relieve animal suffering in pounds and laboratories. Pressurizes authorities to enforce the Animal Protection Law (in which it was instrumental), and also to reform conditions in laboratories, hospitals, zoos, circuses, etc.
Members/Supporters: 1,600.

JEWISH VEGETARIAN AND ECOLOGICAL SOCIETY.*
853–855 Finchley Road, London NW11 8LX. Tel. 081 455 0692. Registered Charity No. 258581. Founded in 1964 by a committee organized by Philip L. Pick.
Aims and Methods. To promote a compassionate and healthy way of life, and to help counter the worldwide war against Creation. Has been responsible for the initiation of many non-Jewish vegetarian societies. Believes that the teachings of Judaism are a complete philosophy for vegetarian living and that special responsibility devolves on to it to take a leading role in the campaign against factory farming and the international trafficking of sentient beings. Campaigned successfully against the introduction of Portuguese bullfighting to Israel. At above HQ has restaurant, library, naturopathic centre and an information service. Youth membership. Publishes the *Jewish Vegetarian*. Members/Supporters: 17,000.

L

LABORATORY ANIMALS PROTECTION SOCIETY (LAPS).
16 Thistleworth Close, Osterley, Middlesex TW7 4QQ. Tel. 081 847 3628. Founded in 1983 by Mrs J. Beckett-Terrell.
Aims and Methods. To further the interests and welfare of laboratory animals. Disseminates information to educate the general public as to what is involved for laboratory animals used in scientific research. Believes that the 1986 Animals (Scientific Procedures) Act [page 123] offers less protection to laboratory animals than before (i.e. under the Cruelty to Animals Act 1876). Continues to campaign for more humane conditions for animals and for a decrease in the number of animals used in experimentation.

LAWSON TAIT TRUST.
Brook House, 29 Bramhall Lane South, Bramhall, Stockport, Cheshire SK7 2DN. See Humane Research Trust [page 188].

LEAGUE AGAINST CRUEL SPORTS (LACS).*
83–87 Union Street, London SE1 1SG. Tel. 071 403 6155. Fax. 071 403 4532. Founded in 1924 by Henry B. Amos and Ernest Bell.
Aims and Methods. To abolish bloodsports. Initiated the UK's first organized hunt sabotage in the 1950s, although such tactics are no longer part of the League's work. Main approach now is to campaign for parliamentary legislation to prohibit hunting with dogs and also some forms of shooting. Condemns the hunting with hounds of deer, fox, hare, and also hare coursing [pages 14–19]. Encourages landowners to prohibit hunting with dogs and unnecessary shooting on land they own/control, with the Co-op (CWS) and approx. 120 local authorities having done so. LACS buys land for wildlife

sanctuaries in Devon and Somerset where red deer are hunted with dogs. Offers a free legal service to farmers and property owners who have suffered trespass, livestock worrying, crop damage and other problems caused by the invasion of hounds and mounted followers [page 17]. Local groups. Publishes *Wildlife Guardian*.

LIBERAL DEMOCRAT ANIMAL PROTECTION GROUP.*

2 Houldsworth Avenue, Timperley, Altrincham, Cheshire WA14 1SS. Tel. 061 929 1157. Founded in 1988 by a merger of the Liberal Animal Welfare Group and the Social Democrat Party Animal Protection Group.
Aims and Methods. To influence the policy of the Liberal Democrats. Organizes seminars involving animal welfare organizations; piloted a wide ranging policy motion through party conference in 1989, and lobbied for a policy working group on animal protection. Publishes *Animal Protection News*.

LIGUE INTERNATIONALE MÉDECINS POUR L'ABOLITION DE LA VIVISECTION (International League of Doctors for the Abolition of Vivisection).*

UK Office, Lynmouth, Devon EX35 6EE. Fax. 0271 88 2235. Founded by the Swiss Anti-Vivisection Society.
Aims and Methods. To fight for the total abolition of animal experiments on scientific and medical grounds, by the dissemination of information, and by exposing weaknesses in the establishment's arguments. Publishes the *European Medical Journal*.
Members/Supporters: 750 doctors plus many supporters.

LONDON GREENPEACE.*

5 Caledonian Road, London N1 9DX. Tel. 071 837 7557. Founded in 1971 by activists from *Peace News* and War Resisters International, originally campaigning against nuclear bomb tests. Not related to Greenpeace [page 214].
Aims and Methods. An independent collective encouraging people to think, organize and act for themselves, to fight the State and capitalism (which London Greenpeace sees as responsible for the oppression and exploitation of humans, animals and the environment). Works for ecological and social revolution to abolish money and bosses, and for a free, co-operative anarchist society. Has co-ordinated worldwide campaigns against McDonalds Hamburger Corporation since 1985.

LORD DOWDING FUND.

Ravenside, 261 Goldhawk Road, Hammersmith, London W12 9PE. Tel. 081 846 9777. Fax. 081 846 9712. A wing of the National Anti-Vivisection Society [page 196]. Raises money in order to sponsor research into alternatives to animal experiments.

LYNX.*
PO Box 300, Nottingham NG1 5HN. Tel. 0602 403211. Fax. 0602 873084.
Founded in 1985 by Mark Glover and Lynne Kentish.
Aims and Methods. Dedicated to changing society's attitude towards fur, and aims to create a new climate of public opinion where the wearing of fur is no longer acceptable. Actively campaigns within parliament to introduce or update laws that affect fur-bearing animals and to close down all fur factory farms in the UK. Uses billboard and bus shelter advertising and cinema commercials. Lynx has shops at 79 Long Acre, London WC2; Quayside, Bridge Street, Cambridge, and 14 Cheapside, Nottingham. Publishes Lynx Newsletter.

M

MOVEMENT FOR COMPASSIONATE LIVING (MCL).
47 Highlands Road, Leatherhead, Surrey KT22 8NQ. Tel. 0372 372389. Founded in 1985 by K. and J. Jannaway and C. and D. Yates.
Aims and Methods. Seeks to spread compassionate understanding and to simplify lifestyles by promoting awareness of the connections between the way we live and the way others suffer, and between development, consumption and the destruction of the planet. Publishes *New Leaves* journal.

N

NATIONAL ANIMAL RESCUE ASSOCIATION (NARA).
8 Waterpump Court, Thorplands, Northampton NN3 1XU.
Aims and Methods. To rescue animals. Trained team of volunteers operate a twenty-four-hour rescue service for sick, trapped and injured wild and domestic animals. Has an ambulance and high-powered rescue boats. Carries out patrols in the Wash to rescue abandoned or injured seals, to provide data on the seal population and to prevent poaching of seal pups. Deals with around 1,200 rescues annually; road traffic accidents; snared animals; swans injured by fishing tackle and poisoned with lead weights.

NATIONAL ANTI-COURSING COUNCIL.
PO Box 8, Widnes, Cheshire WA8 0DX.

NATIONAL ANTI-VIVISECTION SOCIETY (NAVS).*
Ravenside, 261 Goldhawk Road, London W12 9PE. Tel. 081 846 9777. Fax. 081 846 9712. Founded in 1875 by Frances Power Cobbe.

Aims and Methods. Campaigns for an end to experiments on live animals. Also aims at encouraging the development and adoption of research techniques not involving experiments on animals, which it does actively through the Lord Dowding Fund. Organizes World Day for Laboratory Animals activities, nearest Saturday to 24 April. Since 1986 has run a Violence-Free Science campaign aimed at helping students to study life sciences without using animals. Operates The AD Shop, 78 Bull Street, Birmingham, selling clothing, cruelty-free cosmetics, stationery. Publishes *The Campaigner*, and *Animals' Defender* for its youth group.
Members/Supporters: 20,000.

NATIONAL ASSOCIATION FOR THE DEFENCE OF ANIMALS.
21 Barclay Avenue, Burnley, Lancashire BB11 5LX. Tel. 0282 411415.
Aims and Methods. Works to bring about an end to bullfighting and all other animal cruelty in Spain.

NATIONAL CANINE DEFENCE LEAGUE (NDCL).*
1 Pratt Mews, London NW1 0AD. Tel. 071 388 0137. Fax. 071 383 5474.
Registered Charity No. 227523. Founded in 1891, in compliance with a request by Lady Gertrude Stock, to meet the needs of the moment; to counter anti-dog scares perpetrated by the Pasteur Institute.
Aims and Methods. To safeguard the welfare of dogs in all situations. Maintains rescue centres throughout the UK. Does not destroy healthy dogs, with those unhomeable staying at the kennels, on a sponsorship scheme. Promotes neutering with NDCL Roadshow. Campaigns for better legislation regarding dogs (supportive of a dog registration scheme); for an international agreement to end the docking of dogs' tails; for more restrictions on dog breeding; to bring puppy farms within the law; for dog ownership identification; for a consolidated Dog Act to update the forty or so Acts on the Statute Book which refer to dogs. Member of JACOPIS [page 215]. Local branches. Publishes *NDCL News*.
Members/Supporters: 107,000.

NATIONAL EQUINE DEFENCE LEAGUE.
Oaktree Farm, Wetheral Shields, Wetheral, Carlisle, Cumbria CA4 8JA.
Tel. 0228 60082.

NATIONAL FEDERATION OF BADGER GROUPS.*
16 Ashdown Gardens, Sanderstead, Surrey CR2 9DR. Tel. 081 657 4636.
Founded in 1986.
Aims and Methods. To promote measures which enhance the welfare, conservation and protection of badgers; to set up and support a network of local and county badger protection groups. Liaises with other interested parties, government and non-government, giving advice and assistance where appropriate. Represented on the Badgers and Bovine Tuberculosis Advisory Panel [page 88]. Monitors court cases involving prosecutions under the Badgers

Acts [page 128, 135], and the Wildlife and Countryside Act and its amendments [pages 120, 130]; and investigates unacceptable interference by fox hunts to badger setts. Instrumental in achieving greater protection for badgers and their setts via the Badgers Act 1991 [page 128]. Seeking legislation to ban use of snares and supportive of Wild Mammal Protection Bill initiatives. Members/Supporters: eighty affiliated badger protection groups.

NATIONAL PET REGISTER.*
Chishill Road, Heydon, Royston, Herts SG8 8PN. Tel. 0763 838329. Founded in 1988 and operated by Wood Green Animal Shelters [page 208].
Aims and Methods. To rescue and reunite lost and stray animals with their owners by referral to a unique identification and fully computerized system capable of holding 80 million registrations. Has facilities to provide methods of identification such as disc, transponder (implant), tattooing and freeze-branding.

NATIONAL PETWATCH.*
PO Box 16, Brighouse, West Yorkshire HD6 1DS. Tel. 0484 722411. Fax. 0484 400104. Founded in 1983, by Joan Wearne, to deal specifically with the growing problem of stolen family pets.
Aims and Methods. To protect pet animals from ill-usage, cruelty and suffering and to further the development and administration of the law by facilitating both the deterrence and investigation of crimes connected with the theft of pet animals for experimentation, export, fur, fighting, breeding and food. Operates a national network of missing pets registers which monitor the patterns and trends of losses at local, then national level, matches lost and found pets, offers practical help and advice to owners of missing pets and works to prevent losses through public awareness campaigns and the provision of preventive measures. Publishes *The Petwatcher*.

NATUREWATCH TRUST.
Austen House, 122 Bath Road, Cheltenham, Gloucestershire GL53 7JX. Tel. 0242 252871.

NETWORK OF INDIVIDUALS AND CAMPAIGNS FOR HUMANE EDUCATION (NICHE).*
c/o Department of Psychology, University of Stirling, Stirling FK5 4LA. Tel. 0786 67677. Founded in 1988.
Aims and Methods. To promote alternatives to animal use in teaching and research, such as video systems and plant materials; to encourage discussion of the ethical issues surrounding animal use in education; to support the right of the student at school or university to conscientiously object. Issues information to potential students detailing which UK universities do/don't demand animal-based practicals. Publishes education packs and NICHE Newsletter. Members/Supporters: 250.

NURSES' ANTI-VIVISECTION MOVEMENT.*
PO Box 32, Matlock, Derbyshire DE4 3YJ. Tel. 0629 824664. Founded in 1983 by Sheila Dickety.
Aims and Methods. The total and immediate abolition of vivisection on medical and scientific grounds, mainly by publicity and through nurses' professional organizations and trade unions. Publishes quarterly newsletter.

O

OPERATION FUR FACTORY.
PO Box 87, Rochdale, Lancashire OL16 1AA.

OTTER TRUST.
Earsham, Nr Bungay, Suffolk NR35 2AF. Tel. 0986 3470.

P

PAGAN ANIMAL RIGHTS.*
23 Highfield South, Rock Ferry, Merseyside L42 4NA. Tel. 051 645 0485. Founded in 1983 by Tina Fox.
Aims and Methods. To assist animals, using magical and spiritual means; to inform the pagan community about animal issues and inform the animal rights community about the pagan religion. Publishes *PAR* magazine.

PEOPLE'S DISPENSARY FOR SICK ANIMALS (PDSA).*
Whitechapel Way, Priorslee, Telford, Shropshire TF2 9PQ. Tel. 0952 290999. Fax. 0952 291035. Registered Charity No. 208217. Founded in 1917 by Maria Dickin to help sick and injured animals in the East End of London at that time.
Aims and Methods. To provide free veterinary treatment (not vaccinations or neuterings) for sick and injured pets of owners who qualify for the Society's free charitable service. Operates fifty animal treatment centres, and a pet-aid scheme in over sixty communities. Provides a twenty-four-hour emergency service.

PEOPLE'S TRUST FOR ENDANGERED SPECIES.
Hamble House, Meadrow, Godalming, Surrey, GU7 3JX. Tel. 04868 24848. Founded in 1977.
Aims and Methods. To inform people about the critical need to protect endangered species, to foster research and to protect threatened wild animals and their habitat. Most of the work is involved with conservation and carried out by hiring experts to work on various projects. Has provided anti-poaching

equipment, such as the light aircraft presented to Uganda National Parks. Campaigns include the Faroe Isles pilot whale slaughter [page 94]; the kangaroo slaughter [page 92]; and the whaling industry in general. Member of the United Nations Environment Programme; the International Union for the Conservation of Nature [page 214] and the Special Survival Committee of the IUCN; and the International Whaling Commission [page 215].
Supporters: 15,000.

POLITICAL ANIMAL LOBBY (PAL).
The Laurels, Eridge Road, Crowborough, East Sussex TN6 2SJ. Tel. 0892 663374/663819. Fax. 0892 665460. Founded in 1991 by Brian Davies (International Fund for Animal Welfare [page 193]).
Aims and Methods. To raise political profile of animal welfare issues; to lobby Parliament and to press for creation of a single animal welfare ministry or commission (rather than the present ten or so government departments) to deal with all animal issues.

PREVENT UNWANTED PETS (PUPS).
8 Previn Gardens, Marmion Road, Nottingham NG3 2HR. Tel. 0602 505964. Founded in 1986 by Christine Scott.
Aims and Methods. Helps to subsidize the costs of spaying or neutering pets for people on low incomes.

PRO DOGS.
Rocky Bank, New Road, Ditton, Kent ME20 6AD. Tel. 0732 848499/872222. Registered Charity No. 275574. Founded in 1976 by Lesley Scott-Ordish.
Aims and Methods. To promote a better appreciation and understanding of dogs and the ways in which they enrich human life. Branches throughout the UK. Operates a school-visiting service to teach caring ownership to children; Dogs Deserve Better People Scheme, and the Pro Dogs Active Therapy (PAT) Scheme. Campaigns for the end of death by electrocution for unwanted dogs, which led to the cessation in 1984 of this method at the Dogs' Home Battersea [page 185], although other organizations in the UK still use it. Publishes *ARGOS* magazine.

PROTECTION AND CONSERVATION OF ANIMALS AND PLANT-LIFE INTERNATIONAL.
29 Broughton Drive, Grassendale, Liverpool L19 OPB. Tel. 051 494 0470.
Aims and Methods. To achieve worldwide consciousness among human beings, regarding the rights of the members of the animal kingdom and preservation of the world's forests, fauna and flora.

PUPPY WATCH.*
PO Box 23, Neath, West Glamorgan SA11 1QP. Tel. 0639 845755. Registered Charity No. (yet to be allocated). Founded in 1989 by Tricia Roberts and Alan Clark, as Puppy Watch Wales. Became Puppy Watch in 1991.

Aims and Methods. To document and expose the illegal, intensive breeding of puppies on puppy farms. To work towards an end to the breeding or transfer, by means of middlemen or dealers, of any pet animal for profit; to restrict breeding, alleviate suffering and to improve conditions. Initiated amendment to the Breeding of Dogs Act 1973 [page 130] giving local authorities some power of entry to unlicensed premises. Publishes *Puppy Watch News.* Members/Supporters: 700.

Q

QUAKER CONCERN FOR ANIMALS (QCA).*
Webb's Cottage, Saling, Braintree, Essex CM7 5DZ. Tel./Fax. 0371 850423. Registered Charity No. (in process of application at time of writing). Founded in 1891 by members of the Religious Society of Friends.
Aims and Methods. Encourages Friends to try to live without dependence on cruelty and to support efforts to bring in effective legislation to protect animals. Promotion of compassion, sensitivity and awareness for human and animal benefit. Represented on the Christian Consultative Council. Publishes QCA Newsletter.
Members/Supporters: 500.

QUEST CANCER TEST.
Woodbury, Harlow Road, Roydon, Essex CM19 5HF. Tel. 027979 3671/2233. Registered Charity No. 284526. Founded in 1982 by Jean Pitt.
Aims and Methods. To fund medical research into early cancer detection with a policy of not using animals. Believes that animals are unreliable as models for cancers affecting humans, and is concerned at the numbers of animals used in cancer research. Funds research into new methods of diagnosing cancer at three universities in the UK. Aims to set up routine testing centres using a test to detect cancer developed by Quest which has been successful at detecting a number of types of cancer. Publishes Teamwork Newsletter .

R

REDWINGS HORSE SANCTUARY.*
Hill Top Farm, Hall Lane, Frettenham, Nr Norwich, Norfolk NR12 7LT. Tel. 0603 737432. Fax. 0603 738286. Registered Charity No. 295763. Founded in 1984 by Wendy Valentine.
Aims and Methods. To rescue horses, ponies, donkeys and mules from neglect and slaughter and provide them with a caring, permanent home. Operates a

veterinary unit. Runs an Adopt a Rescued Horse, Pony, Donkey scheme. Regional Welfare Officers.
Members/Supporters: 150,000.

REPTILE PROTECTION TRUST.*
College Gates, 2 Deansway, Worcester WR1 2JD. Tel./Fax. 0483 417550. Registered Charity No. 802433. Founded in 1989 by Clifford Warwick, Catrina Steedman and Richard Peters.
Aims and Methods. To tackle all inhumanities to reptiles; to encourage people to view reptiles sympathetically. Has focused initially on rattlesnake round-ups in the USA and the international trade in red-eared terrapins, the latter campaign resulting in several countries banning their import. Aiming for public rejection of exotic pet trade in general.

ROYAL SOCIETY FOR THE PREVENTION OF CRUELTY TO ANIMALS (RSPCA).*
Causeway, Horsham, West Sussex RH12 1HG. Tel. 0403 64181. Fax. 0403 41048. Registered Charity No. 219099. Founded in 1824 by Revd Arthur Broome.
Aims and Methods. To promote kindness and prevent cruelty to animals. Operates an Inspectorate covering England and Wales, maintains animal homes and clinics. Lobbies throughout Europe for legal reform for the protection of animals, and much of today's animal welfare legislation is due to such activity. Special Investigations Department conducts discreet surveillance of activities such as the transportation of livestock abroad, dog fighting, cock fighting, and the wild bird trade. Takes in and re-homes (or destroys when thought necessary) stray and unwanted dogs and cats. Funds research into animal welfare. In 1980 initiated the Eurogroup for Animal Welfare [page 186] joining together animal welfare organizations in the EC [page 213]. Overseas Department maintains links with over 400 affiliated and independent organizations. Local branches. Publishes *Animal Life* and, for junior members, *Animal World*.
Members: 21,000/Supporters: 450,000.

ROYAL SOCIETY FOR THE PROTECTION OF BIRDS (RSPB).
The Lodge, Sandy, Bedfordshire SG19 2DL. Tel. 0767 680551. Fax. 0767 692365. Founded in 1889.
Aims and Methods. Originally to outlaw the practice of ornamenting ladies' dresses and hats with birds and their plumage. Campaigns to protect wild birds and their habitats; to prevent egg stealing, and the poisoning of raptors by game estates. Buys up land to maintain or establish habitats. Protects and encourages rare, endangered species. Over 100 nature reserves. Inspectorate. Publishes *Birds* magazine, and *Bird Life* for junior section.
Members/Supporters: 860,000.

S

ST ANDREW ANIMAL FUND.
10 Queensferry Street, Edinburgh EH2 4PG. Tel. 031 225 2116. Fax. 031 220 6377. Registered Charity No. 47073. Founded 1969 by the Scottish Society for the Prevention of Vivisection (now Advocates for Animals [page 174]).
Aims and Methods. To advance and encourage humane methods of study and research for the advancement of knowledge in the natural and medical sciences; to foster and encourage humane attitudes towards animal life; to organize, encourage and support educational activities designed to create a proper understanding and appreciation of animals and wildlife; to take appropriate measures for the protection of animals from cruelty and the infliction of suffering, and to provide funding or other assistance in support of animal welfare projects in Scotland and throughout the world.

SCOTTISH SOCIETY FOR THE PREVENTION OF CRUELTY TO ANIMALS (SSPCA).*
19 Melville Street, Edinburgh EH3 7PL. Tel. 031 225 6418. Fax. 031 220 4675. Registered Charity No. CR2244. Founded in 1839 by Sir James Forrest of Comiston, the Lord Provost of Edinburgh. Covers all Scotland, including islands, except Aberdeen area (see Aberdeen Association PCA [page 174]). Independent of the RSPCA.
Aims and Methods. To prevent cruelty to animals and to promote kindness and humanity in their treatment. Inspectorate investigates cruelty cases, routinely visits slaughterhouses, pet shops, stables, kennels, etc., and rescues animals in distress. Operates animal welfare centres, taking in injured and abandoned animals and re-homing where possible. Lobbies for improved and new animal welfare legislation. SSPCA Education Officers visit schools. Local branches. Youth membership. Publishes *Scottish SPCA News* and *Animal Express.*
Members/Supporters: 2,800.

SEA SHEPHERD UK.
PO Box 5, Ashford, Middx TW15 2PY. Tel. 0784 254846.
Aims and Methods. Campaigns against marine-life abuse. Operates two sea-going vessels. Takes direct action against seal culls, illegal whaling, drift-nets.

SEA TURTLE SURVIVAL.*
PO Box 790, London SW16 3NJ. Tel. 081 764 9186. Founded in 1990 by a group of British conservation volunteers.
Aims and Methods. To raise awareness of the plight of turtles worldwide. Campaigns to protect nesting beaches against, e.g., tourism at Laganas Bay, Zakynthos, Greece, and the abuse of turtles for food, trade and shells. Works closely with other conservation groups, tour companies, schools and political

parties. Launched report on conservation of the loggerhead turtle in 1991. Publishes Sea Turtle Survival Newsletter.

SEA WATCH FOUNDATION.*
7 Andrews Lane, Southwater, West Sussex RH13 7DY. Tel. 0403 731679/0865 727984. Fax. 0403 730049/0865 727984. Registered Charity No. (yet to be allocated). Founded in 1991 by Paul Vodden and Peter Evans.
Aims and Methods. To support the network of over 1,000 individuals and groups recording sightings of cetaceans in UK waters, collecting and disseminating data. Public education. Advises government and others regarding protection of whales, dolphins and porpoises against marine pollution, fishing nets, etc. Affiliated to the Mammal Society [page 215]. Local groups.
Members/Supporters: 1,000 plus network members.

SOCIETY FOR THE PROTECTION OF ANIMALS IN NORTH AFRICA (SPANA).
15 Buckingham Gate, London SW1E 6LB. Tel. 071 828 0997. Founded in 1923 by Mrs F. Hosali and daughter.
Aims and Methods. To promote animal welfare in North Africa. Raises money in the UK to support animal refuges and provide free veterinary treatment in Morocco, Algeria and Tunisia. Publishes *SPANA News*.
Members/Supporters: approx. 200.

SOIL ASSOCIATION.*
86 Colston Street, Bristol BS1 5BB. Tel. 0272 290661. Fax. 0272 252504. Registered Charity No. 206862. Founded in 1946 by Lady Eve Balfour.
Aims and Methods. To research, develop and promote sustainable relationships between the soil, plants, animals, people and the biosphere, in order to produce healthy food and other products while protecting and enhancing the environment. Produced the first Standards for Organic Agriculture in 1973; brought soil erosion on to national agenda in late 1980s; secured government support for organic food production in early 1990s. Publishes Soil Association News and *Living Earth* magazine.
Members/Supporters: 6,000.

STUDENT CAMPAIGN FOR ANIMAL RIGHTS (SCAR).*
PO Box 155, Manchester M60 1FT. Tel. 061 953 4039. Founded in 1987.
Aims and Methods. Co-ordinates animal rights groups in colleges across UK.

SUSTAINABLE AGRICULTURE, FOOD AND ENVIRONMENT ALLIANCE (SAFE).*
21 Tower Street, London WC2H 9NS. Tel. 071 240 1811. Fax. 071 240 1899. Founded in 1991. A coalition of over twenty-five organic, farming, consumer, animal welfare, environmental and Third World development groups.
Aims and Methods. The groups are linked by a concern about the malaise of conventional farming and the Common Agricultural Policy. Lobbies parlia-

ment for agricultural reform. Consumer concerns about intensive systems, including the widespread opposition to factory farming of livestock and the patenting of life forms, lie at the heart of its farm-support blueprint, *Farming for the Future*.

T

TEACHERS FOR ANIMAL RIGHTS (TFAR).
29 Lynwood Road, London SW17 8SB.
Aims and Methods. To change attitudes towards animals through the educational system.

TETTENHALL HORSE SANCTUARY FOUNDATION.*
Jenny Walker Lane, Old Perton, Wolverhampton WV6 7HB. Tel. 0902 764422/380370. Registered Charity No. 513386. Founded in 1978 by the Wilson family.
Aims and Methods. To prevent and relieve cruelty to horses (including ponies, mules and donkeys) and other animals by the provision of a home of rest and grazing. To prevent the illegal export of horses to the continent for slaughter. To abolish lifetime tethering of horses. Runs a Horse Home Register to match horses that cannot be admitted to the shelter, with people offering good homes. Participates in humane education of deprived children from cities, riding for the handicapped, and runs a Jodhpur Club for youngsters. Maintains a burial ground for pets.
Members/Supporters: 9,000.

TRAFFIC INTERNATIONAL.
219c Huntingdon Road, Cambridge CB3 0DL. Tel. 0223 277427.
Aims and Methods. To enhance, in accordance with the principles of the World Conservation Strategy, the conservation of biological diversity by monitoring and reporting on trade or other forms of utilization of animals and plants and their derivatives. Identifies areas of such utilization that may be detrimental to any species, and assists the Secretariat of, and parties to, the Convention on International Trade in Endangered Species of Wild Fauna and Flora (CITES) [page 213] and other appropriate bodies in facilitating the control of trade and in curtailing possible threats to species created by trade or other forms of utilization. Publishes *TRAFFIC Bulletin*.

TRUST FOR URBAN ECOLOGY (TRUE).*
PO Box 514, London SE16 1AS. Tel./Fax. 071 237 9165. Registered Charity No. 278601. Founded in 1979.
Aims and Methods. To promote the development of knowledge and expertise in the fields of urban ecology and nature conservation. To develop the means to conserve, create and enhance natural elements of the urban landscape; to

stimulate public interest in and appreciation of nature in towns and cities; to promote the use of urban nature areas; to provide information, advice and expertise on the design, creation and management of urban greenspaces. Runs nature parks for education.

U

ULSTER SOCIETY FOR THE PREVENTION OF CRUELTY TO ANIMALS (USPCA).*

11 Drumview Road, Lisburn, County Antrim BT27 6YF. Tel. 0232 813126. Fax. 0232 812260. Registered Charity No. XN 45066. Founded in 1836 by Belfast clergy and businessmen. Independent of the RSPCA.

Aims and Methods. To obtain justice for animals, to endeavour by every means to put an end to cruelty to animals and to encourage kindness and humanity in their treatment. To provide protection, care and housing to all stray, unwanted and injured animals. To investigate allegations of cruelty. To advise, admonish and where necessary prosecute offenders. Runs a uniformed inspectorate dealing with complaints of cruelty from the public, visiting fairs, markets, shows, abattoirs, circuses, etc., and answering emergency calls to road accidents, etc. Re-homes animals after spaying/neutering. Participates in education, visiting schools and other groups, and runs the Junior Branch for young members. Local branches.

Members/Supporters: 1,000.

UNIVERSITIES' FEDERATION FOR ANIMAL WELFARE (UFAW).

8 Hamilton Close, South Mimms, Potters Bar, Herts, EN6 3QD. Tel. 0707 58202. Founded in 1926 by C. Hume.

Aims and Methods. To promote humane behaviour towards animals and, in the pursuance of this aim, to enlist the energies of members of universities and professional men and women. To obtain and disseminate relevant information; to help teachers to provide humane education; to co-operate with governmental departments, parliament, the Churches, the learned societies and other bodies, and to pursue any other charitable activities conducive to the end in view and appropriate to the character of a university organization.

V

VEGAN SOCIETY.*

7 Battle Road, St Leonards on Sea, East Sussex TN37 7AA. Tel./Fax. 0424 427393. Registered Charity No. 279228. Founded in 1944.

Aims and Methods. To encourage the development and use of alternatives to all

commodities normally derived wholly or partly from animals. To further knowledge of and interest in nutrition and veganism and in the vegan method of agriculture as a means of increasing the potential of the earth to the physical, moral and economic advantage of humankind. Promotes a vegan way of life which seeks to exclude, as far as is possible and practical, all forms of exploitation of, and cruelty to, animals for food, clothing or any other purpose, dispensing with all animal flesh, fish, eggs, fowl, animal milks, and their derivatives. Licenses use of its (sunflower) logo on consumer product packaging. Co-organizer of the Great British MeatOut campaign. Local contacts. Publishes *The Vegan*.
Members: 4,000.

VEGETARIAN SOCIETY OF ULSTER.*
66 Ravenhill Gardens, Belfast BT6 8GQ. Tel. 0232 457888. Founded in 1932.
Aims and Methods. The promotion of vegetarianism in Northern Ireland. Investigates source of foods and their production methods. Promotes compassion to all creatures; health and fitness; world economics and environmental concern based on vegetarian land use.

VEGETARIAN SOCIETY OF THE UNITED KINGDOM (VSUK).*
Parkdale, Dunham Road, Altrincham, Cheshire WA14 4QG. Tel. 061 928 0793. Fax. 061 926 9182. Registered Charity No. 959115. Founded in 1847.
Aims and Methods. To promote vegetarianism in the UK in order to save animals, benefit human health and protect the environment and world food resources. Dedicated to fundraising to drive its programmes in campaigning, education, information and research. Supports epidemiological research with volunteers, examining their medical and nutritional status, etc. Organizes demonstration against the annual Royal Smithfield Show. Co-organizer of the Great British MeatOut. Licenses use of its vegetarian (green V-shaped seedling) logo on consumer product packaging. Publishes *The Vegetarian* magazine. Runs two clubs for Junior members, who receive *Greenscene* magazine; the Green Gang club for under 12s, and Club VI for 12–17s. Local groups.
Members: 21,000.

VEGFAM.*
The Sanctuary, Nr Lydford, Okehampton, Devon EX20 4AL. Tel. 0822 82203 and 0462 456294. Registered Charity No. 232208. Founded in 1963 by Christopher and Janet Aldous.
Aims and Methods. To feed the hungry without exploiting animals. Provides plant-based foods, or the means for their production (land reclamation, seeds, irrigation, etc.), to hungry people. Finances various projects, e.g. leaf protein schemes, aimed at the relief of famine and drought in the Third World.

VEGGIES.
The Rainbow Centre, 180 Mansfield Road, Nottingham NG1 3HU. Tel. 0602 585666. Founded in 1984. [See page 158].

W

WHALE AND DOLPHIN CONSERVATION SOCIETY (WDCS).*

19A James Street West, Bath, Avon BA1 2BT. Tel. 0225 334511. Fax. 0225 480097. Registered Charity No. 298656. Founded in 1987 by Sean Whyte and Kieran Mulvaney.

Aims and Methods. To work towards the total abolition of all scientific and commercial whaling; to raise general awareness of the ways in which cetaceans of all kinds are being needlessly slaughtered; to alert the public to the continuing need to protect them in their natural habitat. Has funded over forty conservation and research projects and gained the release of captured dolphins and whales into the wild. Puts pressure on government and maintains presence at proceedings of the International Whaling Commission [page 215] to counter at source any propaganda disseminated by whaling nations. Local groups. Publishes *SONAR* magazine and the WDCS newsletter.

Members/Supporters: 35,000.

WILDLIFE HOSPITAL TRUST.

1 Pemberton Close, Aylesbury, Bucks, HP21 7NY. Tel. 0296 29860. Founded 1978.

Aims and Methods. Rescues sick and injured wild animals and birds which are returned to the wild or kept in as natural habitat as possible. Has a hedgehog hospital willing to take in casualties from all over the UK. Organizes toad lifts and barn owl re-introductions, etc. Is a licensed rehabilitation centre for the Department of the Environment under the Wildlife and Countryside Act 1981 [page 120].

WOOD GREEN ANIMAL SHELTERS.*

Highway Cottage, Chishill Road, Heydon, Royston, Herts SG8 8PN. Tel. 0763 838329. Fax. 0763 838318. Registered Charity No. 298348. Founded in 1924.

Aims and Methods. To take in and re-home, where possible, unwanted and stray animals; to educate people in responsible pet ownership and husbandry. Has four sites, at Royston, Evesham, London and at Godmanchester where the College of Animal Welfare has been founded [page 183]. Operates the National Pet Register [page 200]. Youth membership.

WORLD SOCIETY FOR THE PROTECTION OF ANIMALS (WSPA).

Park Place, 10 Lawn Lane, London SW8 1UA. Tel. 071 793 0540. Founded in 1981 by the merging of the International Society for the Protection of Animals (established 1959), the World Federation for the Protection of Animals (established 1950), incorporating the International Council Against Bullfighting.

Aims and Methods. To eliminate pain, suffering, injury and abuse to animals wherever possible, worldwide. Offices in Boston, USA and Zurich, Switzerland, and field offices in India, Costa Rica, Brazil and Canada. Campaigns on behalf of farm animals, laboratory animals, companion animals, captive wild animals, and free-living wildlife. Organizes rescue missions to aid animals involved at times of disaster. Publishes *Animal International* magazine. Members/Supporters: Over 350 member societies in sixty countries.

Y, Z

YOUNG INDIAN VEGETARIANS.*
226 London Road, West Croydon, Surrey CR0 2TF. Tel. 081 681 8884. Fax. 081 681 7143. Founded in 1978 by Nitin Mehta.
Aims and Methods. To promote vegetarianism and animal welfare. Organizes programmes in different parts of the country, e.g. the mass vegetarian rally in Hyde Park in 1990. Supports like-minded organizations. Membership open to everyone. Publishes Ahimsa Newsletter.

ZOO CHECK.*
Cherry Tree Cottage, Coldharbour, Dorking, Surrey RH5 6HA. Tel. 0306 712091. Fax. 0306 713350. Registered Charity No. 296024. Founded in 1984 by Virginia McKenna, Bill Travers and Bill Jordan. Zoo Check is now a project of the Born Free Foundation [page 000].
Aims and Methods. To check and prevent all types of abuse to captive animals and wildlife; to phase out zoos and, where appropriate, support conservation centres; to promote international support for the conservation of animals in their natural habitat; to end the taking of wild animals from the wild; to encourage respect for the natural world and an understanding of its interrelationships; to persuade zoos and national and local governments to accept and promote these aims. Has published findings of investigations into zoos; rescued animals; established tiger sanctuary in India; established Operation Wolf in Portugal, and was instrumental in setting up Into the Blue [page 195], returning captive dolphins to a sea sanctuary. Publishes *Zoo Check News*. Members/Supporters: 3,500.

Appendix
OTHER ORGANIZATIONS REFERRED TO IN THE TEXT

Agriculture and Food Research Council (AFRC). Institute of Animal Physiology and Genetic Research, Babraham Hall, Babraham, Cambridgeshire CB2 4AT. Tel. 0223 832132.

Animal Procedures Committee. c/o Home Office, 50 Queen Anne's Gate, London SW1H 9AT. Tel. 071 273 3000.

Association of Circus Proprietors of Great Britain (ACP). Mellor House, Primrose Lane, Mellor, Nr Blackburn, Lancashire BB1 9DN. Tel. 0254 672222. Fax. 0254 681723.

Association for Science Education. College Lane, Hatfield, Herts AL10 9AA. Tel. 0707 267411.

British Association for the Advancement of Science. Fortress House, 23 Savile Row, London W1X 1AB. Tel. 071 494 3326.

British Association for Shooting and Conservation. Marford Mill, Chester Road, Rossett, Wrexham, Clwyd LL12 0HL. Tel. 0244 570881. Fax. 0244 571678.

British Field Sports Society (BFSS). 59 Kennington Road, London SE1 7PZ. Tel. 071 928 4742.

British Fur Trade Association. See Fur Education Council.

British Horse Society. British Equestrian Centre, Stoneleigh, Kenilworth, Warwickshire CV8 2LR. Tel. 0203 696697.

British Poultry Federation. High Holborn House, 52-54 High Holborn, London WC1V 6SX. Tel. 071 242 4683.

British Psychological Society. St Andrews House, 48 Princess Road East, Leicester LE1 7DR. Tel. 0533 549568.

British Small Animals Veterinary Association. Kingsley House, Church Lane, Shurdington, Cheltenham, Gloucestershire GL51 5TQ. Tel. 0242 862994.

British Veterinary Association (BVA). 7 Mansfield Street, London W1M 0AT. Tel. 071 636 6541.

British Veterinary Association Animal Welfare Foundation. 7 Mansfield Street, London W1M 0AT. Tel. 071 636 6541.

Central Committee of Fell Packs. 65 High Brigham, Cockermouth, Cumbria CA13 0TG. Tel. 0900 825205.

Centre for Rural Building (formerly the Scottish Farm Buildings Investigation Unit). Craibstone, Bucksburn, Aberdeen AB2 9TR. Tel. 0224 713622.

Convention on International Trade in Endangered Species of Wild Flora and Fauna (CITES). CITES Secretariat, 6 Rue de Maupas, Postal Box 78, CH-1000 Lausanne 9, Switzerland. Tel. 010 4121 200081. CITES is a United Nations Environment Programme, formed in 1976 to regulate trade in endangered species. There are 113 signatory countries each of which may send a delegation to the biennial meeting and each is entitled to one vote. Observers may attend and participate but not vote. There are three categories for a species listing at CITES. Appendix 1 lists a species as 'endangered', thereby halting international trade in its products. Appendix 2 is 'threatened' and sets limits on international trade. Appendix 3 allows any member country to gather data about the national status of any given species considered worthy of protection which could then be used to form the basis of future population evaluation.

Council of Europe. BP 431, RS 67006, Strasbourg, France. Comprises twenty-three nations, including the twelve members of the European Community, although apart from human rights issues it has no power to enforce its decisions. Draws up Conventions which take effect once they have been adopted by four member states, although a Convention is only binding to those states which have acceded to its terms. Thus a Convention will be opened for signatures, and when a country signs it implies that it agrees with the terms of the Convention and will work towards them. Conventions are frequently used as a basis for the EC draft Directives.

Countryside Council for Wales. Plas Penrhos, Ffordd Penrhos, Bangor, Gwynedd LL57 2LQ. Tel. 0248 370444.

Cruelty to Animals Inspectorate. c/o Home Office, 50 Queen Anne's Gate, London SW1H 9AT. Tel. 071 213 3000. Inspectorate appointed by Secretary of State to administer the Animals (Scientific Procedures) Act 1986.

English Nature. Northminster House, Peterborough, Cambridgeshire PE1 1UA. Tel. 0733 340345.

European Commission. 200 Rue de la Roi, B-1049 Brussels, Belgium. Tel. 010 32/2/2 35 11 11.

European Community (EC). UK Information Office, 20 Kensington Palace Gardens, London W8 4QQ. Tel. 071 973 1992. Aims to prevent the distortion of trade within its member nations; Belgium, Denmark, France, Germany, Greece, Ireland, Italy, Luxembourg, Netherlands, Portugal, Spain, United Kingdom. Based on the Treaties of Rome 1957 as updated by the Single European Act of 1987, if legislation is passed by this body in the form of a Directive or Regulation, it is binding upon the national government of each of the twelve member countries. The workings of the Community are complex and are governed by the three main Institutions: the Commission (initial drafting, administration); the European Parliament (amendments), and the Council of Ministers (final drafting, adoption). Another body, the Economic and Social Committee, exists purely in a consultative capacity. For further information contact Eurogroup for Animal Welfare [page 186].

Farm Animal Welfare Council (FAWC). Block B, MAFF Government Buildings, Hook Rise South, Tolworth, Surbiton, Surrey KT6 7NF. Tel. 081 330 4411.

Forestry Commission. 231 Costorphine Road, Edinburgh EH12 7AT. Tel. 031 334 0303.

Friends of the Earth (FoE). 26–28 Underwood Street, London N1 7JQ. Tel. 071 490 1555.

Fur Breeders Association. See Fur Education Council.

Fur Education Council. PO Box 1EW, London W1A 1EW. Promotes fur trapping, farming and wearing.

Game Conservancy. Burgate Manor, Fordingbridge, Hants SP6 1EF. Tel. 0425 652381.

Greenpeace. 30–31 Islington Green, London N1 8XE. Tel. 071 354 5100. Founded in 1971, originally to campaign against nuclear testing on the Aleutian Islands which are now a bird sanctuary. Campaigns to save whales; to stop nuclear weapons tests; to protect seals, dolphins, porpoises and sea turtles; to stop the disposal of radioactive waste and dangerous chemicals at sea; to close down nuclear power stations and nuclear reprocessing plants; to stop acid rain and protect the atmosphere; to reduce the trade in endangered species products; for stricter control over chemical waste disposal on land; and to declare Antarctica a World Park – free of military and industrial exploitation. Started anti-fur campaign, later transferred to LYNX [page 198].

House of Commons Select Committee on Agriculture. House of Commons, London SW1A 0AA.

House of Commons Information Office. House of Commons, London SW1A 0AA. Tel. 071 219 4272.

International Union for the Conservation of Nature and Natural Resources. (IUCN). UK office: 219c Huntingdon Road, Cambridge CB3 0DL. Tel. 0223 277314 (World Conservation Monitoring Unit) and 0223 277427 (Wildlife Trade Monitoring Unit). HQ: Avenue du Mont Blanc, CH-1196, Gland, Switzerland. Possibly the most powerful conservation organization in the world. Has a World Wildlife Convention which specifies criteria for the slaughter of wildlife, which Care for the Wild [page 181] considers most commercial slaughterers do not meet. IUCN established the Conservation Monitoring Centre (CMC) in 1983 to provide information service on global conservation for governments, agencies, media, etc. and the World Wide Fund for Nature [page 217], its sister organization, which funds the quarterly TRAFFIC *Bulletin*. CMC is under contract to the Secretariat of the Convention on Trade in

Endangered Species of Wild Fauna and Flora (CITES) [page 213] to manage data on such trade. Gathers information worldwide and disseminates through database output, publications such as the IUCN *Red Data Book* on plants and animals, and through special reports. Also maintains an Environmental Law Centre and the Trade Records Analysis of Flora and Fauna in Commerce (TRAFFIC) which has offices in several countries monitoring wildlife trade.

International Whaling Commission (IWC). The Red House, Station Road, Histon, Cambridge CB4 4NP. Tel. 0223 233971. Fax. 0223 232876. Comprises thirty-six member nations. Meets annually to regulate the number of whales caught. Operates on conservationist basis.

Jockey Club. 42 Portman Square, London W1H 0EN. Tel. 071 486 4921.

Joint Advisory Committee on Pets in Society (JACOPIS). 1 Dean's Yard, London SW1P 3NR. Tel. 071 799 9811. Founded in 1974 as a result of a symposium Pet Animals and Society organized by the British Small Animals Veterinary Association [page 212]. Investigates the changing relationship between humans and companion animals, making recommendations to government and others as to how the changes might best be managed in the interests of animals, their owners and the rest of society.

Joint Nature Conservation Committee. Monkston House, Peterborough, Cambridgeshire PE1 1JY. Tel. 0733 62626. Co-ordinates work of English Nature, Scottish Natural Heritage and Countryside Council for Wales and operates internationally.

Kennel Club. 1–5 Clarges Street, Piccadilly, London, W1Y 8AB. Tel. 071 493 6651. Fax. 071 495 6162. Promotes the improvement of dogs, dog shows, field trials, working trials and obedience tests. Stud Book authority for pedigree dogs, involved in the registering of pedigrees of dogs and licensing of all forms of competitions in which they compete. Disciplines those who offend against Rules and Regulations or are convicted in the civil courts on matters related to the well-being of dogs. Liaises with the British Veterinary Association [page 212] and the Royal Society for the Prevention of Cruelty to Animals [page 202] over welfare matters related to dogs. Has shown concern over dogs being exported to other countries such as Japan [page 79], where the animals may suffer, and have advised members to ensure that they sell to *bona fide* owners/breeders, known to the seller. Holds data on breeders, clubs, training centres and rescue/welfare societies.

Mammal Society. Business Offices, 141 Newmarket Road, Cambridge CB5 8HA. Tel. 0223 351870. Founded in 1954. To promote the study of mammals. Caters for professionals and amateurs with an interest in mammals. Represented at a range of meetings with government departments, Nature Conservancy Council [page 216], Forestry Commission [page 214] and voluntary bodies, giving authoritative advice. Holds two symposia per year, with additional occasional meetings. Conducts surveys on British wild mammals; provides information for the distribution maps of British mammals. Has a number of specialist groups with a working party to co-ordinate tasks. Publishes, with Blackwell Scientific Publications, the journal *Mammal Review* and has played a major part in the production of *The Handbook Of British Mammals*.

Masters of Foxhounds Association. Parsloes Cottage, Bagendon, Cirencester, Gloucestershire. Tel. 028 583 470.

Ministry of Agriculture, Fisheries and Food (MAFF). Hook Rise South, Tolworth, Surbiton, Surrey. Tel. 081 330 4411.

National Farmers Union (NFU). Agricultural House, 25–31 Knightsbridge, London SW1X 7NJ. Tel. 071 235 5077.

National Federation of Zoological Gardens of Great Britain and Ireland. Zoological Gardens, Regent's Park, London NW1 4RY. Tel. 071 722 3333.

National Sheep Association. National Sheep Centre, Malvern, Worcestershire WR13 6PH. Tel. 0684 892661.

Nature Conservancy Council. Now split into English Nature, Scottish Natural Heritage and the Countryside Council for Wales, *q.v.* See also Joint Nature Conservation Committee [page 215].

Research Defence Society (RDS). 58 Great Malborough Street, London W1V 1DD. Tel. 071 287 2818.

Royal College of Veterinary Surgeons (RCVS). 32 Belgrave Square, London SW1X 8QP. Tel. 071 235 4971.

Royal Society. 6 Carlton House Terrace, London SW1Y 5AG. Tel. 071 839 5561.

Royal Society for Nature Conservation. The Green, Witham Park, Waterside South, Lincoln LN5 7JR. Tel. 0522 752326. Founded in 1912 as the Society for the Promotion of Nature Reserves. Is the national association for forty-six local Nature Conservation Trusts. Aims to halt and reverse the decline of wildlife in the UK. Cares for over 1,500 nature reserves. Tries to ensure that changes to the countryside do the least harm to animals and wild flowers. Aims to achieve a united response to legislation and government policy. Advises government on wildlife issues. Alerts government and the public to damage to nationally important wildlife sites, gives evidence at planning enquiries and reponds to proposals for river improvements by Water Authorities. Promotes education through visitor centres, trails, activities and events for the public.

Scottish Farm Buildings Investigation Unit. See Centre for Rural Building.

Scottish Natural Heritage. 12 Hope Terrace, Edinburgh EH9 2AS. Tel. 031 447 4784.

Social Audit. PO Box 111, London NW1 8XG. Tel. 071 586 7771. Examines the operations and impacts of major organizations whose decisions and actions shape our lives.

State Veterinary Service. Hook Rise South, Tolworth, Surbiton, Surrey KT6 7NF. Tel. 071 330 4411.

World Wide Fund for Nature (WWF). Panda House, Weyside Park, Catteshall Lane, Godalming, Surrey, GU7 7XR. Tel. 0483 426444. Registered Charity No. 201707. Founded in 1961. Aims to stop human destruction of the natural environment on which all human, animal and plant life depends. Raises money for worldwide conservation projects to ensure the wise use of renewable natural resources which, according to WWF, include wild animals, plants and their habitats. Is represented in twenty-five countries, with the emphasis of its work on threatened species and habitats.

INDEX OF AUTHORS AND TITLES

Organizations are indexed here as authors only where no individual appears to be responsible for the publication in question. Such organizations will also be found listed in the alphabetically-arranged Directory [page 173].

Key: (S) = Slides; (S/T) = Slides/Tapes; (T) = Tapes. All other titles are publications; magazines being followed by (M).

INDEX OF SUBJECTS

Organizations indexed here will also be found listed in the alphabetically-arranged Directory [page 173].